PERFORMING ARTS

CAREER DIRECTORY

Gale Research Inc. proudly presents the first edition of the *Performing Arts Career Directory*. The hallmark of this volume, part of Gale's Career Advisor Series, is the essays by active professionals. Here, industry insiders describe opportunities and challenges in many fields related to the performing arts, including:

- Acting
- Improvisational comedy
- Broadway musicals
- Opera administration
- Choreography
- Dance instructing
- Ballet

- Concert composing
- Theatre design and technology
- Opportunities for the disabled
- Fundraising and development
- Internships
- Working in the cruise industry

In fully up-to-date articles, they describe:

- What to expect on the job
- Typical career paths
- What they look for in an applicant
- How their specialty is unique

Provides Excellent Job Hunting Resources

Once this "Advice from the Pro's" has given you a feel for performing arts careers, the *Directory* offers even more help with your job search strategy:

- **The Job Search Process** includes essays on determining career objectives, resume preparation, networking, writing effective cover letters, interviewing, and auditioning. With worksheets and sample resumes and letters. FEATURES: Resumes are targeted to the realities of performing arts careers.

- **Job Opportunities Databank** provides details on hundreds of companies that hire at entry-level. FEATURES: In addition to the entry-level information, entries also include information on all-important internship opportunities.

- **Career Resources** identifies sources of help wanted ads, professional associations, employment agencies and search firms, career guides, professional and trade periodicals, and basic reference guides and handbooks. FEATURES: Resource listings include detailed descriptions to help you select the publications and organizations that will best meet your needs.

Master Index Puts Information at Your Fingertips

This *Directory* is thoroughly indexed, with access to essays and directory sections both by subject and by organization name, publication title, or service name.

ISSN 1074-2840

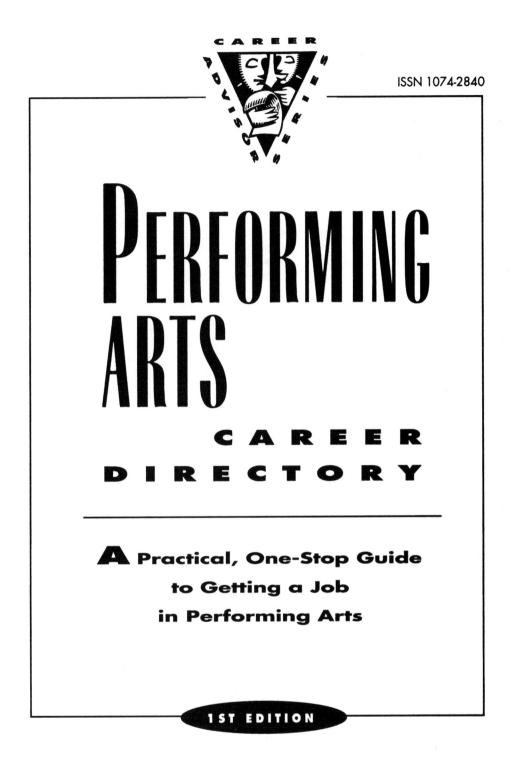

PERFORMING ARTS

CAREER DIRECTORY

A Practical, One-Stop Guide
to Getting a Job
in Performing Arts

1ST EDITION

**Bradley J. Morgan and
Joseph M. Palmisano, Editors**

Diane M. Sawinski, Associate Editor

Gale Research Inc.

DETROIT • WASHINGTON, D.C. • LONDON

Editors: Bradley J. Morgan and Joseph M. Palmisano
Associate Editors: Ned Burels and Diane M. Sawinski
Assistant Editors: Catherine C. DiMercurio and Wendy H. Mason
Aided by: Shawn Brennan, Sara Burak, Kristine Carl, Scot Ferman,
Kristin Kahrs, Debra M. Kirby, Richard Lawson, Deborah Morad,
Kathleen Lopez Nolan, Christopher P. Scanlon, Maria L. Sheler,
Christine Slovey, Wendi Sweetland, and Gwen E. Turecki
Senior Editor: Linda S. Hubbard

Research Manager: Victoria B. Cariappa
Research Supervisor: Gary J. Oudersluys
Editorial Associate: Tracie A. Wade
Editorial Assistants: Melissa E. Brown, Andreia L. Earley, Charles A. Jewell,
Michele L. McRobert, Michele P. Pica, Amy T. Roy, and Phyllis N. Shepherd

Production Director: Mary Beth Trimper
Production Assistant: Shanna Philpott Heilveil

Technical Design Services Manager: Art Chartow
Art Director: Cindy Baldwin
Graphic Designer: Mary Krzewinski

Manager, Technical Support Services: Theresa Rocklin
Programmer: Timothy Richardson

Data Entry Services Manager: Benita L. Spight
Data Entry Supervisor: Gwendolyn S. Tucker
Data Entry Associates: Merrie Ann Carpenter, Tara Y. McKissack,
Frances L. Monroe, Nancy K. Sheridan, and Constance J. Wells

ISBN 0-8103-9160-0
ISSN 1074-2840

Printed in the United States of America

Published simultaneously in the United Kingdom
by Gale Research International Limited
(An affiliated company of Gale Research Inc.)

I(T)P

The trademark **ITP** is used under license.

10 9 8 7 6 5 4 3 2 1

Contents

PART ONE

Advice from the Pro's

v

PART TWO

The Job Search Process

PART THREE

Job Opportunities Databank

PART FOUR

Career Resources

PART FIVE

Master Index

Acknowledgments

The editors would like to thank all the "pro's" who took the time out of their busy schedules to share their first-hand knowledge and enthusiasm with the next generation of job-seekers. A special thanks to Kathleen M. Daniels, Assistant Director of the Career Planning and Placement Office at the University of Detroit Mercy, who provided much needed help with the job search section.

Thanks are also owed to the human resources personnel at the companies listed in this volume and to the public relations staffs of the associations who provided excellent suggestions for essays. Chuck Linker, Stage Manager at Walt Disney World, and Rose Marie Floyd, Artistic Director and Choreographer at the Contemporary Civic Ballet Company, deserve special mention.

Introduction

It is a well-known fact that getting into show business is a challenging and competitive process. To beat the competition, job seekers need information. By utilizing the *Performing Arts Career Directory,* job seekers gain all the information they need to make the best possible decisions about their job search. The *Directory* is a comprehensive, one-stop resource that includes:

- Essays by industry professionals that provide practical advice not found in any other career resource
- Job search guidance designed to help you get in the door in a performing arts organization
- Job and internship listings from leading companies in the United States
- Information on additional career resources to further the job hunt
- A Master Index to facilitate easy access to the *Directory*

The *Directory* is organized into four parts that correspond to the steps of a typical job search—identifying your area of interest, refining your presentation, targeting companies, and researching your prospects.

Advice from the Pro's: An Invaluable Tool

Instead of offering "one-size-fits-all" advice or government statistics on what the working world is like, the *Performing Arts Career Directory* goes into the field for first-hand reports from experienced professionals working in many segments of performing arts. This "Advice from the Pro's" is offered by people who know what it's like to land that first job and turn it into a rich and rewarding career. Learn about:

- what it takes to be a successful actor from Dick Moore and Helaine Feldman of Dick Moore Associates. Dick (better known as Dickie) Moore has appeared in over 100 films and many of the *Our Gang* comedies.
- opportunities in the performing arts for people with disabilities from William E. Rickert, Co-Founder and Board Member of the Association for Theatre and Disability.

- beginning your performing arts career through an internship program from Darrell Ayers, Internship Program Manager of the John F. Kennedy Center for the Performing Arts.

- and 10 other areas of specialization, including:

Improvisational comedy	Ballet
Broadway musicals	Concert composing
Opera administration	Theatre design and technology
Choreography	Working in the cruise industry
Dance instruction	Fundraising and development

The essays cover the most important things a job applicant needs to know, including:

- What college courses and other background offer the best preparation
- Specific skills that are needed
- What people look for in an applicant
- Typical career paths
- Salary information

The Job Search Process: Making Sense of It All

What is the first thing a new job-hunter should do?

What different types of resumes exist and what should they look like?

What questions are off-limits in an interview?

These important questions are among the dozens that go through every person's mind when he or she begins to look for a job. Part Two of the *Performing Arts Career Directory*, **The Job Search Process**, answers these questions and more. It is divided into five chapters that cover all the basics of how to aggressively pursue a job:

- **Getting Started: Self-Evaluation and Career Objectives.** How to evaluate personal strengths and weaknesses and set goals.

- **Targeting Companies and Networking for Success.** How to identify the companies you would like to work for and how to build a network of contacts.

- **Preparing Your Resume.** What to include, what not to include, and what style to use. Includes samples of the three basic resume types and worksheets to help you organize your information. Also covers the use of head shots and the auditioning process.

- **Writing Better Letters.** What letters should be written throughout the search process and how to make them more effective. Includes samples.

- **Questions for You, Questions for Them.** How to handle an interview and get the job.

Job Opportunities Databank: Finding the Job You Want

Once you're ready to start sending out those first resumes, how do you know where to start? The **Job Opportunities Databank**, Part Three of the *Directory*, includes listings for more than 360 commercial and nonprofit performing arts centers, companies, and festivals; Broadway, off-Broadway, regional, and community theatres; opera companies; music ensembles; dance companies and troupes; and theatre production companies in the United States that offer entry-level jobs. These listings provide detailed contact information and data on the companies' activities, hiring practices, benefits, and application procedures—everything you need to know to approach potential employers. And since internships play an increasingly important role in the career research and employment process, information on the internship opportunities offered by the companies listed is also included.

It should be noted that the companies found in the *Directory* are primarily larger or more well-known performing arts organizations. Since there are many other small, private, or community performing arts companies or organizations, students should not limit their job or internship search to the companies listed, but instead, should investigate all companies of interest.

For further information on the arrangement and content of the **Job Opportunities Databank**, consult "How to Use the Job Opportunities Databank" immediately following this introduction.

Career Resources: A Guide to Organizations and Publications in the Field

Need to do more research on the specialty you've chosen or the companies you'll be interviewing with? Part Four of the *Directory,* **Career Resources,** includes information on the following:

- Sources of help wanted ads
- Professional associations
- Employment agencies and search firms
- Career guides
- Professional and trade periodicals
- Basic reference guides and handbooks

Listings contain contact information and descriptions of each publication's content and each organization's membership, purposes, and activities, helping you to pinpoint the resources you need for your own specific job search.

For additional information on the arrangement and content of **Career Resources**, consult "How to Locate Career Resources" following this introduction.

Master Index Speeds Access to Resources

A **Master Index** leads you to the information contained in all four sections of the *Directory* by citing all subjects, organizations, publications, and services listed throughout in a single alphabetic sequence. The index also includes inversions on significant keywords appearing in cited organization, publication, and service names. For example, the "National Dance Association" would also be listed in the index under "Dance Association; National." Citations in the index refer to page numbers.

Information Keeps Pace with the Changing Job Market

This first edition of the *Performing Arts Career Directory* contains essays in the **Advice from the Pro's** section that were contributed by leading performing arts professionals on subjects of particular interest to today's job seekers. All employers listed in the **Job Opportunities Databank** were contacted by telephone or facsimile to obtain current information, and **Career Resources** listings were obtained from selected material from other databases compiled by Gale Research Inc.

Comments and Suggestions Welcome

The staff of the *Performing Arts Career Directory* appreciates learning of any corrections or additions that will make this book as complete and useful as possible. Comments or suggestions for future essay topics or other improvements are also welcome, as are suggestions for careers that could be covered in new volumes of the Career Advisor Series. Please contact:

Career Advisor Series
Gale Research Inc.
835 Penobscot Bldg.
Detroit, MI 48226-4094
Phone: 800-347-GALE
Fax: (313)961-6815

Bradley J. Morgan
Joseph M. Palmisano

How to Use the
Job Opportunities Databank

The **Job Opportunities Databank** comprises two sections:

Entry-Level Job and Internship Listings
Additional Companies

Entry-Level Job and Internship Listings

Provides listings for more than 360 commercial and nonprofit performing arts centers, companies, and festivals; Broadway, off-Broadway, regional, and community theatres; opera companies; music ensembles; dance companies and troupes; and theatre production companies in the United States. Entries in the **Job Opportunities Databank** are arranged alphabetically by company name. When available, entries include:

- **Company name.**
- **Address and telephone number.** A mailing address and telephone number are provided in every entry.
- **Fax and toll-free telephone number.** These are provided when known.
- **Business description.** Outlines the company's activities. The geographical scope of the company's operations may also be provided.
- **Corporate officers.** Lists the names of executive officers, with titles.
- **Number of employees.** Includes the most recently provided figure for total number of employees. Other employee-specific information may be provided as well.
- **Average entry-level hiring.** Includes the number of entry-level employees the company typically hires in an average year. Many companies have listed "Unknown" or "0" for their average number of entry-level jobs. Because of current economic conditions, many could not estimate their projected entry-level hires for the coming years. However, because they have offered entry-level positions in the past and because their needs may change, we have listed them in this edition.
- **Opportunities.** Describes the entry-level positions that the company typically

offers, as well as the education and other requirements needed for those positions.

- **Benefits.** Lists the insurance, time off, retirement and financial plans, activities, and programs provided by the company, if known.
- **Human resources contacts.** Lists the names of personnel-related staff, with titles.
- **Application procedure.** Describes specific application instructions, when provided by the company.

Many entries also include information on available internship programs. Internship information provided includes:

- **Contact name.** Lists the names of officers or personnel-related contacts who are responsible for the internship program.
- **Type.** Indicates the type of internship, including time period and whether it is paid, unpaid, or for college credit. Also indicates if a company does not offer internships.
- **Number available.** Number of internships that the company typically offers.
- **Number of applications received.** Total number of applications received in a typical year.
- **Application procedures and deadline.** Describes specific application instructions and the deadline for submitting applications.
- **Decision date.** Final date when internship placement decisions are made.
- **Duties.** Lists the typical duties that an intern can expect to perform at the company.
- **Qualifications.** Lists the criteria a prospective applicant must meet to be considered for an internship with the company.

Additional Companies

Covers those organizations that either elected to provide only their name, address, and telephone number for inclusion in the *Directory* or that only rent out their space for performance purposes. Entries are arranged alphabetically by company name.

How to Locate
Career Resources

The **Career Resources** chapter contains six categories of information sources, each of which is arranged alphabetically by resource or organization name. The categories include:

▼ Sources of Help Wanted Ads

- **Covers:** Professional journals, industry periodicals, association newsletters, placement bulletins, and online services that include employment ads or business opportunities. Includes sources that focus specifically on performing arts concerns, as well as general periodical sources such as the *National Business Employment Weekly*.
- **Entries include:** The resource's title; name, address, and telephone number of its publisher; frequency; subscription rate; description of contents; toll-free and additional telephone numbers; and facsimile numbers.
- **Sources:** *Job Hunter's Sourcebook* (published by Gale Research Inc.) and original research.

▼ Professional Associations

- **Covers:** Trade and professional associations that offer career-related information and services.
- **Entries include:** Association name, address, and telephone number; membership; purpose and objectives; publications; toll-free or additional telephone numbers; and facsimile numbers. In some cases, the publications mentioned in these entries are described in greater detail as separate entries cited in the Sources of Help Wanted Ads, Career Guides, Professional and Trade Periodicals, and Basic Reference Guides and Handbooks categories.
- **Sources:** *Encyclopedia of Associations* (published by Gale Research Inc.) and original research.

▼ Employment Agencies and Search Firms

- **Covers:** Firms used by companies to recruit candidates for positions and, at times, by individuals to pursue openings. Employment agencies are generally geared towards filling openings at entry- to mid-level in the local job market, while executive search firms are paid by the hiring organization to recruit professional and managerial candidates, usually for higher-level openings. Also covers temporary employment agencies because they can be a method of identifying and obtaining regular employment. Includes firms that focus specifically on performing arts, as well as some larger general firms.

- **Entries include:** The firm's name, address, and telephone number; whether it's an employment agency, executive search firm, or temporary agency; descriptive information, as appropriate; toll-free and additional telephone numbers; and facsimile number.
- **Sources:** *Job Hunter's Sourcebook.*

▼ Career Guides

- **Covers:** Books, kits, pamphlets, brochures, videocassettes, films, online services, and other materials that describe the job-hunting process in general or that provide guidance and insight into the job-hunting process in performing arts careers.
- **Entries include:** The resource's title; name, address, and telephone number of its publisher or distributor; name of the editor or author; publication date or frequency; description of contents; arrangement; indexes; toll-free or additional telephone numbers; and facsimile numbers.
- **Sources:** *Directories in Print* and *Video Sourcebook* (published by Gale Research Inc.) and original research.

▼ Professional and Trade Periodicals

- **Covers:** Newsletters, magazines, newspapers, trade journals, and other serials that offer information to performing arts professionals.
- **Entries include:** The resource's title; the name, address, and telephone number of the publisher; the editor's name; frequency; description of contents; toll-free and additional telephone numbers; and facsimile numbers. Publication titles appear in italics.
- **Sources:** *Gale Directory of Publications and Broadcast Media* and *Newsletters in Print* (published by Gale Research Inc.) and original research.

▼ Basic Reference Guides and Handbooks

- **Covers:** Manuals, directories, dictionaries, encyclopedias, films and videocassettes, and other published reference material used by professionals working in performing arts careers.
- **Entries include:** The resource's title; name, address, and telephone number of the publisher or distributor; the editor's or author's name; publication date or frequency; description of contents; toll-free and additional telephone numbers; and facsimile numbers. Publication titles are rendered in italics.
- **Sources:** *Directories in Print, Video Sourcebook,* and original research.

ADVICE FROM THE PRO'S

CHAPTER ONE

So You Want to Be an Actor?

Dick Moore and Helaine Feldman, Dick Moore Associates

Every week our office receives dozens of inquiries from youngsters wanting to break into "show business," to become "stars" and to be rich and famous. Alas, many of the people who aspire to careers as actors or entertainers see only the successful few who make it—those who become stars, earn tremendous salaries, ride in limousines and have homes with tennis courts and swimming pools. They do not see the other side: the struggle, the constant search for employment, the lack of job security, the rejection and the heartbreak.

A U.S. government survey conducted several years ago actually confirmed several common notions about performing: performers work considerably less than full time at their profession because not enough work is available; employment is very sporadic and most performers work for many employers during a year; performers have to and do leave home in order to work at their profession; most performers work at other or "survival" jobs at some time during the year and, contrary to popular belief, when performers do get other jobs, the jobs are usually not related to acting.

In short, most people who earn their living in some area of entertainment would advise newcomers to give serious thought to acting as a profession. They might even add that if there is anything else they can do that would make them happy, they should do it.

Still Interested? Then Read On . . .

Actors' Equity Association, the union of professional actors and stage managers in the United States, publishes a statistical summary each year of employment and earnings of its more than 30,000 members. The figures for 1991-92, the latest that are available, show a paid membership of 33,516. Of these, only 14,451 worked at some time during that period and then only for an average of 16.7 weeks, earning an average of $10,676 for the year.

Acting is tough. Unemployment is inevitable and job security is nonexistent. Even *A Chorus Line*, which ran on Broadway for 15 years, eventually closed and the actors had to move on and look for new jobs. And what about the Broadway shows that begin with great promise and close within a week or even after just one performance? This lack of job security makes it very difficult for actors to make long range plans—to get married, start a family, buy a home or a car or even go on vacation. People in other jobs take these things for granted. Then there's the constant rejection. When each job ends (and they all do) the task of job hunting begins again. The process never seems to end.

Playwright Neil Simon has called actors the bravest souls he knows. Honored by Actors' Equity Association for providing countless jobs for actors is his more than 20 plays, Mr. Simon once said:

> *It's hard to be an actor. I know of no greater act of courage than to walk out on an empty stage, seeing the silhouette of four ominous figures sitting in the darkened theatre, with your mouth drying and your fingers trembling, trying to keep the pages in your hand from rattling and trying to focus your eyes on the lines so you don't automatically skip the two most important speeches in the scene, and all the while trying to give a performance worthy of an opening night with only four pages of a play, the rest of which you know nothing about . . . and then to finally get through it, only to hear from the voice in the darkened theatre, 'Thank you . . . ' It has got to be the most painful, frustrating, and fearful experience in the world. Because with it comes a 90 percent chance of rejection. And to do it time after time, year after year, even after you've proven yourself in show after show, requires more than courage and fearlessness. It requires such dedication to your craft and to the work you've chosen for your life, that I'm sure if Equity posted a sign backstage that said, 'Any actor auditioning for this show who gets turned down will automatically be shot,' you'd still only get about a 12 percent turnaway.*

Everything you've read to this point illustrates the down side of acting. Suppose you ignore all of this and still want to be an actor, what then?

Well, if you "make it," if you can earn a living as an actor, there are several obvious advantages. There is the possibility of greater earnings than in other areas. There is also fame and celebrity. And freedom from routine. While the study of acting or playing the same part for months or even years may be tedious, the overall lifestyle is not. There is no nine-to-five routine; opportunities for travel are great, as are opportunities for creativity and learning. Depending on the role, actors have had to learn everything from horseback riding to sign language to playing the piano—skills they might not have developed otherwise.

Knowing all these pros and cons, you've made your decision—you must be an actor. What now? How do you go about getting a job? What do you do first?

The 10 Most Powerful People in American Theater

Ranked by criteria such as: authority to green light a project; influence on the future of theater; how fast phone calls are returned; size of audience generated; cash flow; and where they dine regularly.

1. Andrew Lloyd Webber
2. Frank Rich
3. Cameron Mackintosh
4. Bernie Jacobs/Gerald Schoenfeld
5. Hal Prince
6. George C. Wolfe
7. Rocco Landesman
8. Neil Simon
9. Jerry Zaks
10. Andre Bishop/Bernie Gersten

Source: *Theater Week*

How to Get Started

First, you must learn about acting. There are many acting schools and teachers throughout the country, plus colleges and universities that offer advanced training. It is important to know your way around a stage, to learn the terminology and how to take direction. Do you know that "down stage" is towards the audience and "up stage" toward the rear. Stage right is to the actor's right and stage left to the actor's left. It is also important to have a good memory. On the stage, whole scripts must be committed to memory, rather than portions as in the movies or television. If you sing and/or dance, it is important to study these skills as well.

Next, you'll need some pictures and a resume. These are essential tools of your trade. The photograph must show you off to best advantage and, most of all, should look like you. If it doesn't look the way you do when you walk in the door, then it is not doing its job. Your choice of photographer is also very important. You should shop around, talk to friends, and examine the photographer's work before deciding which one to use. It is important to use someone whose work you like and with whom you feel comfortable. Then work out the arrangements. What is the cost? Who keeps the negatives? How many enlargements do you get? How much time and film will be used? Where will the photo session take place? How long will you have to wait for the session and how long will it be before you get your pictures?

Your resume should be limited to a single page and should include all your vital statistics: name, address, telephone number, height, weight, color of eyes and hair, and experience. It should also be typewritten and neat. A word about your telephone number: you should have an answering service or a machine attached to your home phone so that you can receive messages at all times. You should also return any calls you get as quickly as possible.

Armed with a photo and resume, it is now time to start "making the rounds." There are several trade newspapers which contain casting information. Among these are *Back Stage* in New York and Los Angeles, and *Ross Reports* in New York. There is also the weekly *Variety*. In Los Angeles, there's also *Daily Variety*, the *Hollywood Reporter*, and *Drama-Logue*. Making the rounds is the process of going from office to office looking for work. Don't expect too much at first. Showcases are good places to be seen and it's always better to have a casting person see you work rather than just see your photo and resume.

There are many venues for acting work. Dinner theatre, regional theatre, summer stock, theatre for young audiences—all will provide valuable experience and contacts. Who knows? Perhaps an actor or director you work with will get another job and recommend you to be a part of the new project. Although this work can be discouraging, keep at it. Persistence often pays off. Once you get a job, you probably will have to join the Actors' Equity Association union for stage performances.

What About College?

The advantages of a college education are as obvious in the acting profession as they are anywhere else. Regular liberal arts courses broaden your general knowledge. Special theatre courses can provide a training ground for an acting career along with experience and skills that can be valuable in any number of careers. Besides, valuable theatre experience, college can also help when you have to accept nonacting jobs that every actor must take.

A final word. Acting is not an easy life, but success in the field can bring great rewards. Whether your involvement leads to a full-time career or just to a pleasurable and stimulating avocation, if that's what you really want, go for it.

An actor from the age of 11 months, **DICK MOORE** was known as Dickie Moore and appeared in over 100 films, including such screen classics as *Oliver Twist, Sergeant York, The Life of Louis Pasteur, Blonde Venus, Heaven Can Wait*, and many of the *Our Gang* comedies. As an adult, he added radio, television, summer stock, Broadway and Off-Broadway to his credits, both as an actor and director. Today, he is president of a New York-based public relations firm that bears his name and lists among its clients several organizations prominent in the performing arts. Mr. Moore is listed in *Who's Who in the American Theatre, Who's Who in the East*, and *Who's Who in Hollywood*.

HELAINE FELDMAN is a senior associate with Dick Moore Associates; a member of the Drama Desk, an association of New York theatre critics, editors, and reporters; and a member of the League of Professional Theatre Women/NY.

In the Trenches: Working as a Professional Actor

John Keith Miller, Actor

Picture yourself on stage. Hundreds of people are watching you—looking right at you. You have their undivided attention. How they feel for the next few hours hinges on *you* and anyone else with you on stage. Is that a frightening feeling or a desirable one? Or both? It's okay to say both, because if you are to become any kind of a performer, you should have a healthy nervous energy—it means you care about your performance. Now picture yourself doing this for a living. Dare I say, picture yourself working as an **actor** or **actress** for a living. That might be a desirable thought to you and a frightening thought to your loved ones, but if that ends up to be a goal, then you had better start with the nuts and bolts so those nervous loved ones know you mean it.

The Nuts and Bolts

When I moved to Chicago, I had a bachelor of arts degree in radio/television and a minor in theatre. I didn't realize *then* what a major seed that minor in theatre had planted. My first play was in a community theater in a suburb of Chicago, and I remember driving back after the first rehearsal feeling more exhilarated than ever before. Community theatre was *my* start and one I would suggest for anyone wanting to get into acting. You *have* to start somewhere, and more often than not it will be in a small venue like community or underground theatre in the city. But it means getting your feet wet without having to pay for a class. It forces you to fit several rehearsals a week into your busy schedule. It gives you the opportunity to learn and pick apart a script, and eventually—if everything goes right—to perform it. You get involved, and you get on stage. Always remember that there is absolutely no substitute for being on stage. That's how you learn, and that's how you get better.

The Nuts

Now remember, acting is a business like any other (I know... "there's no business like show business") but some guidelines do apply. You need to start with a calling card—a way to leave something along with the memory of your fabulous audition performance so the powers that be can call to offer you the part. Your resume fills this role. You also need a head shot—an 8 x 10 black and white picture with your resume attached. There are different kinds of head shots used in acting, whether it be the smiling shot for commercials or the 3/4 (most of your body visible) shot used for film and theatre. Your photographer will take a lot of every kind so, when you look at your proof sheet you will have many good options. Always make sure, however, that the head shot you choose is not only a very natural expression of your personality but a shot that really looks like you. If you have long red hair in your head shot and drop it off while auditioning with your new short blond haircut, the casting personnel will not be happy. **Look like your head shot.** And don't spend a lot of money on your photographer the first time around. Remember that once you and several people with a good eye look at your proof sheets and pick out shots, those shots go to the printer to have your name put on them and for copies to be made—and that costs money.

The Bolts

Okay, we now have our head shots and have attached our resumes detailing any experience we may have garnered in high school productions or community theatre, so let's hit the beat even harder. Peruse the local trade papers, which are usually found at theatre bookstores, for auditions and hotline numbers. Any major acting community will have hotline numbers that provide audition information. Do this with the knowledge that making money is not a factor at this point—you may not make *any* money at acting for a long time, so don't even consider it as a way to *make a living* for yourself—for now, anyway.

What can you expect from your agent? A good one (it may take a couple before you find the right one for you) will get you in to meet the casting directors in town. A good agent will submit your head shots and get you auditions—and the rest, as you can probably guess, is up to you.

So how do you get all this experience by auditioning for plays and still find the time and money to eat? I can't help you with the time problem because I don't have any myself, but what I *can* help you with are suggestions concerning the dreaded *day job*.

I won't spend much time on this because you'll just have to try several until you find the right situation, but there are several things to keep in mind. One is flexibility. There are jobs that offer great flexibility, like waiting tables at a restaurant or working through a temporary employment agency. You need a job that is flexible not only to allow you to rehearse nights and weekends but to cut away for auditions during the day. And that means auditions for commercials, television, and film.

How to Use Them to Get Work

How do you get these auditions? I knew you were going to ask that. You get an agent—look at the theatre bookstores for listings. There is a protocol to how an agent operates, and it will differ from one to the next. Once you've figured out how and when to contact them, send copies of your head shot (with resume attached). You can write a cover letter but keep it short and don't get cute. Get your resume cut down to 8 x 10—any copy store can do this. Then attach your resume to the back of your picture with one staple at the upper left and right hand corner. Look at other actors and actresses resumes for ideas, and find books in theatre bookstores for reference.

Now the process involves more than just dropping off your materials at prospective agencies. You have to *work* to get an audition or reading with them and even if they sign you, you should keep in close contact. Too many people drop off their resume and head shot and wait for the phone to ring—it won't. You must keep in contact. Stop by and say hello. Check in by phone each week to see if any opportunities are available for you and your many talents, and don't give up. No one gets discovered by sitting at home waiting for the phone to ring. If you're currently in a show, send them a flyer. It shows them you're working and that you're serious.

Keep performing on stage, and continue your training with classes that sharpen your scene study and audition skills. If you have a master's degree in theatre, that's wonderful, but it's not essential. There are many other ladders to the top. Stay positive. Keep yourself physically fit and believe in what you're doing. You will be hit with rejection on a regular basis, and if you can't handle that and keep it in perspective, this probably isn't the business for you. Always know, however, that if you stick with it long enough, your break will come. Just be ready when your chance arrives. A teacher of mine once said that plays are called "plays" for a reason—you're a player playing a part in a play. So play and have fun, and you just might make a living at it—and then some.

JOHN KEITH MILLER is an actor in Chicago. He is currently studying and performing at The Second City conservatory. He has done theatre, stand-up, and improvisation in Chicago. Mr. Miller founded his own improvisational troupe and is one of the first members of The Moveable Feast Theater Company.

Mr. Miller is a graduate of Southern Illinois University in Carbondale. He just began performance on the original work *The Big Conspiracy.*

CHAPTER THREE

There's More to Stage Acting than Broadway

Robert J. Bruyr, Executive Assistant, Communication and Education, Actors' Equity Association

For most people, being a professional **actor** means performing on Broadway. Glamour. Bright lights. If being a Broadway star is what you want, great. But there are hundreds of professional actors all over the United States who have never played on Broadway and who live a comfortable and fulfilling life working in regional, stock, and dinner theatres.

Acting, however, is unbelievably hard work, not very glamorous, emotionally and physically exhausting, and often just plain difficult. However, there is probably no other job that offers the excitement and exhilaration equal to sharing with an audience the life of a character that the actor has helped create. Entertaining, educating, and moving an audience to either laughter or tears makes the actor's job one of the most rewarding in the world.

An Actor Is . . .

What qualities should an actor possess? Since they must bring their entire wealth of life experience to each role, the ability to observe people and remember small details is crucial to success within the industry. A good memory is essential, not only for memorizing lines, but for instantly recalling an infinite number of gestures, facial expressions, and line readings that will assist in bringing a character to life. A love of reading is essential, since an actor is constantly studying the world's theatrical literature, both present and past. An enjoyment of language is helpful, since actors deal primarily with the words of the playwright's characters. Being competitive will assist an actor through the myriad auditions, and a healthy positive attitude will aid in fighting off the constant rejection resulting from those auditions.

A professional actor should be trained, either at a professional theatre school or at a university which specializes in professional theatre arts education. It doesn't really matter which—both are appropriate. And while training is essential, it will never assure stardom. There is that other something called talent. The cliche is true—you either have it or you don't. Training will not make a great actor. There must also be talent. That is not to say that an actor of limited talent won't get work. There are many creditable actors working in regional, stock, and dinner theatres, but chances are they won't end up a regular player on Broadway, nor will they be remembered for brilliant acting performances long after they are dead!

Just Do It

While training is important, the most important thing an actor can do is to actually perform, constantly testing skills and growing with each work experience. Once you begin performing, the question of when to join the Actors' Equity Association (the labor union for professional actors and stage managers in the United States) arises. For the non-Equity actor (i.e., nonunion) many job opportunities are available. However, the actor who is a member of the association may not work in nonequity productions. Equity actors are considered professionals, and as such, must be protected by an Equity contract. Thus, it is essential for the young nonunion actor to build a strong, substantial resume, and to perform many major roles before joining Equity. There will be fewer job opportunities after joining Equity; however, the benefits of Equity jobs are much greater. It is worth solidly building the non-Equity resume in order to prove that you are a fine, dependable, professional actor.

▼

The Top Five Most Powerful Actors in American Theater

Ranked by criteria such as: authority to green light a project; influence on the future of theater; how fast phone calls are returned; size of audience generated; cash flow; and where they dine regularly.

1. Bernadette Peters
2. Julie Harris
3. Kevin Kline
4. Everett Quinton
5. Chita Rivera
   Source: *Theater Week*

Early on in your career, don't be too choosy about the part. Remember the adage, "there are no small parts, only small actors." Each and every job will add something new to your experience that will serve you well in your future. Producers want to know that the actors they hire have the experience to efficiently create their roles and the discipline (that comes only from experience) to deliver the same performance eight times a week.

You're a Professional

Once you are ready to become an Equity member, and are offered an Equity contract, you will be in that exclusive league of 40,000 other Equity actors, each of whom is always ready to prove that he or she is better suited for a role than you are. The competition will be severe. You will need professional pictures and resumes, and probably an agent (perhaps more than one) in order to keep your name in front of producers and directors. You will need to be in good physical shape, as acting is a physically demanding job. You cannot be dismayed by the constant rejection at auditions. You must know, quite simply, that you are the finest actor in the world, and that soon, some lucky producer will discover this—and give you the opportunity to prove it!

Acting is different front most jobs, where once you've obtained your degree, you're basically done with the educational process. Actors are constantly training. The professional actor studies throughout his or her life. Dancing, singing, and acting lessons are a necessary and a regular part of a successful acting career, and they all cost money.

Further, actors must be able to work in film and television as well as on stage. They must work in all three mediums in order to make a living, which means knowing, among other things, how to adjust performance size to the audience—whether it is an auditorium full of people or a camera lurking only a few feet away.

Finally, an aspiring actor should also have a second job, one that will sustain him or her throughout at least the early part of an acting career. Many actors work as waiters or word processors in order to earn enough money to live as actors.

Joshua Logan, the well known American theatre director, once advised, "If anyone can talk you out of going into the theatre, let them." Actors must be able to accept constant rejection, going to audition after audition, with little hope of actually getting a job. It is quite common to go to over 100 auditions before finding any work at all. Then, after one job which is finished (usually in four to seven weeks), the actor must go back to auditioning . . . another 100 failed auditions!

The chance of great success in the theatre is minimal. Talent and being in the right place at the right time are of equal importance. Acting is definitely not the profession for the easily disillusioned.

Considering all the negatives and the positives, for the right person, acting is a career that offers an unparalleled sense of accomplishment and rewards far beyond money that cannot be found in any other profession.

ROBERT J. BRUYR worked for 25 years as a stage manager for on- and off-Broadway, stock, opera, and ballet productions. He was a Councillor of the Association before coming to the staff of Actors' Equity Association. Previous to his current position with the union, he was senior business representative, supervising the contracts of stock, League of Resident Theatres (LORT), Theatre for Young Audiences, dinner theatre, cabaret, and developing theatres, and served as chief negotiator for most of the Equity contracts employed outside of New York City.

CHAPTER FOUR

So You Think You're Funny?

Angela Shelton, The Second City—Detroit

The sound of hundreds of hushed, anxious voices filled the stagnant air of the elegant room. I leaned against an ornately decorated wall, trying to look unconcerned, confident. My palms were sweating, my muscles felt like they were hardened knots, and my heart seemed to be racing against the clock; I had never wanted anything as much as I wanted this. I had always wanted to be an actor, and I loved performing—but until this audition I never had the courage or chutzpa to try. The opportunity that this audition represented was just too great to let my lame insecurities and fears stop me from making the attempt. I had read the announcement in the newspaper just like the other 800 people at the audition, and we all knew that less than 10 of us would make it. In the end only 7 were chosen. The Second City had never held cattle call auditions like this before. This kind of opportunity comes along perhaps once in a lifetime, the chance to skip a lot of steps and jump into acting—into the greatest improvisational theater company in this country—with both feet.

For the next two months of auditioning (an extraordinarily long process, since most auditions last only a day, or perhaps a few more for call backs) I repeated my own audition mantra over and over in my head, before every exercise and during every free moment:

- be loud
- follow directions
- don't be afraid of anything

I had no real prior experience in professional theatre. In fact, the Second City audition was my first *real* audition. I knew very little about the theatre in general, and even less about the kind of improvisational comedy Second City is famous for, but I just kept repeating to myself, "Be loud, follow directions, and don't be afraid of anything." Two months later, with no professional credits, experience, or training I became a member of the first resident company of the new Detroit Second City, and a full-time, paid, professional **actor.**

Auditioning to Win

The three simple ideas I repeated over and over to myself were without a doubt the only clutch I had during this draining process. Without the background in theatre that might have helped me to feel more prepared, I could count on only these basic rules to calm myself and focus my efforts.

Be Loud

It may seem simple, but the mistake many nervous people make is simply not speaking loudly and clearly enough to be understood by the director. Always try to fill the space with your voice and energy, without yelling if it isn't necessary, showing the director that you can work in any space and still be heard.

Follow Directions

This is the most important thing to remember in any audition, and it got me through mine. If the person conducting the audition says jump—you jump, if he/she says to speak louder—speak louder. Believe it or not, in talking to producers and directors, I found out that many times the first cut in a large audition is made based on who followed simple directions—and who didn't. It is also important to ask questions when something is unclear. The director will appreciate your desire to understand what they need to see.

Don't Be Afraid of Anything

This is perhaps the most difficult rule to follow, but it is also the only one that will free you from any insecurities and allow you to perform to the best of your ability, with your own unique flair and style. Don't be afraid of the space you're in—use it to your advantage, and use your body. If you're auditioning with other people, don't be afraid to use them, or to touch them if your characters needs to interact with them. No one is confident at an audition, but if you can concentrate on the scene or the exercise, and not on the people who are watching and judging your performance, then you will have overcome your greatest barrier— **fear**.

The only way to break into the acting business is to audition. School and special training programs are helpful, and in many cases necessary. However, there are opportunities out there that require only that you come to the audition and try. The only way to get a part, or develop a stand-up routine, or break into a company like Second City, is to audition. There are tons of auditions being held daily in most cities. If the acting scene in your area isn't thriving, then you can always audition in a nearby city. The point is—you have to audition! The most difficult part of acting, whether it is dramatic or comic, is the audition. Nothing will tie you up in knots, or make you feel more insecure or less confident. That's why keeping in mind the simple things that I mentioned above will be so helpful during any audition.

Career Preparation

When I auditioned for Second City, I had no theatrical experience. I had a BA in history and a strong desire to act. In my case, going to acting school, or having a lot of experience wasn't necessary. I had a natural ability that the directors recognized to learn and perform improvisational satire. However, having educational and practical performing experience could only have helped me in my audition as well as in my career, and in any other auditions I might choose to go on. While it is not necessary to study acting in college, if you plan on being an actor, then it is highly recommended that you at least enroll in acting programs, if not in a university. If you don't want to study acting and would rather just jump into the field, then you'll have to learn as you go, picking up whatever experience you can and waiting and surviving through failure after failure. Big breaks are few and far between in theatre. Waiting for yours will require perseverance, commitment, and dedication.

The Second City

The Second City started in Chicago over 33 years ago as the only theatre of its kind—a theatre company that developed all of its material through the art of improvisation in front of an audience. Improvisational comedy (improv) is theatre without a safety net. Most of the time when we go on stage we have only a suggestion from the audience, such as healthcare, to guide our scene. In improv, the actors have to work together, in unison, as one organism working towards a common goal. The improvisational ensemble brings material to life on stage in front of an audience without any idea of where that material may lead them or how successful it might be.

Improv is a very serious art form that requires a great deal of work and practice, and the best place to study it, in this country today, is still The Second City.

Since our shows run at night, our "free time" is during the morning and afternoon, and rehearsal time is usually pre-show. On a typical show day I have to read the local and national press, watch the news, and read any popular magazines or informative journals that might help me prepare a higher reference level for the show. Because we come to the audience for suggestions to use in our improvisational games and scenes, it is important that we all know about what is going on in the news, what issues or questions are on people's minds, and understand something (if not a lot!) of a variety of topics.

The Second City has developed a reputation over the years of being on the cutting edge of political and social satire, and one of the only theatres in the world in which audience participation was a necessary part of every show. Working for The Second City is a one of a kind opportunity. Members of Second City casts have gone on to a variety of television, film, and theatre opportunities. The training that you receive at Second City will develop your skills as an actor, director, and writer. It will also eat up every spare moment of your life—but like any dream, it requires real dedication.

Being a well-rounded person is essential to acting. An actor who knows only about acting is useless in many roles, but an actor with knowledge of history or art has access to information, references, and experiences that can only enhance his/her performance. Every performance depends upon physical condition as well as the intellectual preparations we make. We have a very rigorous performance schedule at Second City with eight or more shows a week, and this requires that we be well-rested and in good physical condition. Before every show the cast engages in a physical and vocal warm-up, to stretch out all of our muscles and vocal chords. Then, to warm up our minds and get our energy level up, the cast often plays a game, usually some form of tag or duck- duck-goose. As simple as these games are, they really help our concentration and energy level. Every performance at Second City can be different, as the improvisation allows us to be new and inventive every single night, even when we don't want to. And, a lot of times, like any job, you won't feel like being funny, or you will be sick of everyone else in the cast. In an ensemble, you spend a lot of time with the other members of the cast, usually in the cramped quarters backstage or in the dressing room. While the mood backstage is usually relaxed but nervous, upbeat but exhausted, wild but restrained, it is always definitely work.

Contrary to what a lot of people might think, comedy is work. Any form of acting is hard work with little financial reward. Making the decision to be an actor or comedian means deciding to work for the love of the craft, not for huge financial rewards or instant fame. For most performers, neither fame nor fortune ever arrives at all during their careers. It takes a special kind of love for performing, a real spiritual need to entertain and create to be involved in any type of theater. You won't get paid a lot, and you won't always get the parts you want to—or even be considered for them—but you will still have to give each performance your all. An actor has to be vigilant; you must go on every and any audition, and be prepared to spend a lot of time in jobs you don't like just so that you can act and pay your bills. You have to be strong enough to take rejection and criticism and keep trying. A strong sense of your goals will help you through all of the rough times when work isn't coming your way. One of the most important traits you need to develop as an actor is independence, whether its stand-up, improv, or theater, for most of your career you will most likely be your own agent and manager. You will need to understand the operation of the different unions—Screen Actors' Guild (SAG), American Federation of Television and Radio Artists (AFTRA), and Actors' Equity Association (AEA)—and how or if you need to join them for certain kinds of work. Understanding what you're entitled to under a contract, or what deductions your eligible for on your taxes as an actor will keep you from missing the financial rewards and concessions you're allowed.

Most of all, what you need to be an actor is the ability to do it, and to say it. Every morning when you wake up say to yourself, "I am an Actor." And every single day possible, go on an audition, take a class, read a book on the history of acting, anything-just devote yourself, your soul, and your energy to your craft, and the opportunities will present themselves.

ANGELA SHELTON is a current member of the first cast of The Second City—Detroit.

Ms. Shelton studied history at the University of Michigan in Ann Arbor. She is 22 years old and was born in Cambridge, MA, and raised in Detroit, MI.

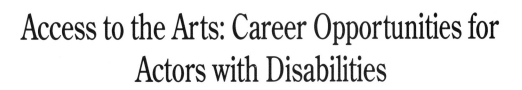

CHAPTER FIVE

Access to the Arts: Career Opportunities for Actors with Disabilities

William E. Rickert, Co-founder and Board Member, Association for Theatre and Disability

Nearly one person in six has a disability. That's over 40 million people in the United States—people who deserve to see themselves as participants in our diverse culture—people who want their own stories told. Today, in increasing numbers, actors using wheelchairs, walking with crutches, or communicating in American Sign Language are seen in professional theatre, films, television shows, and commercials for everything from fast food to pet food.

As an aspiring actor with a disability, you are hoping to join a fairly small, but growing number of nontraditional performers who are emerging to assume these roles. You bring unique qualities to the stage or screen, and they just might open up opportunities for you. That's the good news. Your disability will also present challenges that will be difficult—maybe even impossible—to overcome.

A career directory for the performing arts 10 years ago would probably not have offered advice for people with disabilities. In the past, there were few roles for persons with disabilities—and they were usually performed by nondisabled actors. Though still severely limited, opportunities for performers with disabilities have greatly increased and are still getting better. Today, if you have talent, solid training, and persistence, you have a legitimate chance to find work. However, it is *still* almost impossible for you to earn your living *strictly* as a performer with a disability. In the future, if circumstances continue to improve as they have, the outlook is likely to be brighter.

Are You Tough Enough?

Acting is hard work. It is physically taxing and emotionally draining. For every moment spent basking in the applause of an appreciative audience, there are many hours of training, auditions, and rehearsals. In addition, there is rejection and criticism—a lot of it—that you must endure. Are you tough enough? Do you have the mental and physical stamina? Can you put your all into an audition, be rejected, and do it all over again for another part? If you hesitate in answering "yes" to any of these questions, then you probably should not pursue a career as a performing artist.

All actors need to be tough, dependable, and resilient. As an actor with a disability, however, you may need to prove yourself even more than most. You might be the first person with a disability who has auditioned for a particular director—and that is likely to raise fears and concerns. Can you arrive on time and keep pace with the others? Are you prone to accidents or illness? What special needs will you have? If you have doubts about your ability, the director will, too, and you will not be cast. If you are confident, however, and openly explain any accommodations you might need for your disability, then you are much more likely to calm fears and gain trust. Fortunately for you, others have come before and proven that they can *take it* just as well as their nondisabled counterparts.

Making Your Own Rules

This is a time of transition for persons with disabilities. Attitudes are changing, and architectural barriers are coming down. The Americans with Disabilities Act (ADA) became law in 1992, and it holds great promise for citizens with disabilities to participate more fully in all aspects of society. Public facilities, schooling, and jobs that were inaccessible only a few years ago, are now open. These are exciting times, and opportunities for persons with disabilities are expanding rapidly in many fields—including the performing arts. That's good news, but the changes are happening so rapidly that what would have been good advice a few years ago might be inappropriate by the time you read this.

Therefore, rule number one is that *there are no rules*. There is no map to the secret treasure, no *right way* to do it, no fool-proof system for breaking into show business. You need to be the right person in the right place at the right time. You'll need to develop a lot of skills and be in as many places at as many times as you can. Don't just sit back and hope for a lucky break—make your own.

Good News and Bad News

The good news is that opportunities have never been better for performers who have disabilities. The bad news is that they are still extremely limited.

The good news is that persons with disabilities are getting many more parts than they used to. The bad news is that they tend to be supporting—not starring—roles.

The good news is that the number of professional actors with disabilities (your competition) is rather low. The bad news is that the number of parts actually available to them is low, too.

Neil Marcus is an artist who has made his own luck. His disability, called *dystonia,* results in muscle spasms and slowed speech that can be very hard to understand. He uses a motorized wheelchair and is certainly not a *traditional* actor. Yet Neil plays the lead role in an award-winning stage production that has toured from coast to coast and internationally since 1988. How did this happen? Neil Marcus wrote the play, *Storm Reading.*

Victoria Ann-Lewis is another actor who has made her own luck. In the 1970s, when she sought admission to acting school, she was told that she had no chance of becoming an actress because of her disability, the result of polio. Rather than accept rejection, she forged ahead with her career. You may have seen her as Peggy on *Knots*

Landing. Many others know her through her work at the Mark Taper Forum in Los Angeles, where she has developed workshops for actors and writers with disabilities.

Rick Curry, a Jesuit brother, had been discouraged from pursuing an acting career because of his physical disability. So, in 1977, he founded the National Theatre Workshop of the Handicapped (NTWH) in New York City. NTWH continues to train performers and playwrights with disabilities and to mount productions that feature their work.

The lesson to be learned from Neil Marcus, Victoria Ann-Lewis, and Rick Curry is the same; develop your own opportunities, tear down the obstacles, and find a way— any way—to get what you need. Write the script, develop the training program, produce the play.

Training and Performance Opportunities in Accessible Theatres

Necessity is indeed the mother of invention. The lack of training and performance opportunities in the 1960s and 1970s led to the development of accessible theatre companies, which offer training and performance opportunities for persons with disabilities. The NTWH is one such organization. A second is Access Theatre of Santa Barbara, CA, which has trained and employed actors with disabilities since 1979. Neil Marcus' *Storm Reading* is one of many access productions featuring performers with disabilities. Performing Arts Theatre of the Handicapped (PATH) of Carlsbad, CA, is a third such organization directly committed to training actors with disabilities.

Others—some professional, some amateur—exist in various places around the country. If there is one nearby, you should probably check it out. If there is not one nearby, then maybe you should start one!

Some of the most widely known programs to employ performers with disabilities are *theatres of the deaf.* The National Theatre of the Deaf in Chester, CT has performed in all 50 states and 24 other countries since 1967. The Fairmount Theatre of the Deaf has thrived in Cleveland, OH since 1975. Other successful theatres of the deaf are located in New York, Boston, Los Angeles, and elsewhere. In addition to these organizations, university training has long been available at the National Technical Institute for the Deaf (NTID) in Rochester, NY and at Gallaudet University in Washington, DC.

How Do You Get Started?

You definitely need actor training, and you definitely need to gain experience performing—but there is no one right way to proceed. Specialized training is available at the accessible theatre organizations mentioned above, but do not be limited to these. College and university theatre programs may have limited experience working with actors who have disabilities, but this shouldn't deter you from working with them.

There's a great deal that they can learn from you, and your unique presence will enrich their program. Other actor training programs are also available, just as they are for any nondisabled actor. Advice for performing artists found elsewhere in this volume and in other sources applies to you, too.

What Roles Can You Play?

First, it seems reasonable that persons with disabilities be cast in roles that call for a disability. If you are deaf or hearing impaired, you should certainly audition for roles wherein the character is deaf. If you have a physical disability, you should pursue roles that call for a person with limited mobility, and so on. Chicago-based actress Diana Jordan says, "I would not be working if all I did was sit around waiting for the next good disabled role to be written." While a person who uses a wheelchair is not likely to be cast as a professional football player, he/she could portray a former player, a lawyer, factory worker, or any of the countless roles that persons using wheelchairs assume in real life.

When you audition for a role that does *not* call for a disability, you may get some strange looks. You may be turned down before you ever read for the part—but read for it anyway. And come back to the next audition, and the next, and the next. Keep knocking on the door. Each time you come, your presence will seem a bit more normal to everyone (including yourself). Each time you come, you make it a somewhat easier on yourself—and on every other performer with a disability who follows.

So, should you do it? Should you, as a person with a disability, pursue a career as a professional performer? The answer is **yes**—but only if: you really understand the enormous odds against you, the frustration and rejection you will undoubtedly experience, and the sacrifices you will have to make; you are prepared to work hard, often for little pay and no security, while waiting for the *big break* that will probably never come; you have the talent, the energy, the stamina to persevere. If you accept the challenge, the journey can be as exciting and rewarding as any other I can even imagine. Ask those who are doing it—they'll tell you.

WILLIAM RICKERT, PhD, is a professor and chair of the communications department at Wright State University, Dayton,OH. He received a PhD in 1974 from the department of speech and theatre at the University of Michigan. Between 1979 and 1986, he directed numerous productions with integrated casts of actors with and without disabilities. He was co-founder of the Association for Theatre and Disability (ATD) and continues to serve on its board of directors. From 1986 to 1992, he developed and maintained the ATD data bank of information about people and programs in the field of theatre and disability.

The Broadway Musical: A Performer's Perspective

Duane Bodin, Actor

The Stage Bug Bites

kay, so you're neurotic and have a long-term ego problem to work out; you played the lead role in the last community college or high school production of *Fiddler on the Roof.* Everyone said you were brilliant— and you were. Now you need to work for a living, but the local tire plant just closed down. There *are* options: run for president or become a professional **actor.** Sounds like Robin Williams as the genie in Disney's *Aladdin,* right? Careers often begin in such a crazy way—at least in theatre.

It's been said that Broadway performers are children who refused to grow up— rebels who want to *stand out* from the crowd—to win applause, party late, sleep until noon, make big bucks, and go on the *Late Show with David Letterman* to teach him how to whistle through the space in his front teeth. This is true, in part. But Broadway is a *business,* and you're the commodity that's up for sale.

The Company Structure

The *boss* of a Broadway production is the **producer.** He's the head honcho, the money man. He hires the writer, director, choreographer, designers, and composers. Some of them, in turn, hire the performers in the time-honored process known as the *audition.* The audition procedure is not unlike the early Christians in Rome facing a hungry lion's mouth. Both the **principal (lead) actors** and the **chorus** must *audition*—there is no avoiding it. The stage and film versions of *A Chorus Line* illustrate this procedure in a heart-rendering way. I suggest you see the film.

Preparing for Success

Every craft has its tools. You may have majored in theatre in college, sang in the church choir, or taken a dance class at a local studio. In musical theatre, all of these techniques are necessary.

Because most musicals open in New York City, it should be your target. Hundreds of acting and dance schools can be found there—voice *coaches*/teachers as well. It costs money to improve your craft, so you'll need a job in the meantime. You should take dance lessons five times a week, work on scene studies, and take voice lessons at least twice a week. You could do this for months or years. As in athletics, only the best win. Your future union competition as a *pro* will be from 50 to 300 persons for each job! You must be talented, energetic, and very persistent. If you *cop-out* on these odds, be assured that most of the others won't. Faith in yourself is your engine.

First Breaks

The route to professional status in musical theatre usually begins with *summer stock*. There are about 30 of these union, summer theatres spread across the country. They often hire nonprofessionals—providing the talent is excellent. One summer of this work will get you an Actors' Equity union card, which is the passport you need to audition for future Broadway productions. However, it does not *guarantee* employment on Broadway. You can also work at nonunion stock theatres—they build experience at little pay. Summer stock producers hire/audition at the local level as well as in New York City. A professional 8 x 10 photograph and a resume detailing your experience and study should be presented at all auditions.

The Top Five Most Powerful Producers in American Theater

Ranked by criteria such as: authority to green light a project; influence on the future of theater; how fast phone calls are returned; size of audience generated; cash flow; and where they dine regularly.
  1. Andrew Lloyd Webber
  2. Cameron Mackintosh
  3. Hal Prince
  4. Rocco Landesman
  5. The Dodgers (Sherman Warner, Michael David, Ed Strong)
Source: *Theater Week*

How to Survive the Audition

Lead actors and actresses must sing well and *move* a little. These top performers are promoted by agents. Agents usually require you to have a lot of experience and talent—and prefer to see your work on stage *in action* before they will sign or represent you. Many a chorus person serving as an **understudy** has become upwardly mobile by calling an agent and offering free tickets for the night they substituted for the star or lead actor. Since salaries are negotiated by agents, actors are eager for representation. *All About Eve* is a classic film on the subject and should not be missed.

Chorus auditions on Broadway (or in summer stock) are broken into *Singers Calls* and *Dancers Calls*. **Both** types of performers are assumed to have acting ability. From hundreds, the dancers are eliminated until a dozen or so of each gender remain. The same applies for singers. The remaining singers will then dance—and the dancers will sing. This is why both disciplines must be studied. Some will be chosen to read for minor roles and understudies to the lead actors.

Physical type is important to a production. The writer and director *see* what is needed in the script. You may be a superb dancer, singer, or actor, but are too tall, short, fat, thin, or your hair may be the wrong color. You then simply go on to the next audition. Always remember that the people you audition for are only human. They can't always know the depth of your talent.

If you get chosen for the show, you will sign a Broadway Equity minimum contract in the area of $800-plus per week. If the show wins a *Tony* award, you'll have a guarantee of 2 to 10 years of further employment.

Casting Directors

Gaining influence every day is the **casting director.** Most used to work directly in the producer's office. They now have their own offices and work as *independents.* From photos and resumes, talent directories such as the *Players Guide,* and just plain networking over the phone, they sift through hundreds of professional actors who might be *type-near* what the show demands—they are the FBI of the talent world. Many casting directors were performers themselves—they know the business well.

Crossovers: Wearing Many Hats

One of Broadway's finest directors today, Hal Prince, began as a stage manager. Gene Saks is an actor, but also a director of many hit comedies and musicals. Jerry Robbins began as a dancer, then became choreographer/director for *West Side Story, Fiddler on the Roof,* and many other hit musicals. One fine lady I know crossed back and forth: she was in one show as a dancer, another as a stage manager, and yet another as the *star* of the production. She developed her career with talent, curiosity, and courage. From stage, you might cross over to film or television; from musicals to drama or comedy. A wonderful girl I worked with in *Fiddler* went on to tough days in cabaret, then became the famed *Bette Midler* of concert and film. Of course, I am citing the exceptions here—not the rule. But what's to prevent you from becoming the exception?

Those successful in theatre have ambition. In nontheatre life, they could easily have been the head of General Motors, or at least a member of Congress. Yes—that's how much energy and drive it takes to lead in the entertainment field. Few people understand this. You can and must evaluate this reality. And remember: *you are your own entrepreneur.* It ain't all rosy. What will you give up to hit your targets—a family of your own until age 35?

The Casting Couch: Sex in Show Biz

Many believe that you need to use sex to succeed on Broadway. Sure, many have. Some zoomed to the top, others fell. It's a cheap way to travel—and you don't need it. Promiscuity is a thing of the past for good reasons. There's an old Sinatra song, *I Did It My Way.* Male or female, never prostitute your talent for ambition by using beauty as barter. Some will tempt you—say no, but politely. In a corporation or in show-biz, sex has no place in your long-term career. People on Broadway aren't concerned with your sexual orientation or lifestyle. They want to create a product—that product is a smash hit.

Professional Temperament

A bad temper on Broadway can be a disaster—it has destroyed careers at star and chorus level. Broadway is known for despotic directors and choreographers—they are often cruel and insulting. Oftentimes, performers want to lash back—especially in rehearsals or just prior to opening. There may be good reason; however, one must look at the intense pressure facing the director or choreographer. With you and the rest of the cast, they must get it *just right*. They will chastise and "nanny" you. Their reputations are at stake—the critics will praise or roast them in the papers. **No one** gets a second chance on opening night. You must rise above criticism during this trying period. No matter what you may think, the creative team wants the best for you. After all, they chose you from a large number of applicants at the audition. If you are a great talent but difficult to work with, Broadway will shun you. People would rather have less talent and less headache.

What About Behind the Scenes?

The Stage Manager

The **stage manager** has one of the most stressful jobs in the theatrical production. The job requires fast reflexes and quick decision making in emergency situations. They know Murphy's Law—if something *can* go wrong, it eventually *will*. With a cast of 40, hundreds of lighting and sound cues, costumes, sets, stagehands, plus orchestra—all working together in split-second timing—the stage manager is the person who keeps it all running performance after performance. It is interesting to note that many women now hold jobs in this once male-dominated profession.

Stage managers also conduct understudy rehearsals and must not stray from the director's work. They police the running time of the show: if the curtain comes down five minutes late, the producer might have to pay hundreds of dollars of overtime to backstage workers. Special talents include steel nerves, good humor, and the ability to placate the star, stage hand, or chorus performer. If he/she is good, the stage manager usually has tenure (rare in theatre) and does the producer's next new show. They usually train at university, regional, or summer theatres. Performers often cross over to such jobs, beginning as assistants. Salaries for stage managers are excellent.

The Designers: Set, Costume, and Lighting

Set, costume, and **lighting designers** are the unsung geniuses of the theatre. Their contribution often dictates or reveals the paths that both director and performer must or can take. In doing so, they are the *silent* directors. They begin at the university level, and when their training is complete, become assistants. Producers rely on the most successful and proven designers. Actors can easily be let go, but having cost many thousands of dollars to build, it's difficult to "fire" the sets if the show gets in trouble prior to opening. Today, a Broadway musical may well cost over $4 million.

To Sum

My concentration here has been the musical stage worker. Careers in the area of music itself are an entire separate area and best left to a musician. Nor have I mentioned the many job opportunities in regional theatre, which supplies a lot of work for the *non*musical actor. In addition, in every stage production, there are wardrobe workers, stagehands, publicists, box office workers, and company managers. One comment for all: this is a very competitive business with great satisfaction—if you can land the job. If you can't, you can always become a lawyer— that's an actor without a union card.

Duane Bodin has performed in four Tony-winning shows on Broadway, and his career has spanned some 25 years of musical theatre in New York City. He has worked as a dancer, singer, stage manager, director, and choreographer. Prior to theatre, he worked in other entertainment media, and traveled from the Far East to Europe under cultural exchange programs via the State Department. He currently resides in New York City.

Preparing for a Career as a General Director in Opera

Richard Marshall, DMA, Director,
Center for Contemporary Opera

I n the past 20 years, there has been dramatic growth in the number of professional opera companies in the United States, thereby increasing opportunities for employment in opera production. Despite this growth, however, the field is small and openings are few. A company may use an orchestra of 40, but there is only one **general director** (GD). Out of a field of perhaps 96 companies offering full- or part-time employment, there will be only 96 GDs. Only a small number of these positions, if any, open up in any given year, as a result of either retirement, movement to another position, or termination. The best way to find out about these openings is by networking in the opera community, since positions are often filled by the time they are announced. A good avenue for networking is attendance at opera conferences, particularly those of OPERA America.

The Director Does It All

A GD of an opera company should have thorough knowledge of all areas of opera production and management: repertory, singing, stage directing, designing, technical directing, conducting, fund-raising, budgeting, bookkeeping, promoting, and marketing; and becoming acquainted with the community in which the opera company is located is a must. In a very small company, the GD may have to assume many of these responsibilities personally. However, in large companies, entire departments may exist for each area. If the GD also acts as the artistic director, choosing the repertory for each season is an additional responsibility. This requires knowing which singers will be needed, deciding on the basic concept behind the production, and hiring the personnel to carry out each part of the production. This includes: the stage director, music director, production manager, scenic designer, costume designer, and all other necessary personnel. In larger companies, many of these people are regular employees. In addition, the GD is responsible for preparing

27

budgets, establishing personnel policies, bargaining with unions, assuring that proper accounting practices are followed, and preparing an annual report.

Fund-raising

The GD is also responsible for assuring the company's financial security. In some companies, this becomes the GD's dominant role. For instance, Beverly Sills, the former head of the New York City Opera, was primarily a fund-raiser. This involves everything from personal solicitation of donors to conducting basic research of foundations, government programs, and cultivation of individuals. Again, the smaller the company, the more the responsibility rests directly on the GD's shoulders. Also, the company's board of directors should have a development committee that is involved directly in fund-raising or that helps to supply the contacts needed for the GD and production staff to carry out this work. Without money, a company ceases to exist.

The Board of Directors

The board of directors determines the major boundaries in which the GD works—but the GD has the ultimate responsibility for running the company. Therefore, he/she *must* run a tight ship. Often, the GD is more adventuresome than the board, which tends to be conservative. The GD must be careful that any innovations that have been undertaken have been carefully thought out and discussed with the board of directors. Franklin D. Roosevelt knew that to lead, he had to follow. Remember to *bring the board along with you—or they will move the company along without you.*

Getting Started

If your community supports any performing arts organizations, become involved as a volunteer. Anyone hoping to administer an arts organization must have the initiative and willingness to work hard at whatever areas are open and learn everything possible. The more areas of expertise you have, the more likely you are to secure a position.

Some arts administration programs now exist in several universities, which can provide some preparation, while regular business courses can provide training in business skills. It is not necessary to be professionally competent in *all* areas, but one must have basic understanding of each skill. Above all, one must understand the politics of working with a board of directors. Failure to master this skill may shorten the term of employment drastically, no matter how well other tasks are being carried out. Life experience and learning to be sensitive to the needs of others are the best training ground for this.

OPERA America provides information on available apprenticeship programs for beginners needing administrative experience. OPERA America is a membership organization for opera companies in North America. It is a good place to start looking when searching for a position, since it has listings of all of its member companies along with the names of the directors, and its newsletter announces openings. There is also ArtSEARCH, the National Jobs Bulletin for the performing arts, which lists more than 6,000 jobs per year from more than 1,000 advertisers. Universities with arts administration courses may also assist in finding apprenticeship openings.

Once you have a job, promotion may be slow or non-existent. But openings do occur in other companies, allowing you to upgrade your employment. Again, the more you network and get acquainted with the operatic world, the more successful you will be in finding jobs.

If you are interested in a 9-to-5 job, the arts are not the place to be, especially if you wish to become the GD. Small companies run the risk of burning out their staff, who are often extremely dedicated. Because of limited funds, it is often impossible to hire the personnel needed, and workers must take on extra assignments.

GDs typically come from a variety of backgrounds, but usually from either a business or performance concentration. GDs that serve in both a business and artistic capacity must have a thorough background in both disciplines. Some boards prefer that the GD not be involved in the performance work itself, believing the GD has enough to do in running the company. Be sure you are clear about your own desires and those of the board before you assume a directorship. Conflicts in these areas can be devastating. In the end, what the board wishes usually prevails.

Salaries

There are occasional surveys indicating salary levels for general directors in opera companies. You will probably start out earning around $15,000 to $20,000, although rates are extremely variable. The larger the company, the higher the salary is apt to be—but salaries and benefits will always be on the low side, not comparable with those in business. Opera is a labor-intensive art form, therefore very expensive, and as most money must be raised through contributions and grants, there is never enough. Most opera companies run deficits and have little ability to offer high salaries. In fact, star performers usually earn more than the GD.

Be Your Own Boss

Another avenue to becoming a GD is to start your own company. Several companies in the United States today were started by one individual with the tenacity and skill to make it successful. Unless you intend to become a commercial business— such as a Broadway production company, where you locate investors who wish to *profit* from their investment, you should register as a not-for-profit organization. To do this, you should find out what the Internal Revenue Service (IRS) and state registration requirements are for setting up a charity organization. An attorney can help with this procedure.

Starting your own company requires first forming a not-for-profit corporation. You must also have a board of directors. This usually means three or more persons and can include yourself. The board of directors oversees the operation of the company—but may not receive compensation. (You can be paid for your administrative and artistic work, but not your board work.)

Then, you must write by-laws designating how your company is to operate. Use another company's by-laws for reference and ask a lawyer for help. These by-laws should contain a mission statement, which states what the company is in business to do. It should state whether or not it is a membership corporation. It also determines the terms of office of board members, how you hire and fire employees, where the lines of authority are drawn, the parameters of your fiscal year, and what happens to the company's assets if it ceases to exist. On the basis of these by-laws, the IRS will make an initial determination of whether or not it is a public charity. Later, they will review your reports and make a final decision. After setting up your business, you have to raise money, find a place to perform, hire performers, and sell your product.

Do It Now

There are no guarantees of success in this field. But the more dedicated you are, the more skills you have, and the more resourceful you are, the more you are apt to succeed. This is a job for an entrepreneur. If you *do* make it, it can be most exciting and rewarding. Interest in the art form is burgeoning, so this is a good time to start a career in opera.

RICHARD MARSHALL is founder and general director/artistic director of the Center for Contemporary Opera in New York City. He was formerly general director of the Charlotte (NC) Opera, head of opera at the Boston Conservatory of Music, founder and director of the New England Regional Opera in Boston, and head of opera and choral music at the University of Buffalo (NY). He has a doctor of music in opera degree from Indiana University.

Marshall has produced, conducted, and staged over 60 operas. In Charlotte, he commissioned, produced, and conducted the world premiere of *Abelard and Heloise* by Pulitzer Prize-winning composer Robert Ward, which was taped for presentation on national television. He brought several first productions of American works to Boston and New York. Marshall was presented with the Award for Service to Opera by the Performing Arts Association for his work in New England.

The Choreographer: Who Are They? What Do They Do? How Can You Become One?

**Norman Walker, Director,
Adelphi University Dance Program**

magine that you are a playwright and that you have to teach each line to your actors as you are creating those words. *Now* imagine that you also have to direct these actors in the whys and wherefores of what they are saying. In other words, you are functioning as the playwright and the director at the same time. This is what a **choreographer** does, using movement, not dialogue, as a means of communication. This dual function is what makes the choreographer a unique and special person in the field of dance. It makes no difference whether you work in classical ballet, contemporary dance, jazz, broadway, or television—your job is the same. You are responsible for creating the steps and movements, teaching them to the performers, and then directing them in such a way that what you are trying to get across is clear, direct, and holds the interest of your audience.

An Act of Creation

Young people sometimes confuse choreography with staged movement. A **choreographer** invents movement and steps, and puts them together in new and surprising ways. Someone who stages movement borrows from a lot of stock steps, movements, and gestures, and arranges them in familiar ways. The creation of new and original dances is not a part of this work, and the result is what you see in many television dance routines—something ordinary, common, and everyday. When we talk about a choreographer we are talking about someone who is constantly exploring the new, the unusual, and the exciting. Of course, a very good television director can, with the aid of technological tricks, make an ordinary routine look better than it is.

Laying the Groundwork

Becoming a successful choreographer requires preparation in many areas. First of all, you must have been a dancer yourself. The experience of having performed is essential if you are to communicate that to another person. It is not necessary that you be a *great* dancer, but rather that you have gone through the discipline that makes a dancer. This includes: the daily schedule of classes for many years, the discipline of rehearsals under a diverse number of choreographers, the preparation for performance, the wearing and use of costumes, the manipulation of props, the application of makeup, and finally, the performance itself. As a choreographer you will often have to guide young dancers through all of these areas, as well as play confidant, therapist, and father/mother figure. Are you ready for all of that? Well, if you are, and you have a burning need to express yourself through the creation of dance, then perhaps you are ready to think about a career as a choreographer.

Now that you have been—or are—a dancer, you are beginning to feel that insatiable desire to do more than just perform—perhaps you want to create dances of your own. What should you know about choreography before you try it on your own? You must first realize that there is a craft involved. It is not just talent and inspiration—there is a lot of hard work to go through first. You have to learn how to use music, how to listen to music, and how to count with the music so that you can make use of its inherent rhythms and beat. You have to discover space and its properties. You also need to acquire a familiarity with the concept of time and how it is perceived. You have to gain a certain mastery over form, or the shape of the entire work. And you have to discover the best means to project what it is you want to say—this means you must first have something to say.

There are many aspiring choreographers and very few successful ones. This is true in all of the various fields. In the ballet and concert field, the rewards are seldom monetary. You enter these fields because you love them so much that nothing else will satisfy you. In musical theatre, film, and video the monetary rewards are much greater. There are a number of successful choreographers in these areas who make very comfortable livings.

Go Back to School

One of the best places to get this training is in a good dance department in a university. There you have the most concentrated education for potential choreographers available. In a university setting you have the opportunity to learn about music, theatre, painting, sculpture, costuming, design, and almost any other area of knowledge that is helpful to the development of a young creative artist. In a university setting you will also have the opportunity to see and study the works of other choreographers, both the masters in the field and the up-and-coming. Many successful choreographers have started their careers in university dance departments.

Another advantage of attending and studying at a good dance department is the possibility of presenting your initial endeavors in a professional atmosphere. Here you can choose your dancers, have costumes designed and made for the work, collaborate with a lighting designer to enhance the look of your creation, and afterwards learn from critical discussion and feedback. This is invaluable as it will stimulate your own critical faculties and assist you in your future work. It is possible for you to get *some* of this education from a few of the private dance studios. It is *not* possible for you to get *all* of the above in one place outside of a university.

Learn From the Masters

It is also possible for you to get your initial opportunities if you are a member of a permanent dance company (e.g., the New York City Ballet, the San Francisco Ballet, the Martha Graham Dance Co., the Paul Taylor Dance Co., etc.). There are many more that often conduct workshops for their dancers, so that they might try their hand at choreographing. They will often give workshop (informal) performances of some of these attempts. The problem here is that no formal training is usually involved. The advantage is that as a young, aspiring, choreographer you will be working closely with some of the greatest choreographers of our time and learning by being involved in the creation of new works. Sitting at the feet of the masters is a great spark that will help kindle the flame of creative impulse.

Getting Your Feet Wet

Young choreographers in the concert field often have to design their own costumes, so a knowledge of fabric and materials is essential. It is also a good idea to have a practical knowledge of lighting, as you will frequently be incorporating lighting ideas into the choreography itself. If you don't know what is possible, you may end up frustrated at not seeing your vision come alive on stage as you imagined. But if you are knowledgeable about these ideas then you will truly be able to realize your vision.

In the areas of film and video you will need to know as much about camera and editing techniques as a director does. With the constant advances in the area of video technology, it is also important for you to learn and experiment with new developments so that you can incorporate them into your work. There is also the possibility that soon you will be able to choreograph video dance right at the control console without the use of live dancers. Fortunately, that is still in the future.

Once you have choreographed several pieces it is a good idea to enter a choreographic competition. *Dance Magazine* is the best source of information for this. Not only will it be helpful to your ego if you win, but it will also give your work wider exposure, as many company directors attend these competitions. It is essential that you try to obtain high quality videos of your work, as this is the most convenient means by which you can send your work to competitions and possibly dance companies. No one will hire you until they have seen your work—if not in person, then on a good video presentation. Finding the opportunity for your choreography to be seen by company directors—and finally by the public—is what will bring you more and more work. And constant choreographing is the best way to improve your work.

Your Future

In the ballet and concert fields the successful choreographer commonly becomes, after many years, the artistic director. This is a natural progression, as the personal vision of the company's choreographer often becomes the artistic vision of the company itself. Martha Graham, Paul Taylor, Bruce Marks (Boston Ballet), George Balanchine, and now Peter Martins (New York City Ballet) are examples of such success. In musical theatre, choreographers often become directors, just as Jerome Robbins, Bob Fosse, Michael Bennett, Gower Champion, and Tommy Tune went on to do. This is also true for film and video.

It is not uncommon for the future choreographer to work for a period of years as an assistant to a successful choreographer. This has many advantages, especially in the commercial fields. You will get to work with someone who is established , you will meet others who are in the field, and most important of all, many times you will be recommended by your boss for a job that he/she is too busy to take work on. It is a very effective way of getting started.

If you must choreograph then you will find the way to do so. There is no greater joy than seeing your vision realized in a beautifully mounted and performed production. It's what keeps us all going. Good luck!

NORMAN WALKER is presently director of the dance program at Adelphi University. He is the choreographer of over 180 produced works which have been seen all over the United States, South America, Canada, Europe, Russia, China, Southeast Asia, etc. His works have been mounted by such diverse companies as the Joffrey Ballet, the Harkness Ballet, the Alvin Ailey Dance Theatre, Dennis Wayne's Dancers, Ballet Philippines, the Central Ballet of China, Norman Walker Dance Co., and many more.

Mr. Walker is also an internationally renowned teacher of dance technique and choreography. He was born, and presently resides, in New York City.

CHAPTER NINE

So You Want to Be a Ballet Dancer?

**Jan Hanniford Goetz, Director,
Huntington School of Ballet**

f the soul stirring sounds of magnificent music have always made you dream of the day when you might bring that music to life, bathed in the warm glow of a spotlight, soaring through the cavernous emptiness of a stage, then in the words of the late great American icon, Agnes De Mille, "(So) . . . you want to be a dancer." Chances are, if classical ballet is the career path you have chosen, you made that decision very early in life. Ironically, most budding professionals decide they will dance when they grow up long before they have any knowledge of what a dancer's life is like. My personal experience was very much an odyssey into the exotic unknown. While my odyssey culminated in a fine and rewarding performing career, I strongly recommend that serious dance students do a bit of career planning.

Training

It is a generally accepted rule of thumb that 10 years is required to train a fine ballet dancer. Since most professional ballet dancers begin their careers between the ages of 18 and 20, they must begin their serious training at a respectable school somewhere around age eight. Indeed, many children begin training as early as age three or four with creative movement classes. While these classes offer children a delightful taste of musicality and movement, they are hardly a requirement for an ultimate career.

Hopefully, by the time students reach the ripe old age of 13, they will be studying five to six days a week—one and one-half hours on days when a technique-only class is offered to six hours per day on days with varied classes and rehearsal. If your course of study is not this rigorous, don't panic. However, do pause to evaluate your goals. The field of professional ballet is extremely competitive and success requires serious training.

Now you're a junior in high school, have studied hard and still love the strenuous work and long hours associated with ballet dancing. How do you make the all-important transition from student to professional? I recommend that my students make a dream list of which ballet company they would like to work for (if they could choose) in order of preference. Compiling this list requires a bit of research. Aspiring young dancers should know as much about various ballet companies as possible. This knowledge can be gained by seeing professional companies perform live, as well as renting video tapes from the local library and reading dance publications such as *Dance Magazine*. What you are looking for is an understanding about what differentiates one company from another. Is the "style" of the company classical, modern, or eclectic? Does the company appear to have rigid body requirements, (i.e., all the female dancers are long limbed, tall, and thin)? Is the company relatively large (50 dancers or more) or rather small? Does the company perform the works of many choreographers or predominantly one? Answering these questions will provide two important impressions: one, does the company provide the career opportunities you are looking for, and two, will your qualities as a dancer fit into this homogeneous group of professionals?

Professional ballet companies often have affiliations with official schools that offer wonderful training programs for serious students. If, for example, you live in Iowa City and aspire to dance with Boston Ballet, you might consider auditioning for the Boston Ballet summer school program. In fact, it was in a Joffrey Ballet summer program that I first became affiliated with the Joffrey Ballet School. I was invited back with a full scholarship the following summer, seen in class by Mr. Joffrey, and invited to join the Joffrey Ballet Company.

Once you've narrowed your "A" list down to six or eight companies, it is time to do some specific research. Call the company in question and let them know you are interested in auditioning. Very often ballet companies do "audition tours" to major U.S. cities. However, I feel, if possible, that it's far better to be seen in a company's own environment. Ask if you can take "company class" in the company's hometown. That way the artistic director gets the opportunity to see you dance with the company dancers rather than at a cattle call with hundreds of other hopefuls. If the company is full or you are not quite strong enough, the director may offer you a scholarship to study at the school with which the company is associated. This is a definite indication of interest in you as a dancer. In fact, this is another viable method of being seen by the company of your choice.

Performing

The magic moment has arrived, you too have been invited to join the company of your choice. You are elated and just a little frightened. A bit of knowledge should help calm your new dancer jitters. If the company is in the middle of a performing season you may be required to understudy a role in one or many ballets. Don't take this responsibility lightly. Unexpected things often happen in the theatre and you may be "on" long before you expect. A typical performance day schedule includes class in the morning, usually between the hours of 9:00 and 10:00 a.m., for approximately one and a half hours, followed by up to three hours of rehearsal. Rehearsals usually end by 6:00 p.m., allowing just enough time to prepare for an 8:00 p.m. performance. Considering that performing seasons may run as long as six to eight weeks, six days a week of this schedule can get to be very debilitating. Rehearsal periods can also be quite strenuous. An average day begins with a one and one-half hour class (ballet dancers never stop taking class) followed by up to six hours of rehearsal five days per week.

Professional ballet companies usually alternate rehearsal and performance periods, with the rehearsal periods taking place in the company's hometown. Most companies also do at least one performing season in their hometown followed by out of town tours. For me, touring was one of the magnificent fringe benefits of working for a ballet company. I've traveled extensively throughout the United States, visited Mexico and the U.S.S.R. with the Joffrey Ballet, seen most of Italy and Switzerland with A.T.E.R. Balletto, and, I think, every square inch of Holland with the Netherlands Dance Theatre (not to mention Prague, Vienna, and Paris). Working in a city allows a dancer a much different view of the city than that of a tourist and can be a wonderfully enriching life experience.

Salaries

Now we will consider the issue of money, which brings to mind a song from the much loved Broadway show, *A Chorus Line*, entitled "What I Did for Love." While love is indeed the primary motivator for most dancers, the financial picture is far more optimistic than it once was. Dancers' salaries are governed by collective bargaining agreement between the American Guild of Musical Artists (AGMA), the union that represents dancers and individual companies. Entry-level salaries vary greatly from company to company. A major ballet company such as the American Ballet Theatre (ABT) offers its new dancers (dancers with no professional experience) $509 per week. However, due to ABT's desperate financial situation, the 1993 contract guaranteed only 25 weeks of work. Principal dancers' salaries start at $1,275 per week. Principal dancers are free to negotiate salaries above the minimum rate based upon their personal prestige as well as the importance of the roles they perform. Ultimately, principal dancers can expect to earn a salary in the range of $70,000 per year. Generally, ballet companies guarantee their dancers at least 36 weeks of employment, with the best contracts offering 44 to 45 weeks of work.

Conclusion

Most dancers dream of one day performing leading roles. How long it might take for a dancer to transition from corps member to soloist and then to principal is highly individual and, of course, there are no guarantees this transition will take place at all. It is not unusual for a dancer to spend four to six years in the corps de ballet of a large company, while another dancer may be offered a soloist contract in their second year of employment.

Career information is vital to making informed decisions. However, dancing is more than just a career. For those who succeed, it is the stuff of which life itself is made. Stay healthy, keep your goals in focus, work hard, and the world will indeed become your stage. Good luck and happy dancing.

JAN HANNIFORD GOETZ began her international career at the age of 17 when she was invited to join the Joffrey Ballet, performing principal roles in ballets choreographed by many of the world's best-known and best-loved choreographers. After leaving the Joffrey, she joined the A.T.E.R. Balletto in Italy with the coveted title of Prima Ballerina. From here she moved to Holland as a member of the Netherlands Dance Theatre. In May of 1992, Ms. Goetz was given the Saraband Award for "Service to Youth in the Arts," in recognition of the dedication to nurturing and inspiring her young dancers.

Ms. Goetz has trained students who dance with internationally recognized ballet companies such as the National Ballet of Canada, the Pittsburgh Ballet Theatre, the Cleveland Ballet, the Joffrey II, and the St. Louis Ballet. Her students have appeared in productions with the Royal Ballet and the New York City Ballet, and received numerous scholarships to such prestigious summer programs as New York State Summer School of the Arts at Saratoga, the Boston Ballet, the Pacific Northwest Ballet, the Washington Ballet, the Joffrey Ballet, and the School of the American Ballet.

Careers in Dance: Working as an Artistic Director, Instructor, or Choreographer

Debra Jean White-Hunt, Founder and Artistic Director, Detroit-Windsor Dance Academy/Company

s artistic director and founder of a dance academy and company, my responsibilities are endless. However, the rewards of my job are what makes life exciting and fulfilling.

Artistic Directors Wear Many Different Hats

As **artistic director,** one is responsible for the overall artistic quality of everything on the stage—from the dancers' readiness and choreography to the quality of the lighting, sound, set, costumes, instructors, etc. In addition, the artistic director must oversee the artistic quality of written programs, photographs, or anything that represents the organization. As the visionary, motivator, and many times the driving force behind the school and company, the artistic director must be dedicated, hard working, and determined to succeed.

Other hats that the artistic director may wear include that of choreographer, dance instructor, and performer. These jobs require somewhat different skills and preparation, though they combine to best complete the whole.

Choreographer

The function of a **choreographer** is to create and arrange dances. This person must have a vision to bring to life through the art of dance. Many times as choreographer, I am motivated by music to create movement. Music becomes the catalyst that touches something deep within and gives birth to motion.

Dance Instructor

A **dance instructor** is responsible for teaching students the art of dance. Instruction includes teaching technique, theory, performance skills, history, self-discipline, building self-esteem, and much more. Many dance companies—though not all—have a school that acts as the training facility for future performers, both amateur and professional.

Performer

As a **performer,** the artistic director may be just one of many other dancers. They may have to work with other choreographers or cast themselves in *their own* choreography. The artistic director must be flexible.

Steps to a Career in Dance

Becoming an artistic director is generally the result of many years of success in the art of dance. The typical path to a dance career includes first being a student. Some students then move on to a dancer apprenticeship position (where those with great potential are selected to work along with professionals to receive more training). The final step is to become a **professional dancer,** one who earns a living—though sometimes slight—through dance. Formal education is very helpful but is not necessarily required.Many artistic directors have not been formally educated. A good course of study for those who wish to attend college, however, would be classes in dance and theatre, as well as education, administration, business, public speaking, and writing.

An ideal candidate for this position is some one with basic and advanced dance skills who is dedicated to the art form, capable of working long hours, has had a background in successful choreography (or recognizes good choreography), has good people skills, is organized, has political savvy, and has a decent personal performance record. A person in this position must also be well-groomed and articulate.

Choreographer

As a choreographer, good people skills are an asset. You may work with various companies and with many different personalities—including dancers who are extremely gifted and talented, but who may have been pampered and show signs of diva-ism (and otherwise potentially irritating traits).

Dance Instructor

As a teacher, it is imperative to learn as much as possible about *many* dance forms, though many teachers choose to *specialize.* In today's market, many dance forms overlap, and the more experience one possesses in a variety of forms, the better he/she will be able to give students an interesting and well-rounded dance education and experience.

In most states, a college degree and teaching certificate are necessary to teach in the public schools. Some school systems require dance teachers to be certified in physical education as well. Dance teachers in public schools are not usually given a full schedule of dance classes, due to curriculum or budget constraints. The public school system where I have taught for more than 20 years includes more than 22 high schools. Full dance programs exist in most, as well as in many district middle and elementary schools. This reality, however, does not exist in many states. It is important to research your school district of interest prior to applying for a position to see what is available and what the state requirements are—they do vary. A student matriculating in college will find this knowledge most valuable for future employment.

A teacher in a private dance studio is generally hired as a result of his/her individual background and preparation. Referrals are also important. Teachers of dance should always have a resume and background materials available to present to potential employers. Teachers should be careful not to be *bridge burners*—the dance community typically is quite small and can often be harmfully competitive. No matter what area a person chooses for a dance career—professional or educational—having a love for people, children in particular, is a necessity for happiness and success.

The Typical Day of an Artistic Director

The career of an artistic director can be quite unpredictable. A *typical* day is *atypical*. An artistic director has many responsibilities, so it is important to be well-organized, as one's role may need to shift from artist to businessperson. Being a businessperson sometimes requires being shrewd and stern. On the other hand, as an artist, one must be in touch with the emotional self, be compassionate, warm, and open.

Being an artistic director requires dedication, perseverance, and commitment. A day in the life of an artistic director can include choreography conducting rehearsals, media interviews, planning fund-raisers and concerts, meeting with costume designers, returning telephone calls, addressing irate parents, researching

To prepare for a career in dance, one should seek out a mentor to work with, or volunteer in a dance school/company and learn the business from the ground up. Getting involved at a young age definitely has its advantages—though I have found that those who have waited until after high school or college generally are more serious, focused, and able to advance quickly.

music, writing grants, and coping with adult staff needs and conflicts. Most artistic directors are also founders of their own companies. Some have taken over companies whose artistic director has passed away or left for other reasons. Artistic directors have a burning desire to be in control of their artistic yearnings and to have the vehicle to express that need. This is not always to be thought of as egotistical, but more as a spiritual longing. Many times, a person cannot be at peace until they get this creative energy expressed or channelled.

What About Money?

Salaries in dance careers vary. As my company is a nonprofit organization, it is dedicated to providing a service to the community. We work with a minimum budget, and though we would all love to be financially independent, we sometimes seem to be working at a poverty level. That surely doesn't sound very exciting, but this business has such potential for financial growth, that a high salary is totally dependent on one's willingness to work, be innovative, and create new income sources.

There are many fringe benefits that parallel this job. One of *my* favorite is traveling. There are many opportunities to travel domestically and internationally. Most performances are underwritten, so they are at no cost to the company and staff. In this field, there is no limit to growth potential. In five years one's salary can double or triple. In 10 years, it can do the same—it just depends on the artistic excellence of the dance company and one's willingness to work hard. Conversely, one's salary can drop if one does *not* produce.

Artistic directors/founders of a dance company typically start with no regular income.Once the organization grows, one can expect an income of $200 per week or more. Once established in a fairly large, well-known company of national status, the yearly income can rise into the high five or six figures. Dance academies and companies typically work in seasons. Therefore, one has to be prepared to also *live* during the off-season (usually the summer months) and should prepare and budget accordingly. Many professional dancers line up at the unemployment office during off-season.

Moving on

If one were to leave the position of artistic director, it is possible to be hired for other creative positions on name recognition alone, as often times the artistic director of a successful dance company is very visible and considered a celebrity in the community. Related industries include other arts fields and college and/or university professorships. As most dancers must struggle financially to make ends meet, one would be wise to have another career interest. Though we, as artists, may have financial desires, we usually are not motivated by the dollar. There is a greater motivation for us and this is what makes us who we are.

After reading this chapter, one may wonder why anyone would want to pursue an artistic directing career, but for me and other artistic director's that I know, the answer to that question is, "You just don't always have a choice—sometimes it's a *calling*".

DEBRA WHITE-HUNT, founder and artistic director of the Detroit-Windsor Dance Academy and the Detroit-Windsor Dance Company, is a native Detroiter who has danced, taught, choreographed, and performed on stage, television, and video. After attending public schools in Detroit, she went on to receive her BA in theatre and dance from Michigan State University and her master's in education from Wayne State University. Ms. White-Hunt has taught dance for more than 20 years in the New York and Detroit public school systems and has completed dance residencies in Australia, New York, California, Minnesota, Michigan, Canada, and Bermuda.

As a result of her work, Debra has received numerous awards. In 1987, she was one of seven Americans selected by the Kennedy Center to travel to Australia to study the Aborigines and their dance forms. She also choreographed and set an American jazz piece on Australian dancers, as well as taught and danced. In 1990, Debra received the *Nobel Prize of Education*, the Michigan and National Educator Award. Ms. Hunt was the 1990 *Detroit News* Michiganian of the Year and has been recognized by the Detroit City Council, state senators and representatives, the mayor, the Detroit Board of Education and others.

In 1988, she was selected as Dance Teacher of the Year by the Michigan Dance Association. In January, 1992, she was again saluted by the Detroit City Council and The Development Centers for her ability to rise against the odds. Most recently, (November, 1993) Ms. White-Hunt was awarded the Payne Pulliam Door Opener's Award.

Ms. White-Hunt is married to Bruce Hunt and has a step-daughter, Alise.

Composing Concert Music: The Joys and Hardships

David Cleary, DMA, Composer

Being a **"classical"** or **concert music composer** is very rewarding. The act of composing—solving complex and engrossing musical issues, watching your compositional dreams materialize on paper, shaping a wonderful little world of your own in the privacy of your studio—holds a unique appeal. It is most stimulating to hear your ideas take shape while coaching or conducting your work with sympathetic musicians. And there is nothing more exhilarating than hearing your newest compositions played inspiringly by savvy, well-rehearsed performers before an appreciative audience. Numerous problems and frustrations come with this career too, such as long hours of isolation, a conspicuous lack of financial backing and mass audience support, dealings with the occasional unsympathetic or incompetent performer/conductor, the unbelievable level of competition for scarce opportunities, and the impossibility of earning a steady living in the field.

Expertise You Will Need

Innate abilities most conducive to a concert music composing career include the following:

- **A good ear**—defined as the ability to hear music perceptively and critically. Without this you cannot effectively write music at all.

- A burning **desire to create music**—this must be stronger than the desire to earn a lot of money or have constant ego support, as you will get precious little of either.

- Extraordinary **patience** and **perseverance**—since there are few opportunities and the field is highly competitive.

- Good **interpersonal skills** (or the desire to cultivate them)—you will gain many of your opportunities through personal contacts and you will need to effectively rehearse the musicians who play your pieces.

Acquired skills necessary to concert music composers include:

- The **ability to play an instrument**, preferably piano or a similar keyboard instrument. This is needed in order to reproduce your music for yourself and others.

- **Knowledge of music theory, orchestration,** and **compositional techniques,** obtained ideally through a university program or perhaps private study. Normally, one or more degrees in music composition is considered mandatory.

- A deep **familiarity with** both the standard and current **concert music literature.**

Getting Started

A career path for concert music composers typically begins with attempts to write music at a young age (in a sense, few people choose to compose—composing chooses them). Those who are serious about the discipline attend music colleges and study with one or more composition teachers while there. Building useful contacts is crucial, so start now; make sure your teacher will not only instruct you in composition but will also help you with such real-world matters as resumes, reference letters, supportive phone calls, and practical advice. Be active and known among performers and fellow composers at your school; such contacts can be invaluable to you after graduation.

Your composition degree(s) will give you basic credence as a composer; a doctoral degree in the field will also qualify you for college teaching jobs (if you can find any). Unfortunately, these diplomas are highly specialized and do not transfer well to other disciplines. If you want to work as a nonmusic professional, you must get appropriate degrees or certification for that field, separate from your music diploma(s).

Supplementing Your Composition Income

At this juncture, you must hear the bad news: no concert music composer can adequately support himself from his works alone. If you want to eventually earn a living composing music, you must do so by:

- Writing jingles or other commercial music
- Writing music for movies and other soundtracks
- Writing rock-and-roll or other popular music that sells

The market for all these options is even more competitive than that for concert music. If you hope to pursue one of these other careers while writing the music you really want "on the side," you will instead find yourself swamped with the demands of your money-making composing, likely having little time or energy left to write good concert music. You will also run the risk of having other concert music composers not take your art music seriously because you are a "popular composer." Leonard Bernstein was one of very few composers able to successfully combine popular and concert music careers.

Even the most prestigious concert music composers today must have a second, more reliable source of income. The two types of adjunct jobs most useful to composers are:

▼

The Money Jobs Ranking

Listed below are the rankings of 11 out of 100 jobs as evaluated by *Money* in 1992.
1. Biologist
2. Geologist
3. Physician
4. College math professor
5. High school principal
6. Sociologist
7. Pharmacist
8. Urban planner
9. Civil engineer
10. Veterinarian
23. **Orchestral musician**
Source: *Money*

- Less-taxing posts that will leave a maximum of time and/or mental energy to compose (e.g., working as a free-lance recording engineer who tapes live recitals; copying music; teaching private students; working in the service industry as a store clerk, library assistant, cab driver, bartender, etc.). Unfortunately, most such jobs pay poorly or sporadically—or both. Some of these posts can also be physically or emotionally draining.

- Positions that offer strong side benefits, such as performer contacts or free photocopy machine access, that are useful to a composing career (e.g., college teacher, free-lance performer, music editor, radio production or technical worker, recording industry employee, music critic, conductor). Unfortunately, most of these posts are unbelievably competitive or time-demanding—or both.

Many composers combine two or more of these adjunct jobs to earn an adequate living.

Money Matters

How meager is the money for concert music composers? Most grants/fellowships range from $100 to $5,000, contests $200 to $2,500, commissions $100 to $5,000 (a few prestigious grants, like the Guggenheim, will pay enough money to live on for a year). If you are an unknown in the field, you might obtain one lower-end grant or commission every other year. As your reputation increases, you may average one grant or contest and two or more commissions per year. Unless you are a top name in composition, you will not likely make more than $1,000 per year in royalties. Very well-established composers can make as much as $8,000 per year (though amounts vary considerably each year even for them).

Conversely, your expenses as a composer will be considerable, including (but not limited to) copying and reproduction charges, mailings, contest entry fees, performer and hall rental payments, festival and travel costs, and organization dues. You will wind up paying out several thousand dollars a year if you are active.

After Graduation

Once you get out of school, you need to build a career for yourself. To do so, be aggressive! Apply for all the grants, fellowships, arts colony residencies, and contests you possibly can; reapply every year and don't worry about the mountain of rejection letters you will get. Join all the composers' guilds and similar organizations you can afford, being sure to take advantage of the opportunities they offer. Attend conferences, festivals, and concerts and meet as many people as you can. Approach established ensembles and hit up your contacts for performances and commissions. Investigate all reasonable recording and publishing opportunities available. Present concerts devoted to your music. Answer calls for scores put out by ensembles, individual performers, festivals, and composers' guilds. Try to give lectures in support of your work. Write as many pieces as you can, getting as much variety into your portfolio as possible. When you start getting professional performances, join a licensing organization like Broadcast Music, Inc. (BMI) or the American Society of Composers, Authors, and Publishers (ASCAP) to obtain the generated royalties.

There is no secret to winning grants, contests, and similar things. Every judging committee is different and unpredictable. All you can do is make sure your application fits the set guidelines, is submitted on time, and does not contain obvious errors like misspellings or poor copy work.

Your biggest priority as a composer is to have your music played. Obviously, you must write the music first during whatever time you can set aside (weekends, evenings, early mornings, lunch hours). Just as performers should practice every day to maintain and improve their abilities, you should try to compose every day, if possible; if you do, your bad days will get better and your productive days will soar. Next, you must prepare a fair copy of the score and parts (plus a piano/vocal reduction score if your piece has singers) for the performers and conductor. This tedious chore can be done with a top-quality music notation computer program or by hand. If the piece has not been commissioned, you must next try to arrange for its performance. Approach as many good ensembles and performers as you can to secure such presentation; also send the piece to calls for scores. If all else fails, give a concert of your own music (perhaps sharing the stage with other fledgling composers) in a local hall; grass-roots groups such as Boston's Composers in Red Sneakers began this way. Once a performance has been arranged, involve yourself in rehearsals or coaching sessions done in preparation for the concert. If necessary, conduct or play the piece yourself. Finally, be sure to get the performance recorded. You will need good quality tapes to submit with grant/contest applications and to send with scores in soliciting future performances.

Think of your career as a rolling snowball—a small snowball gradually gains size and speed as it rolls down a hill. Recognition, performances, and honors tend to attract more of the same—and the chances of getting the most distinguished grants, commissions, and awards often increase as your track record improves. It normally takes many years of inspired composing, dogged perseverance, development of influential contacts, and luck to obtain *real* recognition in this field. As your career gains in prestige, you will begin to secure more esteemed commissions, win more noteworthy grants and competitions, and receive more performances and recordings without as much effort on your part. You will also likely be asked to judge contests and serve on discussion panels. In short, both you and your music will be much more in demand.

A composer's life is both difficult and rewarding. If you choose this career path, you can achieve a measure of success if you are capable and patient. With perseverance and real artistry, you may build a durable reputation in the field. And who knows? With talent and a bit of good luck, your music may outlive you!

DAVID CLEARY received a DMA from the College-Conservatory of Music, University of Cincinnati (1982); MM from the Hartt College of Music, University of Hartford (1978); and BM from the New England Conservatory of Music (1976). His composition teachers included Donald Martino, Malcolm Peyton, Donald Harris, Norman Dinerstein, Mordechai Scheinkman, and Thomas Pasatieri. His works have been performed and broadcast throughout the United States, Europe, and Australia. He has been awarded commissions, grants, and prizes from organizations throughout the United States; these include commissions from Alea III, Dinosaur Annex Ensemble, Northwestern University Trombone Ensemble, Arcadian Winds, and Artaria String Quartet of Boston; grants from the Ella Lyman Cabot Trust, Meet the Composer, Harvard University, and Somerville (MA) Arts Council; and prizes from the Harvey Gaul Contest and Cincinnati Composers' Guild.

He has been performed at the Tanglewood, June in Buffalo, Conductors' Institute, and Warebrook festivals and has received arts colony residencies at Yaddo, Millay, Ragdale, Cummington, and the Virginia Center for the Creative Arts. His *Lake George Overture* will be released on compact disc in 1994 on the Vienna Modern Masters label. Dr. Cleary has also performed many contemporary and standard works (solo and ensemble) on cello in the United States; his cello teachers included Jack Kirstein, Robert Ripley, Michael Rudiakov, and Martin Hoherman.

Dr. Cleary wishes to thank Thomas Lawrence McKinley, James Sellars, and Jan Swafford for helpful comments and suggestions on earlier drafts of this article

CHAPTER TWELVE

Working as a Designer in the Performing Arts

**Donna E. Brady, Executive Director,
Performing Arts Resources, Inc.**

esigning for the performing arts can be one of the most rewarding careers imaginable. The work encompasses both solitary and communal elements, great creativity, and attention to minute detail.

If you are thinking of pursuing a design career in the performing arts—theatre (fairly traditional plays and musicals), dance, opera, and performance art—think carefully about whether or not this is the career for you. This is not a field to consider if you are hoping to make money hand over fist, work short hours, or get a consistent paycheck with benefits such as health insurance or vacation time. In this field, if you don't work, you don't get paid. In fact, you'll work many hundreds of hours just for the privilege of having your name listed on a program as **designer,** and a new line on your resume. All the while, you'll also be working as a technician, temporary office worker, or waiter to pay your rent.

When starting out as a performer, you are often told that you must be prepared to deal with regular rejection. The same is true for designers. Until you are well established professionally (which can take many years), nearly every job will be a new interview process. This means many meetings, showing your portfolio and resume many times over, and many interviews each year. It is good to remember that the best designers are those who involve their hearts in a project, but not their sense of self-worth. Every designer has at least one memory of the design concept they *knew* was right for the production . . . that everyone else hated.

Except for very rare instances, the performing arts are not a democratic working environment. Rather, they are a cooperative effort under a (benign) dictator, commonly known as the director, whose overall vision is what shapes a project. The designer must always *serve* the production.

You'll Be Working With . . .

The producer is generally the person (or company) responsible for pulling all the aspects of a production together. While producers are often spoken of as "money people," it is their belief in and their commitment to a project that drives them to be the person responsible for the financial aspects (i.e., raising the money and controlling its disbursement). The important thing to remember is, that while the director may want the sun, moon, sky, and the stars, and the designer may want to provide them in technicolor, it is the producer who will bring up the hard budgetary realities of how much money is or is not available.

The director of a project is the person who brings all the different areas of production (including the various design departments and performers) together for a common goal or vision. If you envision talking with friends about an article you all have read, or a movie you all have seen, you all may have had different interpretations. The director's job is to ensure that during the preparation of all of the elements that will be seen by an audience, everyone is working toward a common interpretation of the work.

Production or stage management personnel are responsible for keeping track of everything (and everyone). People who follow this career path must be extremely organized. It helps if one also enjoys being a resource for odd bits of information that prove to be unexpectedly essential to the production. In this part of the business one needs to be able to calm the irate, soothe ruffled feathers, and gracefully remind everyone of what they're forgetting to do—in enough time for them to do it well.

How the Designer Fits In

The **designers** are those who work together to provide the total environment. Design in the performing arts has many elements including scenic (set), lighting, sound, and costume. On large projects, or those with particular needs, specialized designers of props, projections, special effects, wigs, and makeup may also be involved. While each area of design involves the use of particular techniques and skills, common to all is the ability to translate the written word into visual and aural (sound) elements.

There are many steps in the design process. Broadly, they involve *production meetings* when the creative team (director, designers, choreographer, writers, etc.) discusses the direction of the project within the context of the vision articulated by the director. The stage management team will also be present to keep track of details as they emerge. Each member of the creative team then works independently on the complex process of translating mental images into tangible realities, all the while communicating with the others to create a unified image. These meetings begin with initial discussions about how to approach the project, including when and where in time and place the production will be placed (realistic or fantasy; future, past, or present). As ideas are developed, sketches are made and shared. When the ideas are agreed upon, the drawings become more formalized and technical. Schedules are made and changed, and the fine points of each designer's input are worked out.

Career Preparation

Although it is possible to work professionally with little or no formal training—many of us did our first designs by the seat of our pants in high school or community theatre—it is generally worth investing in a college or university education. Very rarely, you may meet or hear of a working designer with no formal training. This is the dramatic exception, and these designers usually come to the performing arts from successful careers in other fields with a strong artistic reputation. In such cases companies will make concessions in the qualifications they would normally expect of a designer. Of course, *working* as a professional designer does not equate with *making a living* as a designer.

A BA or BFA in theatre arts is a common starting point. The importance is not the name of the degree, but what you learn. A master's program can provide you with more opportunities to hone your skills. While you may be eager to leave school for the *real world*, treasure your university moments. It will probably be a long time before you again have the time, money, labor, and facilities available to you as a student designer. If you are at all interested in teaching at a university setting someday, you will need to plan on acquiring at least an MA, if not an MFA. Teaching at a university can provide many creative opportunities and is one of the few places in this field with a relatively steady paycheck—although at the rate arts programs are eliminated, there are no guarantees here either. No matter how skilled or experienced you are as a designer, most teaching positions will be closed to you without an advanced degree.

You should walk out of university with the tools to provide a text with a physical reality. These include research skills; a knowledge of historical references; art skills (sketching, drafting, model making); and knowledge of technical elements. Will the marvelous piece you've sketched fall over? Will the lights you've planned on using blow every circuit breaker in the town? What will happen to the lovely colors you've chosen for your costumes when seen in the lights against the backdrop? These are questions you should be able to answer.

Best U.S. Arts Schools

Ranked by: Composite rating in five academic areas. Overall score is based on the school's percentile where measured in the five categories. See article for details.

1. Juilliard School (NY), with a score of 100.0
2. Rhode Island School of Design, 78.8
3. Art Center College of Design (CA), 78.6

Source: *U.S. News & World Report*

Many theatres still use two-scene preset lighting boards. However, in keeping up with technology, many colleges and theatres are equipped with all the newest electronic and computer gadgetry. For this reason, it is important that as a student you acquire as broad a range of experience as possible. Computer skills are increasingly important. Specialized programs for computer assisted design (CAD) are being used with increasing frequency in the professional world. Equipment that can be programmed individually is also becoming more common, and at a faster pace than the people trained to run it. However, be careful not to rely so heavily on the computer that you can do nothing manually!

Another benefit of university programs that is often overlooked is the opportunity to work with visiting artists. Most schools bring in bands, theatre companies, and many other types of performers. Whatever venue they perform in, your university probably needs staffing at the student level. While it may be an opportunity to earn work-study money, most important is the opportunity to meet working professionals and observe their techniques. It is also a way to start building contacts (known as *networking*) for when you leave the hallowed halls of the university. Many professionals will be glad to give you their business card and have you call them for advice. Just be patient if they don't respond immediately, because they may be hip-deep in a production or out on the road.

As you work, keep a record of what you've accomplished. Learn to take your own photographs under theatrical lighting conditions. Any production photographer will focus on shots of the cast, not the perfect light cue or scenic element. Even if they swear they'll remember, the better your work, the more likely fate will step in and they will forget. School projects have a limited credibility in the *real world,* but you have to start somewhere—and showing a professionally oriented portfolio helps. Given the transient nature of our work, you must think early about documentation. You can always edit things out, but you can't recreate the production and your special contribution to it for that one photograph years later.

Going to Work

You've finished school and have come to New York. Its a big town, but like all towns it has its neighborhoods and communities. The theatre community is spread throughout the city geographically, but it is a multi-faceted community with its own methods of communication. Some of these include: publications such as *Backstage, The New York Theatrical Sourcebook* and *The Village Voice;* shops such as Drama Book Shop; and organizations such as Performing Arts Resources, Art/NY, Dance Theater Workshop, and the Association of Theatrical Artists and Craftspeople (ATAC), which serve as resources. This is *not* an all-inclusive listing.

You'll need a basic resume, which is simply a listing of what you've done laid out on the page with visual clarity. Yes, resumes are one of the most beastly things in the world to create, especially for yourself. Remember that there are people and services to help, and you're placing it on paper, not in stone. Resumes are always being updated as you get new experience. There are several things to remember. The information on it should be clear and easy to read. If your resume is more than one page, your name and phone number should be on every page (including your reference listing). Information should include productions you worked on, your contribution (set designer, electrician, etc.), and the theatre company involved. Most importantly, it must be honest. (*See the Job Search Process section of this directory for more information on compiling your resume.–ed.*)

While you're trying to meet people, pay your rent, and get work, see as much as you can. There is a lot of activity off-off-Broadway and in alternative spaces. Some of it is absolute drek, but you can always continue to develop your eye. Many non-Broadway theatres will allow you to watch the show if you volunteer as an usher or in another capacity. Look at the program credits. Learn whose work you like and why. Those are people to approach for advice, for opportunities to assist them, or to volunteer to work as an electrician or carpenter on their next showcase. Don't bother with generic bulk mailings—they are an insult to those who receive them, and a waste of your time and money.

There are two schools of thought about career paths for designers. One suggests that a designer does nothing but design. He/she does not build sets, hang lights, or make costumes. The other suggests that *technical* activities provide experience in the field while teaching elements of the craft. I personally agree with the second philosophy. As you embark on this career, working in technical capacities enables you to watch other designers at work, observing successes and mistakes. You have the opportunity to participate in productions on a larger scale than you probably would as a young designer. And, to be practical, there are more jobs for electricians, carpenters, costume construction, etc., than there are for designers. Working in a technical capacity may be how you pay the rent for many years while building your portfolio and contacts. If you prove yourself to be reliable, simpatico, and committed to doing the best job you possibly can as a technician, someone will know this about you and be more willing to trust you with designing a special project. These qualities are also included in the term *professionalism*, without which you will not often be hired for any position.

A related debate concerns working on *showcases*. These productions are mounted for the purpose of showcasing the talents of those involved. While the focus is usually on the performers, directors, and possibly playwright, it is an excellent opportunity for a beginning designer to work on honing their skills, building contacts, and having their work seen. It is also a project for which all involved receive little—if any—money. If you are offered a showcase, and you can afford to do it, *do*. The same applies to internships and assisting others. Get the experience, get the credit, meet people, and have them get to know you and your work. You help others, they help you. You never know when someone will call on you to design after remembering that they met you when you worked as an electrician. *One-day jobs* fall under the same heading. A scenic artist/lighting/set/costume designer I know took a one-day job painting murals for a department store complex, which turned into a three-year job as staff designer for several on-site performance spaces and all the murals and visual environments in the common areas of the nine-level complex. An added benefit was the opportunity to use their scenic shop for building her outside design projects! As staff designer, she was also able to employ and pay artists who had worked for her without pay on showcases.

In summary, design is a field where luck and fate play a strong role. You'll probably never become wealthy, but it is a universe full of wonderful, creative, generous (and yes, competitive) human beings who respect honesty and hard work (especially mixed with talent). If you pursue this field, it must be because your heart gives you no choice, however long it takes. That said, Good Luck!

DONNA E. BRADY is executive director of Performing Arts Resources (PAR), Inc. in New York City. This nonprofit service organization works extensively with performing arts organizations through a personnel network, set recycling hotline, seminars, consultations, and resource center. Prior to joining PAR, she worked as a lighting designer and stage manager for dance.

Setting the Stage: Careers in Theatre Design and Technology

Konrad Winters, Commissioner, Education Commission, United States Institute for Theatre Technology

Beyond the roar of the crowd and the smell of the greasepaint, standing in the wings or at the back of the theatre, people are waiting and watching—guiding the performance, unseen by the audience, toward the final curtain. A host of stage managers, electricians, technicians, carpenters, painters, tailors and seamstresses, technical directors, and designers all make up what is called a **production team.** They are charged with the responsibility of bringing to completion all of the physical elements of a theatrical production. How can you become one of these individuals? The road is a long one, but not without a lot of interesting moments along the way.

There is something about a live theatrical performance that sets it apart from all other performances. The relationship that the actor has with the audience is unique to the theatre. One brief magical moment captures the imagination in ways they may have never experienced before. All of the creative energy that goes to support such a performance requires skilled and dedicated designers and technicians, working long hours to develop the setting, costumes, lights, sound, and make-up necessary to complement and enhance the performance. All of these physical elements of the play are designed, developed, constructed, painted, and assembled for that particular production.

I occasionally teach an introductory theatre class to students who aren't pursuing a career in theatre. I am asked a great many questions regarding my work and how it is accomplished. Here are a few of the questions most commonly asked:

What Does a Theatre Designer Do?

Basically, a **theatre designer** (set, costume, light, or sound) works with the theatre director to develop a plan for presenting a live theatrical performance to an audience. The designers are responsible for all of the physical elements (sets, costumes, furniture, properties, lights, special effects, sound, and make-up) that the audience sees when they watch a play. They work in collaboration with the theatre director to create a cohesive and unified *world* within which the play and its characters can exist.

What Sort of Training Is Necessary to Work as a Theatrical Designer?

Generally, professional designers have advanced degrees from a college or university in theatrical design. Most often, that degree is a master's of fine arts (MFA) with a specialty in scenic design, costume design, lighting design, sound design, or technical production. **Scenic designers** study design and decoration, drafting, painting, engineering and mechanics, and construction techniques. **Costume designers** study historical fashions, draping and garment construction, textiles, millinery, and sometimes jewelry making. The courses often taken by **lighting designers** include optics and optical engineering, electrical and electronic theory, as well as lighting design. **Sound designers** study acoustics and audio engineering.

What Sort of Skills Would I Need?

Abilities to draw and paint are a plus, yet those skills—like the balance you need to ride a bicycle—can be acquired through practice.

The Top Five Most Powerful Artistic Directors in American Theater

Ranked by criteria such as: authority to green light a project; influence on the future of theater; how fast phone calls are returned; size of audience generated; cash flow; and where they dine regularly.
  1. George C. Wolfe
  2. Andre Bishop/Bernie Gersten
  3. Lynne Meadow/Barry Grove
  4. Don Scardino
  5. Gordon Davidson
Source: *Theater Week*

How Does a Theatre Designer Get Started?

Internships and apprenticeships are available at a wide range of venues. Many students graduating from colleges and universities around the nation apply to regional professional theatres in entry-level positions. Recently, a student of mine graduated and took a position as an intern with Stagewest, a professional theatre company in the Northeast. She worked there for a year doing everything from building sets and properties to hanging and focusing lights. She is now working with another professional theatre company as a resident scenic artist. She plans to continue for another year and then apply to graduate school. With her professional credits on her resume, her ability to attract the top schools in the country will be greatly enhanced.

Another student of mine, upon completing his MFA in scenic design, took a position as an apprentice scenic artist with Steppenwolf, a professional theatre company in the Midwest. He worked there for several seasons, gaining experience under the direction of some of the top professional designers in the country; having left Steppenwolf, he now runs his own professional scenic studio. Other students have been interested in teaching and, upon completing graduate school, apply for teaching positions with colleges and universities. All in all, much of how you get started depends on what type of career you want.

What Can I Expect to Earn as a Theatrical Designer?

Salaries depend upon the path you choose. For those who teach, the annual salary can be quite modest, often between $30,000 to $40,000 for a 9- to 10-month term. That allows for summer work, which can be helpful. For professional designers, it is much more variable. Some designers work in such related fields as television and motion pictures *as well as* the theatre. Other designers work for commercial or industrial clients, theme parks, or as resident designers for a professional regional theatre. On the average, these designers may earn as much as $75,000 or as little as $25,000. If you're in it for the money, theatrical design is not necessarily the best career choice. Simply put, theatre designers and technicians work in the theatre because of their love of the theatre.

What About Unions or Professional Affiliations?

Professional designers must apply for and pass an exam to be included in the membership of the United Scenic Artists. This professional organization has categories for scenic, lighting, costume, and scenic artists (I believe sound is also on the way). You cannot work in the professional theatre on Broadway without a membership in this organization. As a professional technician, membership in the International Alliance of Stagehands, Technicians, and Electricians (IASTE), is strongly encouraged, especially if you want to work on Broadway or in many of the regional professional theatres. As a professional teacher (designer or technician), no union directly represents your field at present. However, membership in the United States Institute for Theatre Technology (USITT) is highly recommended, since it provides considerable opportunities to make vital contacts and keep up with the latest technology and information within your profession.

Is There Anything I Should Be Cautious of as I Pursue This Career?

Competition, stress, and burn-out are common. The performing arts in general are highly competitive. Learning to work with people will be your greatest asset. Collaboration is the nature of the business, and if you are a good team player, you will go far. Stress is, unfortunately, also a key element in the development of the theatre. Deadlines, workloads, and limited resources are great ingredients for stress. Planning and preparation are by far the best weapons to combat stress. And finally, burn-out needs to be considered. Burn-out is usually the result of overcommitting oneself, with the net result of burning the candle at both ends and having nothing to show for it.

The best advice here is to pace yourself. Don't take on too many projects at once—remember to take the time to plan and prepare.

All things considered, a career in theatrical design and technical production can be fascinating and rewarding. It offers you an opportunity to work with some of the most talented artists and craftspeople in the country, and it opens up whole worlds of personal expression for you as an individual creative artist. Good luck!

Konrad Winters is the commissioner of the Education Commission of the United States Institute for Theatre Technology. He is an associate professor of theatre arts and the resident designer and technical director at Old Dominion University in Norfolk, VA. Mr. Winters received his MFA in scenic design from Illinois State University, Bloomington, IL, and taught in Minnesota and Texas before moving to Virginia.

CHAPTER FOURTEEN

Getting Started in the Cruise Industry

Jim Coston, Cruise Ship Entertainer and Author

During the 1980s and 1990s, one of the fastest growing areas for performers has been the cruise ship market. Only a handful of cruise ships operated in the North American market 20 years ago. Now there are over 100 ships—with more being built each year! It is estimated that by the year 2000 there will be eight million passengers sailing annually. Along with the food and the itineraries, entertainment is one of the chief draws for passengers.

The cruise entertainment industry has grown tremendously during the past 20 years. There was a time when ships were considered the *elephant's graveyard* of entertainment. The only people who worked them did so because they couldn't find other work or they traded their performance for a paid cruise for themselves and their families.

That has changed. Currently, top name entertainers, as well as countless journeyman performers, regularly work on cruise ships. In addition to onstage work, many ships now have full-time sound and light technicians, as well as dee jays.

Preparing for Work

Breaking into the cruise industry is not difficult. However, there are many things to be aware of. I will attempt to cover as many of them as possible here.

1. **Have a valid passport.** It is always your best form of identification. Although many Caribbean cruises may not require one, this is a global market, and cruise lines reserve the right to move entertainers to any ship within their fleet. As a result, you may start off on a ship to Nassau and end up on a ship to Bombay. It is also the responsibility of the artist to have all necessary travel visas and inoculations.

2. **Have health insurance that covers you worldwide.** Although all major ships have a doctor on board, you might find yourself ill enough to

disembark in a foreign port. Also be aware that some cruise lines require a health certificate before they will allow you to work. In addition, some require an HIV test.

3. **Read the fine print.** If you are offered a contract with a cruise line, make sure you understand the details.

- How will you be paid? (for example; by cash or check, on board ship or end of contract, etc.) Will they deduct taxes? Will you be paid in U.S. funds?—some ships might not.

- Are airline tickets and transfers to and from the ship paid for?

- Accommodations: Will you have a passenger or staff cabin (passenger is better)? Private or shared?

- Will you eat off the passenger menu or *crew food* in the mess?

- How many different performances will you work a week and at what length?

- Will you be considered to have passenger status or crew? If you are crew, will you be expected to do boat drills?

- What about extra duties? Will you work as an entertainer *only,* or will you be expected to do staff duties, such as selling bingo cards, greeting passengers during embarkation, escorting tours, etc?

Getting Paid

Not only has the status of shipboard entertaining improved—so has the pay and working conditions. It is not uncommon for a variety cabaret act to make $1,000 to $1,500 for two shows a week. Musician salaries can range from $200 to $1,000 a week, and dancers in review shows make from $200 to $500 a week.

Succeeding on Board

Almost every cruise ship contract is written to allow the employer to cancel out if they feel an entertainer's work is inferior or inappropriate. Remember that your performance should reflect the demographics of the ship. Shorter cruises (three to four days) tend to draw a younger crowd, while cruises longer than seven days attract older passengers. Additionally, cruises to the Caribbean and Mexican Riviera generally attract younger passengers, while cruises to Alaska, Europe, Asia, and the Panama Canal appeal to those 20 to 30 years older.

Most cruise ships offer the same show twice an evening. Once after the first dinner seating (around 8:30 p.m.) and again following the second seating (around 10:30 p.m.). Additionally, many ships may offer a midnight cabaret show or a pre-dinner cocktail hour show. Shows on board ship are rarely longer than one hour.

Cruise ships vary from small, 120-passenger yachts to 2,500-passenger super liners. As a result, stage and backstage areas vary drastically. A juggler working a room with a six-foot ceiling or a magician working with spectators on the sides may need to re-block their shows to accommodate the physical limitations of the room.

Most cruise ships try to offer a variety of entertainment. Usually, there is a production company that does two or three shows a week (a salute to broadway or a country hoedown, for example). Depending upon the size of the ship, that group may include 3 to 20 cast members.

Variety acts such as magicians, comics, instrumentalists, and singers round out the showroom entertainment. If your show requires music, remember that most ships use a six-piece (or larger) orchestra usually consisting of piano, bass, drums, trumpet, sax/clarinet, and trombone. Make sure your charts are clean and accurate. Many ships now employ musicians from countries such as Poland—their English may be limited but their musicianship is not.

Musicians are usually part of the show band, which backs the artists and plays dance sets. Additionally, most ships have one or more lounge groups that entertain in other rooms of the ship.

On-board entertainment is coordinated by the cruise director (CD). The CD usually hosts the evening entertainment and is quite often also a performer.

As an entertainer on a cruise ship, you are constantly in the public eye. From the moment you leave your cabin you are on display. As a result, cruise lines have very specific rules of dress and conduct. Most of these are common sense, while others may not be as obvious. You will receive a copy of the ships rules—read them, understand them, and follow them.

Almost all ships require proper attire at night. Formal, informal, and casual nights are scheduled throughout a cruise. It is also advisable to determine if there are *theme nights* such as *country night* or *'50s night.*

Although all cruise ships have stabilizers to limit the motion, **ships do move**—especially during rough weather. Nothing is quite as miserable as seasickness. If you *think* you are susceptible, find out *before* you sign a six-month contract.

Finding the Work

There are several ways to find work on cruise ships. Some cruise lines hire directly. A promotional pack, including a photo/resume/cover letter and demo tape addressed to the entertainment director may be all you will need. Cruise lines that contract out for entertainment will usually forward your material to their agent. In fact, many cruise lines contract their entertainment through an agent. There are several agencies that specialize in this market. Be aware that most agents will take 10 to 15 percent of your pay as a commission.

If you are interested in singing and dancing in a production show, there are several companies that produce ship board reviews. You should contact them and find out when and where they will be auditioning.

Contracts vary in length from cruise ship to cruise ship. If you are a solo cabaret act, you might be flown in for one night or be offered a six-month contract. Musicians and members of review groups are usually required to sign for a minimum of three to six months.

When submitting a promotional pack, remember to keep your demo tape short (no one looks at more than 10 minutes). An edited live performance is usually

▼

Biggest Amusement/Theme Park Attractions+

Ranked by: 1991 attendance.
1. Walt Disney World's Magic Kingdom, EPCOT Center, MGM Studios Theme Park (Lake Buena Vista, FL), with 28,000,000 attendance
2. Disneyland (Anaheim, CA), 11,610,000
3. Universal Studios Florida (Orlando), 5,900,000
4. Universal Studios Hollywood (Universal City, CA), 4,625,000
5. Knott's Berry Farm (Buena Park, CA), 4,000,000
6. Sea World of Florida (Orlando), 3,420,000
7. Sea World of California (San Diego), 3,300,000
8. Six Flags Magic Mountain (Valencia, CA), 3,200,000
9. Cedar Point (Sandusky, OH), 3,000,000
9. Santa Cruz (CA) Beach Boardwalk, 3,000,000+

Source: *Amusement Business*

preferred over a studio tape. Keep cover letters and resumes to one page each and include a recent 8 x 10 photo.

If you follow these basic rules for getting started, your cruise ship career will be ready to set sail for the future! Good luck!

JIM COSTON has been a cruise ship cabaret act for more than 10 years, having performed on over 30 different ships. He is also coauthor of *STARSEARCHER—The Entertainer's Database & Contact Manager* program for DOS.

CHAPTER FIFTEEN

The Business of Performing Arts

**Johanna Humbert, Director of Development,
International Theatre Festival of Chicago**

I f you love the ballet, adore the theatre, admire the opera, or live for the symphony—and you enjoy a steady paycheck—explore the multitude of options available in **performing arts administration.** To the uninitiated this may appear to be desk work. But those familiar with the field know that without producers, fund-raisers, marketers, and managers, the show would not go on.

Deciding where *you* fit into the picture is in part a matter of matching your skills and interests to the job description, just as in any business. If you are serious about establishing your career, however, be willing to experiment. The basic skills cross all boundaries—you may even discover a knack for work you didn't know existed.

If you've never worked at a performing arts organization, you need to know the basic breakdown of responsibilities in each administrative area: production, development, marketing, and business management.

Producing

The **producer** is at the top of the administrative ladder. **Managing director, producing director,** or **executive director** are typical titles in this area. The producer performs the negotiating and contractual functions associated with the talent, be it dancers, actors, musicians, or their unions. The producer also maintains responsibility for budgeting season costs in conjunction with the artistic staff. To the public, the producer is the magician who puts all the pieces of the puzzle together.

A good producer makes everything work during a crisis—and there is always a crisis—because he/she knows the organization forward and backward. Imagine Ardis Krainik, executive director of Lyric Opera Chicago, announcing to the public that she would never again contract world famous tenor Placido Domingo because he'd failed to perform on his contracted dates. At the peak of his career, having Placido Domingo's name mentioned in the schedule sold thousands of tickets. But as a shrewd manager, Krainik knew that the risk of alienating her audience by continuing what was perceived as *bait and switch* advertising far outweighed the pitfalls of challenging a mega-star. In fact, both the public and the opera world applauded her decisiveness. These are the decisions that belong to the producer.

Obviously, unless you start your own company, being the producer is not an entry-level position! If your interests lie in this area, you should consider two paths. You might look for a position as an **assistant to a producer** in order to learn the ropes. You might also consider starting out in development, marketing, or business management. These specialties often lead to top positions.

Development

The development office's central responsibility is to generate contributed income. Some consider it professional begging. Actually, next to the producer's position, development requires the most in-depth understanding of the organization, and provides the greatest range of challenges and opportunities.

Development directors and their staff—associates, assistants, and those who specialize in corporate or foundation giving, planned giving, or research—tap all available resources for gifts and grants. The traditional work day includes researching giving sources in reference books, philanthropic publications, and the business section of the local paper (development directors also read the obituaries carefully to avoid soliciting someone who can no longer give). Once a target list of donors is compiled, contact is made with each of them either by phone or in writing, often with the assistance of a member of the board of directors (see below). Assuming the donor is interested, a proposal is submitted, and eventually a response is received.

Skills required are a passion for the organization, good verbal and written communication skills, and an ability to work with numbers for tallying up the positive results.

Times are changing, however, as is the traditional day. Donors want more for their money. Can the Lexus be displayed in the lobby? Will you accept Visa to the exclusion of American Express? Might you introduce our company president on stage? What about tickets—how many and how good? These days, the development staff juggles the drive for contributions against the artistic integrity of the organization. Finessing agreements among business and the arts is currently one of the most exciting elements of the job.

Development officers, like producers, need to know about every area of an organization. One backer may know the art well, and want to discuss scores and composers. Another may care little for the art, but is fascinated by the challenges facing a set designer working in an odd-shaped theatre. Still another may want details on your finances: "What percentage of the budget is used for newspaper ads versus brochures?" The development staff is prepared to discuss all areas with equal knowledge and enthusiasm.

Entering the development field, depending on the size of the organization, can mean doing everything from secretarial work to acting as the director. If you're fortunate enough to find an organization that will set you up as a "professional beggar," park your ego at home. The downside of fund-raising is that for every request that becomes a gift, many are rejected.

Marketing

The marketing office *promotes* the performances. This can be done through advertising, public relations, or partnerships with other businesses (yes, the performing arts are a business, too). **Marketers** develop campaigns to sell tickets. They keep the important people in the organization in the public eye. Day-to-day challenges include scheduling all of the marketing campaign elements to build on one another. It is far more useful for a brochure to arrive one day, an ad to appear in the paper the next, and an interview conducted with the star the following weekend, rather than for all of these things to occur simultaneously.

More than any other area, the marketing department shapes the public image of an organization. Similar to political spin doctors, public relations directors can change the firing of a star actor(a negative happening) into a special opportunity to witness the debut performance of an up-and-comer (everyone wants to see a new star). Within the realm of image making, the marketing department works with graphic artists to achieve the right advertising look, and represents the organization to the press. They also discover new ways of reaching the public through audience surveys.

A new area of emphasis within marketing is the search for corporate marketing partnerships, often in conjunction with the development office. Marketers are able to develop packages of advertising and visibility perks that entice big businesses to invest their advertising funds in a performing arts organization. Cigarette manufacturer Philip Morris Company, for example, is a major sponsor of the Brooklyn Academy of Music's *Next Wave Festival,* a series of innovative performing arts presentations. For Philip Morris, it is an opportunity to be a good corporate citizen, and to get their message across to a targeted audience who, if they don't smoke, might still be persuaded to feel more positive about a tobacco company in light of this support.

Typical marketing positions include **marketing director** (and associates or assistants), **press** or **public relations director,** and **advertising manager. Group sales** and **telemarketing,** which are strictly sales jobs, also fall within the marketing department. Departments can range from one-person jack-of-all-trades to 5 or 10 people in a major organization. More than any other department, marketing lends itself to free-lance and agency services, often provided *pro bono* (free of charge) by corporate firms that want the artistic challenge and tax deduction of this kind of partnership.

Largest Public Entertainment Companies in Los Angeles County

Ranked by: 1990 revenue, in millions of dollars.
1. Walt Disney Co., with $6,100.0 million
2. LIVE Entertainment, $742.5
3. MGM-Pathe Communications Co., $690.1
4. Carolco Pictures Inc., $269.1
5. Spelling Entertainment Inc., $166.3
6. Westwood One, $145.9
7. United Television Inc., $119.0
8. Republic Pictures Corp., $57.4
9. Imagine Films Entertainment Inc., $57.3
10. Image Entertainment Inc., $48.2

Source: *Los Angeles Business Journal*

Business Management

The **business manager** controls expenses and manages income. He/she oversees the budgeting process with the producer, and then is responsible for insuring that each department remains within those budget guidelines. Should someone, perhaps a greedy marketing director, require additional funds, the business manager either finds them within the existing budget, or alerts the development office of an extra-budgetary need. The business manager tracks financial trends to be able to project the cash flow, and with a bit of expertise, can predict trouble before it hits.

The business manager is also responsible for payroll, including any benefits the organization may provide. He/she frequently negotiates leases on office and performance space, oversees the maintenance of office equipment, and acts as office manager.

In a few organizations, the business manager actually oversees cash reserves or endowment funds, investing responsibly to guarantee ongoing stability. But in a growing number of performing arts agencies, the business manager practices the art of creative financing. It is truly an art, and those talented few with the necessary skills can command their price.

The Board of Directors

The board of directors is ultimately in charge of any not-for-profit performing arts organization. These groups attract intelligent, wealthy directors to their boards. Administrators in all fields work with these board members on committees, shaping the future of the organization. No matter which field you are attracted to, it is critical that a good rapport with the board is established. They can make your job much simpler with expertise and access to support. Consequently, when the time comes for you to move along to another organization, your board of directors can be extremely helpful in your move.

Where to Start

Performing arts people like to work with a known quantity, so networking and inside-hiring is prevalent. *Your* job is to get a foot in the door. Few jobs are available for the many who want in, so make yourself essential!

Internships are an outstanding entry. Many organizations offer paid internships, though the stipends are small, ranging from $50 to $200 per week. Sometimes an organization offers housing or transportation subsidies in addition to, or in place of, a stipend. But many places don't have money to offer—just experience. However, don't rule them out. Frequently, the organization with restricted funds will have the meatiest intern assignments. They have to because they can't afford to hire the needed staff.

When you take on an internship, be sure to agree on your basic tasks up front. A contract between you and your supervisor will assure that you get the kind of responsible work that will help to prepare you for a staff position. At the same time, be willing to chip in wherever there is need in the office.

Money

Don't go into performing arts administration if you want to get rich. Indeed, many arts managers make a bohemian living, clearing under $20,000 per year. At a mid-sized organization (annual budget $750,000 to $2 million), a department director can earn $25,000 to $50,000, and oversee a staff of one to three people. Large organizations (over $2 million annual budgets) have departments as large as 10 to 15 people, and the top departmental people earn $40,000 to $80,000, or more. Producers, as top staff, can earn six figures, but only at the largest organizations.

Where Will It Lead?

Start out as an intern and be diligent—within a year you should have an entry-level staff job. Career growth can be quite steady, reaching the top level within two or three years, though it is not unusual to settle in as a specialist within a department and stay there for years.

Curiously, the administrative staff at small and mid-sized organizations tends to be younger. There is a high burnout rate in the industry because of the pace of life and the pressure. By age 40, many people have opted out of the field for *real jobs* in advertising, banking, education, tourism, etc.

But even here, the industry is changing, professionalizing, and recognizing the value of experience. The next generation of arts administrators will realize a higher standard of living and greater respect in the business world than those who are leading today.

If you have the enthusiasm, the drive, and the desire for an unusual and creative job with a steady paycheck, then performing arts administration may just be for you.

JOHANNA HUMBERT has been director of development for the International Theatre Festival of Chicago since its founding in 1985. As the only regularly scheduled event of its kind in the United States, the Festival offers many unique challenges to its staff and interns. Before joining the Festival, Ms. Humbert was director of development for Court Theatre, the resident professional company at the University of Chicago, as well as a public relations account executive for Universal Pictures.

CHAPTER SIXTEEN

Internships: The Pathway to a Job in Arts Administration

Darrell Ayers, Internship Program Manager, The John F. Kennedy Center for the Performing Arts

How do you get an entry-level position in arts administration? Through experience. As an undergraduate or graduate student, one way to gain experience is through an internship with a performing arts organization. The John F. Kennedy Center for the Performing Arts in Washington, DC, the Music Center of Los Angeles County, and similar arts organizations offer internships in arts administration, education, and related fields. An internship may lead to permanent employment for the organization or can serve as concrete experience for your resume in the arts administration field.

College is *just the beginning* of your lifelong learning experience; an internship tests your skills and knowledge, moving you from the nurturing atmosphere of school to the real world of employment. You gain an insider's view of what it would be like to be involved in this kind of work without having to make a permanent commitment. The internship should be viewed as an opportunity to ask, "Is this what I really what to do? Will this kind of work use my strengths and satisfy my ambitions?"

Your Role as Intern

During your internship, you will be asked to do many different kinds of tasks. Some will not be very challenging—answering the phone, photocopying, or filing—others will demand creativity or provide interesting and exciting experiences—working with artists, attending performances, workshops, and seminars, answering correspondence, and meeting deadlines.

The interns who truly succeed are those who are able to apply their skills to new tasks quickly and easily—they know when to seek advice and when to take the initiative. An internship can be a time for creative thought, planning, and action if the intern works with energy and an open mind, looking for innovative ways to do everyday assignments. Do not be afraid to ask questions. You will get the most out of your internship if you listen carefully, ask concise follow-up questions, and efficiently complete assigned tasks.

Because the performing arts is a deadline-oriented business, it is important to be helpful, open, creative, and flexible; one with a positive attitude and a sense of humor. Great demands are placed on arts administrators and you will be able to observe how many of them deal with the long hours and fast-paced environment.

Every intern at the Kennedy Center is supervised by a full-time arts administrator in his/her specialized field, such as advertising, education, development, government relations, marketing, media relations, programming, and special events. Establishing a good rapport with your supervisor may be your most important task. Interns who do not develop that rapport may become unhappy about the way they are treated or the kinds of tasks they are asked to perform. Unless you find the courage to speak up, your supervisor may not realize that there is a problem. Every person has a different way of working and significant insights can be gained from observing the work habits of your supervisor.

Some interns feel they are not given enough responsibility. An intern must realize that responsibility is not something given easily—it must be earned through hard, successful work.

▼

Top Employee Motivators

Ranked by: Conclusions in article by Frederick Hertzbert as published in the *Harvard Business Review*.
  1. On-the-job achievement
  2. Recognition
  3. Type of work done
  4. Responsibility assigned
  5. Advancement and growth opportunities
  6. Salary
  7. Relationships with other employees
  8. Type of supervision received
  9. Working conditions
  10. Company policies and administration
Source: *Homecare*

What Background or Experiences Should You Have?

Performing arts organizations need good employees who can write a speech or a letter, solve an employee problem, layout a document, and create a budget. Computer knowledge is essential. Interns at the Kennedy Center have been chosen from many majors and fields, such as art, biology, communications, dance, English, music, political science, theater, and general liberal arts. Of primary importance in the intern selection process is experience in the performing arts. Whether it is courses you have taken or extracurricular activities you have participated in, a performing arts intern must have some practical experience before applying for an internship.

Strong letters of recommendation are also important because they provide a sense of the candidate's personality and ability to work with others. The cover letter provides your first impression, so be certain there are no typographical errors in it. Grade point average is also an influential factor.

During your internship, you will be asked to write many documents and deal with many different people. In order to be prepared, interns need to be able to use good grammar, punctuation, and clear and concise language. They need to listen carefully to others decipher what they are trying to communicate, and respond in an appropriate manner. Those interested should consider taking courses in writing, interpersonal skills, communication, and management. Once you have decided which organization you would like to intern for, read everything printed by the organization to understand their written communication style.

As the workplace increasingly becomes a place where technical knowledge is rewarded, it is essential to maintain the ability to communicate effectively in writing and in person. This can help prevent the inordinate amount of time wasted by misunderstandings and miscommunications. The performing arts are a customer service-oriented business. Our product is a performance that people want to see, and it is our intent to give them the best experience possible. Our ability to communicate with our audiences is an integral part of presenting performances, workshops, and other educational events.

Questions to Ask

When applying for an internship, you should ask many of the same questions you would ask when applying for any job:

- What can I hope to learn from this internship?
- What responsibilities will I have?
- What hours will I work?
- Who is my immediate supervisor?
- What, if anything, will I receive in compensation? When will I be paid?
- Can I attend performances, workshops, etc., free of charge?

You should also ask:

- How much of my time will be spent working with my supervisor?
- Is there someone else with whom I will be directly working?
- How long has my supervisor been with the organization?
- Are there other interns with the organization?
- Are there opportunities to interact with staff members from other departments—either through meetings or social events?

Internships at the John F. Kennedy Center for the Performing Arts

The Kennedy Center has been offering internships for more than a decade. Internships are available in many aspects of arts administration, including advertising, education, development, government relations, marketing, media relations, programming, and special events.

Interns are selected through a competitive process and participate in the program for three to four months in either the fall, winter/spring, or summer.

Competition is greater for summer internships, so it is advisable to apply for a fall or winter/spring internship.

Each intern is assigned to a specific department and completes a project during their tenure. During the internship, interns attend the weekly Executive Seminar Series, which involves presentations by senior Kennedy Center staff and executives from other major arts institutions in Washington, DC. They also keep a weekly journal of their experience.

Interns have the opportunity to attend performances in the six theatres of the Kennedy Center free of charge. Monthly financial support is provided to interns during their internship.

More than 300 interns have participated in the Kennedy Center program and many of them now work for such organizations as the Music Center of Los Angeles County, the Alliance Theater Company, Opera Pacifica, Walt Disney World, and the Kennedy Center.

To receive a brochure about the program, write to: Internship Program Manager, Education Department, The Kennedy Center, Washington, DC 20566, or call (202)416-8800 or fax (202)416-8802.

Internships at the Music Center of Los Angeles County

Since 1990, the Music Center of Los Angeles County (L.A. Music Center) has offered numerous internships in the field of arts administration, including community relations, development, education, finance, and marketing. After a 4-to-6-week selection process, interns are assigned to a 10-to-12 week placement (summer—full-time, spring or fall—full- or part- time).

Regularly scheduled informal discussions on arts management issues and career opportunities are provided by Music Center administrative, artistic, and volunteer managers. Interns receive an hourly wage based on their academic level and work experience. A special goal of the program is to target students of diverse ethnic backgrounds to ensure that the future management of the Music Center and other arts institutions will represent the full diversity of the Southern California population.

To receive additional information about the program, write to: Diversity Enhancement Arts Management (BEAM) Internships, The Music Center of Los Angeles County, Community Relations, 135 N. Grand Avenue, Los Angeles, CA 90012, or call (213)972-8013.

Other Internship Opportunities

There are many other organizations that offer internships and list job openings in their newsletters. There are also a number of directories available that list internships—and most can be found at your university library. *(See the Job Search Process and Job Opportunities Databank sections of this book for more information on internships.—ed.)*

DARRELL M. AYERS is currently the internship program manager at the John F. Kennedy Center for the Performing Arts in Washington, DC. He is also responsible for the Grand Foyer Concert Series and is executive assistant to the managing director of education. He began at the Kennedy Center as an intern in January, 1987. Mr. Ayers has a degree in communications from Georgia Southern University, Statesboro, GA and attended the University of Miami, FL, as a music education major. He worked as a mortgage and loan officer for five years while serving on the boards of numerous local arts agencies. He has worked as a stage manager on many productions and his work in theater and music has allowed him to tour the United States, Russia, and England.

THE JOB
SEARCH
PROCESS

CHAPTER SEVENTEEN

Getting Started: Self-Evaluation and Career Objectives

Getting a job may be a relatively simple one-step or couple of weeks process or a complex, months-long operation.

Starting, nurturing, and developing a career (or even a series of careers) is a lifelong process.

What we'll be talking about in the five chapters that together form our **Job Search Process** are those basic steps to take, assumptions to make, things to think about if you want a job—especially a first job in some area of performing arts. But when these steps—this process—are applied and expanded over a lifetime, most if not all of them are the same procedures, carried out over and over again, that are necessary to develop a successful, lifelong, professional career.

What does all this have to do with putting together a resume and portfolio, writing a cover letter, heading off for interviews, and the other "traditional" steps necessary to get a job? Whether your college graduation is just around the corner or a far distant memory, you will continuously need to focus, evaluate, and re-evaluate your response to the ever-changing challenge of your future: Just what do you want to do with the rest of your life? Whether you like it or not, you're all looking for that "entry-level opportunity."

You're already one or two steps ahead of the competition—you're sure you want to pursue a career in performing arts. By heeding the advice of the many professionals who have written chapters for this *Career Directory*—and utilizing the extensive entry-level job, organization, and career resource listings we've included—you're well on your way to fulfilling that dream. But there are some key decisions and time-consuming preparations to make if you want to transform that hopeful dream into a real, live job.

The actual process of finding the right company (i.e., theatre, ballet, opera, etc.), right career path, and most importantly, the right first job, begins long before you start mailing out resumes and auditioning for potential employers. The choices and decisions you make now are not irrevocable, but this first job will have a definite impact on the career options you leave yourself. To help you make some of the right decisions and choices along the way (and avoid some of the most notable traps and pitfalls), the following chapters will lead you through a series of organized steps. If the entire job search process we are recommending here is properly executed, it will undoubtedly help you land exactly the job you want.

If you're currently in high school and hope, after college, to land a performing arts career, then attending the right college, choosing the right major, and getting the summer work experience many companies look for are all important steps. Read the section of this *Career Directory* that covers the particular field and/or job specialty in which you're interested—many of the contributors have recommended colleges or graduate programs they favor.

If you're hoping to jump right into any of these fields without a college degree or other professional training, our best and only advice is—don't do it. As you'll soon see in the detailed information included in the **Job Opportunities Databank,** there are not that many job openings for students without a college degree or training. Those that do exist are generally clerical and will only rarely lead to promising careers.

The Concept of a Job Search Process

As we've explained, a job search is not a series of random events. Rather, it is a series of connected events that together form the job search process. It is important to know the eight steps that go into that process:

1. Evaluating yourself

Know thyself. What skills and abilities can you offer a prospective employer? What do you enjoy doing? What are your strengths and weaknesses? What do you want to do?

2. Establishing your career objectives

Where do you want to be next year, three years, five years from now? What do you ultimately want to accomplish in your career and your life?

3. Creating a company target list

How to prepare a "Hit List" of potential employers—researching them, matching their needs with your skills, and starting your job search assault. Preparing company information sheets and evaluating your chances.

4. Networking for success

Learning how to utilize every contact, every friend, every relative, and anyone else you can think of to break down the barriers facing any would-be performing arts professional. How to organize your home office to keep track of your communications and stay on top of your job campaign.

5. Preparing your resume

How to encapsulate years of school and little actual work experience into a professional, selling resume. Learning when and how to use it.

6. Preparing cover letters

The many ordinary and the all-too-few extraordinary cover letters, the kind that land interviews and jobs.

7. Interviewing

How to make the interview process work for you—from the first "hello" to the first day on the job.

8. Following up

Often overlooked, it's perhaps the most important part of the job search process.

We won't try to kid you—it is a lot of work. To do it right, you have to get started early, probably quite a bit earlier than you'd planned. Frankly, we recommend beginning this process one full year prior to the day you plan to start work.

So if you're in college, the end of your junior year is the right time to begin your research and preparations. That should give you enough time during summer vacation to set up your files and begin your library research.

Whether you're in college or graduate school, one item may need to be planned even earlier—allowing enough free time in your schedule of classes for interview preparations and appointments. Waiting until your senior year to "make some time" is already too late. Searching for a full-time job is itself a full- time job! Though you're naturally restricted by your schedule, it's not difficult to plan ahead and prepare for your upcoming job search. Try to leave at least a couple of free mornings or afternoons a week. A day or even two without classes is even better.

Otherwise, you'll find yourself crazed and distracted, trying to prepare for an interview in the 10-minute period between classes. Not the best way to make a first impression and certainly not the way you want to approach an important meeting.

The Self-Evaluation Process

Learning about who you are, what you want to be, and what you can be are critical first steps in the job search process and, unfortunately, the ones most often ignored by job seekers everywhere, especially students eager to leave the ivy behind and plunge into the "real world." But avoiding this crucial self- evaluation can hinder your progress and even damage some decent prospects.

Why? Because in order to land a job with a company at which you'll actually be happy, you need to be able to identify those ensembles and/or job descriptions that best match your own skills, likes, and strengths. The more you know about yourself, the more you'll bring to this process, and the more accurate the "match- ups." You'll be able to structure your presentation (resume, cover letter, interviews, follow up) to stress your most marketable skills and talents (and, dare we say it, conveniently avoid your weaknesses?). Later, you'll be able to evaluate potential employers and job offers on the basis of your own needs and desires. This spells the difference between waking up in the morning ready to enthusiastically tackle a new day of challenges and shutting off the alarm in the hopes the day (and your job) will just disappear.

Creating Your Self-Evaluation Form

If your self-evaluation is to have any meaning, you must first be honest with yourself. This self-evaluation form should help you achieve that goal by providing a structured environment to answer these tough questions.

Take a sheet of lined notebook paper. Set up eight columns across the top—Strengths, Weaknesses, Skills, Hobbies, Courses, Experience, Likes, Dislikes.

Now, fill in each of these columns according to these guidelines:

Strengths: Describe personality traits you consider your strengths (and try to look at them as an employer would)—e.g., persistence, organization, ambition, intelligence, logic, assertiveness, aggression, leadership, etc.

Weaknesses: The traits you consider glaring weaknesses—e.g., impatience, conceit, etc. Remember: Look at these as a potential employer would. Don't assume that the personal traits you consider weaknesses will necessarily be considered negatives in the business world. You may be "easily bored," a trait that led to lousy grades early on because teachers couldn't keep you interested in the subjects they were teaching. Well, many entrepreneurs need ever-changing challenges. Strength or weakness?

Skills: Any skill you have, whether you think it's marketable or not. Everything from basic business skills—like typing and word processing—to computer or teaching experience and foreign language literacy. Don't forget possibly obscure but marketable skills like "good telephone voice."

Hobbies: The things you enjoy doing that, more than likely, have no overt connection to career objectives. These should be distinct from the skills listed above, and may include activities such as reading, games, travel, sports, and the like. While these may not be marketable in any general sense, they may well be useful in specific circumstances.

Courses: All the general subject areas (history, literature, etc.) and/or specific courses you've taken that may be marketable, enjoyable, or both.

Experience: Just the specific functions you performed at any part-time (school year) or full-time (summer) jobs. Entries may include "General Office" (typing, filing, answering phones, etc.), "Office Assistant," "Retail Clerk" etc.

Likes: List all your "likes," those important considerations that you haven't listed anywhere else yet. These might include the types of people you like to be with, the kind of environment you prefer (city, country, large places, small places, quiet, loud, fast-paced, slow-paced) and anything else that hasn't shown up somewhere on this form. Try to think of "likes" that you have that are related to the job you are applying for. For example, if you're applying for a job at a major theatre company, mention that you enjoy reading the *Backstage*. However, try not to include entries that refer to specific jobs or companies. We'll list those on another form.

Dislikes: All the people, places, and things you can easily live without.

Now assess the "marketability" of each item you've listed. (In other words, are some of your likes, skills, or courses easier to match to a performing arts job description, or do they have little to do with a specific job or company?) Mark highly marketable skills with an "H". Use "M" to characterize those skills that may be marketable in a particular set of circumstances, "L" for those with minimal potential application to any job.

Referring back to the same list, decide if you'd enjoy using your marketable skills or talents as part of your everyday job—"Y" for yes, "N" for no. You may type 80 words a minute but truly despise typing or worry that stressing it too much will land you on the permanent clerical staff. If so, mark typing with an "N". (Keep one thing in mind— just because you dislike typing shouldn't mean you absolutely won't accept a job that requires it. Almost every professional job today requires computer-based work that makes typing a plus.)

Now, go over the entire form carefully and look for inconsistencies.

To help you with your own form, there's a sample on the following page that a job-hunter might have completed.

The Value of a Second Opinion

There is a familiar misconception about the self-evaluation process that gets in the way of many new job applicants—the belief that it is a process that must be accomplished in isolation. Nothing could be further from the truth. Just because the family doctor tells that you need an operation doesn't mean you run right off to the hospital. Prudence dictates that you check out the opinion with another physician. Getting such a "second opinion"—someone else's, not just your own—is a valuable practice throughout the job search process, as well.

So after you've completed the various exercises in this chapter, review them with a friend, relative, or parent—just be sure it's someone who knows you well and cares about you. These second opinions may reveal some aspects of your self-description on which you and the rest of the world differ. If so, discuss them, learn from them and, if necessary, change some conclusions. Should everyone concur with your self-evaluation, you will be reassured that your choices are on target.

Establishing Your Career Objective(s)

For better or worse, you now know something more of who and what you are. But we've yet to establish and evaluate another important area—your overall needs, desires and goals. Where are you going? What do you want to accomplish?

If you're getting ready to graduate from college or graduate school, the next five years are the most critical period of your whole career. You need to make the initial transition from college to the workplace, establish yourself in a new and completely unfamiliar company environment, and begin to build the professional credentials necessary to achieve your career goals.

If that strikes you as a pretty tall order, well, it is. Unless you've narrowly

Strength	Weakness	Skill	Hobby	Course	Experience	Like	Dislike
Marketable?							
Enjoy?							
Marketable?							
Enjoy?							
Marketable?							
Enjoy?							

prepared yourself for a specific profession, you're probably most ill-prepared for any real job. Instead, you've (hopefully) learned some basic principles—research and analytical skills that are necessary for success at almost any level—and, more or less, how to think.

It's tough to face, but face it you must: No matter what your college, major, or degree, all you represent right now is potential. How you package that potential and what you eventually make of it is completely up to you. It's an unfortunate fact that many companies will take a professional with barely a year or two experience over any newcomer, no matter how promising. Smaller ensembles, especially, can rarely afford to hire someone who can't begin contributing immediately.

So you have to be prepared to take your comparatively modest skills and experience and package them in a way that will get you interviewed and hired. Quite a challenge.

There are a number of different ways to approach such a task. If you find yourself confused or unable to list such goals, you might want to check a few books in your local library that have more time to spend on the topic of "goal-oriented planning."

But Is the Performing Arts Industry Right for You?

Presuming you now have a much better idea of yourself and where you'd like to be, let's make sure some of your basic assumptions are right. We presume you purchased this *Career Directory* because you're considering a career in some area of performing arts. Are you sure? Do you know enough about the industry as a whole and the particular part you're heading for to decide whether it's right for you? Probably not. So start your research now—learn as much about your potential career field as you now know about yourself.

Start with the essays in the **Advice from the Pro's** section—these will give you an excellent overview of the performing arts industry, some very specialized (and growing) areas, and some things to keep in mind as you start on your career search. They will also give you a relatively simplified, though very necessary, understanding of just what people who work in all these areas of performing arts actually do.

Other sources you should consider consulting to learn more about this business are listed in the **Career Resources** section of this book.

In that section, we've listed trade associations and publications associated with performing arts professions (together with many other resources that will help your job search. (Consult the front of this directory for a complete description of the **Career Resources** section.) Where possible in the association entries, we've included details on educational information they make available, but you should certainly consider writing each of the pertinent associations, letting them know you're interested in a career in their area of specialization and would appreciate whatever help and advice they're willing to impart. You'll find many sponsor seminars and conferences throughout the country, some of which you may be able to attend.

The trade publications are dedicated to the highly specific interests of performing arts professionals. These magazines are generally not available at newsstands, but you may be able to obtain back issues at your local library (most major libraries have extensive collections of such journals) or by writing to the magazines' circulation/subscription departments. We've also included regional and local magazines.

You may also try writing to the publishers and/or editors of these publications. State in your cover letter what area of the performing arts you're considering and ask them for whatever help and advice they can offer. But be specific. These are busy professionals and they do not have the time or the inclination to simply "tell me everything you can about performing onstage."

If you can afford it now, we strongly suggest subscribing to whichever trade magazines are applicable to the specialty you're considering. If you can't subscribe to all of them, make it a point to regularly read the copies that arrive at your local public or college library.

These publications may well provide the most imaginative and far-reaching information for your job search. Even a quick perusal of an issue or two will give you an excellent feel for the industry. After reading only a few articles, you'll already get a handle on what's happening in the field and some of the industry's peculiar and particular jargon. Later, more detailed study will aid you in your search for a specific job.

Authors of the articles themselves may well turn out to be important resources. If an article is directly related to your chosen specialty, why not call the author and ask some questions? You'd be amazed how willing many of these professionals will be to talk to you and answer your questions, and the worst they can do is say no. (But *do* use common sense—authors will not *always* respond graciously to your invitation to "chat about the business." And don't be *too* aggressive here.)

You'll find such research to be a double-edged sword. In addition to helping you get a handle on whether the area you've chosen is really right for you, you'll slowly learn enough about particular specialties, companies, the industry, etc., to actually sound like you know what you're talking about when you hit the pavement looking for your first job. And nothing is better than sounding like a pro—except being one.

The Performing Arts Are It. Now What?

After all this research, we're going to assume you've reached that final decision—you really do want a career working to preserve the performing arts. It is with this vague certainty that all too many of you will race off, hunting for any company willing to give you a job. You'll manage to get interviews at a couple and, smiling brightly, tell everyone you meet, "I want a career in the performing arts." The interviewers, unfortunately, will all ask the same awkward question—"What *exactly* do you want to do in our company?"—and that will be the end of that.

It is simply not enough to narrow your job search to a specific industry. And so far, that's all you've done. You must now establish a specific career objective—the job you want to start, the career you want to pursue. Just knowing that you "want to get into the performing arts" doesn't mean anything to anybody. If that's all you can tell an interviewer, it demonstrates a lack of research into the industry itself and your failure to think ahead.

Interviewers will *not* welcome you with open arms if you're still vague about your career goals. If you've managed to get an "informational interview" with an executive whose company currently has no job openings, what is he or she supposed to do with your resume after you leave? Who should he or she send it to for future consideration? Since *you* don't seem to know exactly what you want to do, how's he or she going to figure it out? Worse, that person will probably resent your asking him or her to function as your personal career counselor.

Remember, the more specific your career objective, the better your chances of finding a job. It's that simple and that important. Naturally, before you declare your objective to the world, check once again to make sure your specific job target matches the skills and interests you defined in your self- evaluation. Eventually, you may want to state such an objective on your resume, and "To obtain an entry-level position as an assistant stage manager with a major theatre group," is quite a bit better than "I want a career in the theatre." Do not consider this step final until you can summarize your job/career objective in a single, short, accurate sentence.

Targeting Prospective Employers and Networking for Success

As you move along the job search path, one fact will quickly become crystal clear—it is primarily a process of **elimination**: your task is to consider and research as many options as possible, then—for good reasons—**eliminate** as many as possible, attempting to continually narrow your focus.

Your Ideal Company Profile

Let's establish some criteria to evaluate potential employers. This will enable you to identify your target companies, the places you'd really like to work. (This process, as we've pointed out, is not specific to any industry or field; the same steps, with perhaps some research resource variations, are applicable to any job, any company, any industry.)

Take a sheet of blank paper and divide it into three vertical columns. Title it "Target Company—Ideal Profile." Call the lefthand column "Musts," the middle column "Preferences," and the righthand column "Nevers."

We've listed a series of questions below. After considering each question, decide whether a particular criteria *must* be met, whether you would simply *prefer* it or *never* would consider it at all. If there are other criteria you consider important, feel free to add them to the list below and mark them accordingly on your Profile.

1. What are your geographical preferences? (Possible answers: U.S., Canada, International, Anywhere). If you only want to work in the U.S., then "Work in United States" would be the entry in the "Must" column. "Work in Canada or Foreign Country" might be the first entry in your "Never" column. There would be no applicable entry for this question in the "Preference" column. If, however, you will consider working in two of the three, then your "Must" column entry might read "Work in U.S. or Canada," your "Preference"

entry—if you preferred one over the other—could read "Work in U.S.," and the "Never" column, "Work Overseas."

2. If you prefer to work in the U.S. or Canada, what area, state(s), or province(s)? If overseas, what area or countries?

3. Do you prefer a large city, small city, town, or somewhere as far away from civilization as possible?

4. In regard to question three, any specific preferences?

5. Do you prefer a warm or cold climate?

6. Do you prefer a large or small company? Define your terms (by sales, income, employees, offices, etc.).

7. Do you mind relocating right now? Do you want to work for an ensemble with a reputation for *frequently* relocating top people?

8. Do you mind travelling frequently? What percent do you consider reasonable? (Make sure this matches the normal requirements of the job specialization you're considering.)

9. What salary would you *like* to receive (put in the "Preference" column)? What's the *lowest* salary you'll accept (in the "Must" column)?

10. Are there any benefits (such as an expense account, medical and/or dental insurance, company car, etc.) you must or would like to have?

11. Are you planning to attend graduate school at some point in the future and, if so, is a tuition reimbursement plan important to you?

12. Do you feel that a formal training program is necessary?

13. If applicable, what kinds of specific accounts would you prefer to work with? What specific products?

It's important to keep revising this new form, just as you should continue to update your Self-Evaluation Form. After all, it contains the criteria by which you will judge every potential employer. Armed with a complete list of such criteria, you're now ready to find all the companies that match them.

Targeting Individual Companies

To begin creating your initial list of targeted companies, start with the **Job Opportunities Databank** in this directory. We've listed many major theatre, ballet, opera, symphonic, and theme park companies that offer the most potential for those seeking a performing arts career; most of these companies were contacted by telephone for this edition. These listings provide a plethora of data concerning the companies' overall operations, hiring practices, and other important information on entry-level job opportunities. This latter information includes key contacts (names), the average number of entry-level people they hire each year, along with complete job descriptions and requirements.

One word of advice. You'll notice that some of the companies list "0" under average entry-level hiring. This is more a reflection of the current economic times than a long-range projection. In the past, these companies probably did list an average number of new hires, and they will again in the future. We have listed these companies for three reasons: 1) to present you with the overall view of prospective employers; 2) because even companies that don't plan to do any hiring will experience unexpected job openings; and 3) things change, so as soon as the economy begins to pick up, expect entry-level hiring to increase again.

We have attempted to include information on those major firms that represent many of the entry-level jobs out there. But there are, of course, many other companies of all sizes and shapes that you may also wish to research. In the **Career Resources** section, we have listed other reference tools you can use to obtain more information on the companies we've listed, as well as those we haven't.

The Other Side of the Iceberg

You are now better prepared to choose those companies that meet your own list of criteria. But a word of caution about these now-"obvious" requirements—they are not the only ones you need to take into consideration. And you probably won't be able to find all or many of the answers to this second set of questions in any reference book—they are known, however, by those persons already at work in the industry. Here is the list you will want to follow:

Promotion

If you are aggressive about your career plans, you'll want to know if you have a shot at the top. Look for companies that traditionally promote from within.

Training

Look for companies in which your early tenure will actually be a period of on-the-job training, hopefully ones in which training remains part of the long-term process. As new techniques and technologies enter the workplace, you must make sure you are updated on these skills. Most importantly, look for training that is craft- or function-oriented—these are the so-called **transferable skills**, ones you can easily bring along with you from job-to-job, company-to-company, sometimes industry-to-industry.

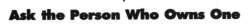

Ask the Person Who Owns One

Some years ago, this advice was used as the theme for a highly successful automobile advertising campaign. The prospective car buyer was encouraged to find out about the product by asking the (supposedly) most trustworthy judge of all—someone who was already an owner.

You can use the same approach in your job search. You all have relatives or friends already out in the workplace—these are your best sources of information about those industries. Cast your net in as wide a circle as possible. Contact these valuable resources. You'll be amazed at how readily they will answer your questions. I suggest you check the criteria list at the beginning of this chapter to formulate your own list of pertinent questions. Ideally and minimally you will want to learn: how the industry is doing, what its long-term prospects are, the kinds of personalities they favor (aggressive, low key), rate of employee turnover, and the availability of training.

Salary

Some industries are generally high paying, some not. But even an industry with a tradition of paying abnormally low salaries may have particular companies or job functions (like sales) within companies that command high remuneration. But it's important you know what the industry standard is.

Benefits

Look for companies in which health insurance, vacation pay, retirement plans, 401K accounts, stock purchase opportunities, and other important employee benefits are extensive—and company paid. If you have to pay for basic benefits like medical coverage yourself, you'll be surprised at how expensive they are. An exceptional benefit package may even lead you to accept a lower-than-usual salary.

Unions

Early in your career in the performing arts, you'll find yourself contemplating unionization. What are the prominent unions in the performing arts industry? Why is there a union? Will I be compelled to join a union?

All labor unions involved in the performing arts in the United States are chartered by the American Federation of Labor and Congress of Industrial Organizations (AFL-CIO). One such union is the Actors' Equity Association—a labor organization that represents actors and stage managers in the legitimate theatre throughout the United States and is a branch of the Associated Actors and Artists of America. There are also numerous professional membership organizations in the arts that serve the functions of unions but are not chartered, such as the Dramatists Guild and the Association of Theatrical Press Agents and Managers (ATPAM). Still other arts professionals, such as filmmakers and talent representatives, have to get licenses or franchises; others must earn stamps of approval from government agencies, labor unions, etc.

As a labor organization, unions negotiate minimum wages and working conditions for its members, administer contracts, and enforce the many provisions of its various agreements with employers. Performing arts unions administer contracts in numerous theatrical venues: Broadway, national tours, productions, bus and truck tours, resident and non-resident dramatic stock, indoor and outdoor musical stock, dinner theatres, resident theatres, business theatres, theatres for young audiences, off-Broadway, theme parks, university theatres, cabaret theatres, developing theatres, and small professional theatres, in addition to guest artist arrangements and special agreements.

Despite common belief, no one can be denied a job simply because he/she does not belong to a particular union having jurisdiction over a job category. However, if you are hired as an actor or musician with a unionized company, you will, in all probability, be asked to join the appropriate union. In fact, you will be obligated to do so in a timely manner. This, however, is not true for stagehands, technicians, managers, and press agents; while you could not be denied such a position if it were offered to you, the union with jurisdiction over that job category is not required to offer you membership. This is because it is legal for unions to set annual quotas on how many new members they will accept.

One last word on unionization. According to guidelines set by the National Labor Relations Board, management cannot be unionized. This is arguable, however, and is not always adhered to throughout the industry. For example, theatrical producers and general managers join unions early in their careers and maintain active membership.

In short, if you seek wide recognition, high position, and maximum union income, it is unlikely that joining an arts-related union or professional association can be avoided for very long.

Making Friends and Influencing People

Networking is a term you have probably heard; it is definitely a key aspect of any successful job search and a process you must master.

Informational interviews and **job interviews** are the two primary outgrowths of successful networking.

Referrals, an aspect of the networking process, entail using someone else's name, credentials, and recommendation to set up a receptive environment when seeking a job interview.

All of these terms have one thing in common: Each depends on the actions of other people to put them in motion. Don't let this idea of "dependency" slow you down, however. A job search *must* be a very pro-active process—*you* have to initiate the action. When networking, this means contacting as many people as you can. The more you contact, the better the chances of getting one of those people you are "depending" on to take action and help you out.

So what *is* networking? How do you build your own network? And why do you need one in the first place? The balance of this chapter answers all of those questions and more.

Get your telephone ready. It's time to make some friends.

Not the World's Oldest Profession, But...

Networking is the process of creating your own group of relatives, friends, and acquaintances who can feed you the information you need to find a job—identifying where the jobs are and giving you the personal introductions and background data necessary to pursue them.

If the job market were so well-organized that details on all employment opportunities were immediately available to all applicants, there would be no need for such a process. Rest assured the job market is *not* such a smooth-running machine— most applicants are left very much to their own devices. Build and use your own network wisely and you'll be amazed at the amount of useful job intelligence you will turn up.

While the term networking didn't gain prominence until the 1970s, it is by no means a new phenomenon. A selection process that connects people of similar skills, backgrounds, and/or attitudes—in other words, networking—has been in existence in a variety of forms for centuries. Attend any Ivy League school and you're automatically part of its very special centuries-old network.

And it works. Remember your own reaction when you were asked to recommend someone for a job, club, or school office? You certainly didn't want to look foolish, so you gave it some thought and tried to recommend the best-qualified person that you thought would "fit in" with the rest of the group. It's a built-in screening process.

Creating the Ideal Network

As in most endeavors, there's a wrong way and a right way to network. The following tips will help you construct your own wide-ranging, information-gathering, interview-generating group—*your* network.

Diversify

Unlike the Harvard or Princeton network—confined to former graduates of each school—your network should be as diversified and wide-ranging as possible. You never know who might be in a position to help, so don't limit your group of friends. The more diverse they are, the greater the variety of information they may supply you with.

Don't Forget...

...to include everyone you know in your initial networking list: friends, relatives, social acquaintances, classmates, college alumni, professors, teachers, your dentist, doctor, family lawyer, insurance agent, banker, travel agent, elected officials in your community, ministers, fellow church members, local tradesmen, and local business or social club officers. And everybody they know!

Be Specific

Make a list of the kinds of assistance you will require from those in your network, then make specific requests of each. Do they know of jobs at their company? Can they introduce you to the proper executives? Have they heard something about or know someone at the company you're planning to interview with next week?

The more organized you are, the easier it will be to target the information you need and figure out who might have it. Begin to keep a business card file or case so you can keep track of all your contacts. A small plastic case for file cards that is available at any discount store will do nicely. One system you can use is to staple the card to a 3 x 5 index card. On the card, write down any information about that contact that you might need later—when you talked to them, job leads they provided, specific job search advice, etc. You will then have all the information you need about each company or contact in one easily accessible location.

Learn the Difference...

...between an **informational** interview and a **job** interview. The former requires you to cast yourself in the role of information gatherer; *you* are the interviewer and knowledge is your goal—about an industry, company, job function, key executive, etc. Such a meeting with someone already doing what you soon hope to be doing is by far the best way to find out everything you need to know—before you walk through the door and sit down for a formal job interview, at which time your purpose is more sharply defined: to get the job you're interviewing for.

If you learn of a specific job opening during an informational interview, you are in a position to find out details about the job, identify the interviewer and, possibly, even learn some things about him or her. In addition, presuming you get your contact's permission, you may be able to use his or her name as a referral. Calling up the interviewer and saying, "Joan Smith in your human resources department suggested I contact you regarding openings for assistant stage managers," is far superior to "Hello. Do you have any job openings at your theatre?"

(In such a case, be careful about referring to a specific job opening, even if your contact told you about it. It may not be something you're supposed to know about. By presenting your query as an open-ended question, you give your prospective employer the option of exploring your background without further commitment. If there is a job there and you're qualified for it, you'll find out soon enough.)

Don't Waste a Contact

Not everyone you call on your highly-diversified networking list will know about a job opening. It would be surprising if each one did. But what about *their* friends and colleagues? It's amazing how everyone knows someone who knows someone. Ask— you'll find that someone.

Value Your Contacts

If someone has provided you with helpful information or an introduction to a friend or colleague, keep him or her informed about how it all turns out. A referral that's panned out should be reported to the person who opened the door for you in the first place. Such courtesy will be appreciated—and may lead to more contacts. If someone has nothing to offer today, a call back in the future is still appropriate and may pay off.

The lesson is clear: Keep your options open, your contact list alive. Detailed records of your network—whom you spoke with, when, what transpired, etc.—will help you keep track of your overall progress and organize what can be a complicated and involved process.

Informational Interviews

So now you've done your homework, built your network, and begun using your contacts. It's time to go on your first informational interview.

A Typical Interview

You were, of course, smart enough to include John Fredericks, the bank officer who handled your dad's mortgage, on your original contact list. He knew you as a bright and conscientious college senior; in fact, your perfect three-year repayment record on the loan you took out to buy that '67 Plymouth impressed him. When you called him, he was happy to refer you to his friend, Carol Jones, a producer at the Avondale Repertory Theatre. Armed with permission to use Fredericks' name and recommendation, you wrote a letter to Carol Jones, the gist of which went something like this:

> *I am writing at the suggestion of Mr. John Fredericks at Fidelity National Bank. He knows of my interest in a stage management career and, given your position at the Avondale Repertory Theatre, thought you might be able to help me gain a better understanding of this specialized field and the career opportunities it presents.*
>
> *While I am majoring in theatre, I know I need to speak with professionals such as yourself to learn how to apply my studies to a professional theatre environment.*
>
> *If you could spare a half hour to meet with me, I'm certain I would be able to get enough information about this specialty to give me the direction I need.*
>
> *I'll call your office next week in the hope that we can schedule a meeting.*

Send a copy of this letter to Mr. Fredericks at the bank—it will refresh his memory should Ms. Jones call to inquire about you. Next step: the follow-up phone call. After you get Ms. Jones' secretary on the line, it will, with luck, go something like this:

> *"Hello, I'm Paul Smith. I'm calling in reference to a letter I wrote to Ms. Jones requesting an appointment."*
>
> *"Oh, yes. You're the young man interested in stage management. Ms. Jones can see you on June 23rd. Will 10 A.M. be satisfactory?"*
>
> *"That's fine. I'll be there."*

Well, the appointed day arrives. Well-scrubbed and dressed in your best (and most conservative) suit, you are ushered into Ms. Jones' office. She offers you coffee (you decline) and says that it is okay to light up if you wish to smoke (you decline). The conversation might go something like this:

You: "Thank you for seeing me, Ms. Jones. I know you are busy and appreciate your taking the time to talk with me."

Jones: "Well it's my pleasure since you come so highly recommended. I'm always pleased to meet someone interested in my field."

You: "As I stated in my letter, my interest in stage management is very real, but I'm having trouble seeing how all of my studies will adapt to the work environment. I think I'll be much better prepared to evaluate future job offers if I can learn more about your experiences. May I ask you a few questions about the Avondale Repertory Theatre?"

Jones: "Fire away, Paul".

Ms. Jones relaxes. She realizes this is a knowledge hunt you are on, not a thinly-veiled job interview. Your approach has kept her off the spot—she doesn't have to be concerned with making a hiring decision. You've already gotten high marks for not putting her on the defensive.

You: "I have a few specific questions I'd like to ask. First, at a company such as yours, where does an assistant stage manager start?"

Jones: "In this company, you would be assigned to an experienced stage manager to work as that person's assistant for the first month of your employment. This gives you a chance to see the way we work and to become comfortable with our facilities. After that, if you had progressed well, you would eventually receive your own projects to work on."

You: "Where and how fast does someone progress after that?"

Jones: "Obviously, that depends on the person, but given the proper aptitude and ability, that person would simply get more responsibilities to handle. How well you do all along the way will determine how far and how fast you progress."

You: "What is the work environment like—is it pretty hectic?"

Jones: "The performing arts are exciting but chaotic, and though we try to keep the work load at a manageable level, flexibility and versatility are the most important qualifications in our business. This is an unpredictable business, and things change sometimes minute-to-minute. It's not a profession for the faint-hearted!"

You: "If I may shift to another area, I'd be interested in your opinion about performing arts careers in general and what you see as the most likely areas of opportunity in the foreseeable future. Do you think this is a growth career area?"

Jones: "Well, judging by the hiring record of our company, I think you'll find it's an area worth making a commitment to. At the entry level, we've hired a number of new people in the past three or four years. There always seems to be opportunities, though it's gotten far more competitive."

You: "Do you think someone with my qualifications and background could get started in stage management? Perhaps a look at my resume would be helpful to you." *(Give it to Ms. Jones.)*

Jones: "Your course work looks appropriate. I especially like the internships you've held every summer. I think you have a real chance to break into this field. I don't think we're hiring right now, but I know a couple of theatres that are looking for bright young people with qualifications like yours. Let me give you a couple of phone numbers." *(Write down names and phone numbers.)*

You: "You have been very generous with your time, but I can see from those flashing buttons on your phone that you have other things to do. Thank you again for taking the time to talk with me."

Jones: "You're welcome."

After the Interview

The next step should be obvious: **Two** thank-you letters are required, one to Ms. Jones, the second to Mr. Fredericks. Get them both out immediately. (And see the chapter on writing letters if you need help writing them.)

Keeping Track of the Interview Trail

Let's talk about record keeping again. If your networking works the way it's supposed to, this was only the first of many such interviews. Experts have estimated that the average person could develop a contact list of 250 people. Even if we limit your initial list to only 100, if each of them gave you one referral, your list would suddenly have 200 names. Presuming that it will not be necessary or helpful to see all of them, it's certainly possible that such a list could lead to 100 informational and/or job interviews! Unless you keep accurate records, by the time you're on No. 50, you won't even remember the first dozen!

So get the results of each interview down on paper. Use whatever format with which you're comfortable. You should create some kind of file, folder, or note card that is an "Interview Recap Record." If you have access to a personal computer, take advantage of it. It will be much easier to keep you information stored in one place and well-organized. Your record should be set up and contain something like the following:

> *Name: Avondale Repertory Theatre*
> *Address: 333 E. 54th St., Rochester, NY 10000*
> *Phone: (212) 555-4000*
> *Contact: Carol Jones*
> *Type of Business: Repertory theatre*
> *Referral Contact: Mr. Fredericks, Fidelity National Bank*
> *Date: June 23, 1993*

At this point, you should add a one- or two-paragraph summary of what you found out at the meeting. Since these comments are for your eyes only, you should be both objective and subjective. State the facts—what you found out in response to your specific questions—but include your impressions—your estimate of the opportunities for further discussions, your chances for future consideration for employment.

"I Was Just Calling to..."

Find any logical opportunity to stay in touch with Ms. Jones. You may, for example, let her know when you graduate and tell her your grade point average, carbon her in on any letters you write to Mr. Fredericks, even send a congratulatory note if her company's year-end financial results are positive or if you read something in the local paper about her. This type of follow up has the all-important effect of keeping you and your name in the forefront of others' minds. Out of sight *is* out of mind. No matter how talented you may be or how good an impression you made, you'll have to work hard to "stay visible."

There Are Rules, Just Like Any Game

It should already be obvious that the networking process is not only effective, but also quite deliberate in its objectives. There are two specific groups of people you must attempt to target: those who can give you information about an industry or career area and those who are potential employers. The line between these groups may often blur. Don't be concerned—you'll soon learn when (and how) to shift the focus from interviewer to interviewee.

To simplify this process, follow a single rule: Show interest in the field or job area under discussion, but wait to be asked about actually working for that company. During your informational interviews, you will be surprised at the number of times the person you're interviewing turns to you and asks, "Would you be interested in...?" Consider carefully what's being asked and, if you *would* be interested in the position under discussion, make your feelings known.

If the Process Scares You

Some of you will undoubtedly be hesitant about, even fear, the networking process. It is not an unusual response—it is very human to want to accomplish things "on your own," without anyone's help. Understandable and commendable as such independence might seem, it is, in reality, an impediment if it limits your involvement in this important process. Networking has such universal application because **there is no other effective way to bridge the gap between job applicant and job.** Employers are grateful for its existence. You should be, too.

Whether you are a first-time applicant or reentering the work force now that the children are grown, the networking process will more than likely be your point of entry. Sending out mass mailings of your resume and answering the help-wanted ads may well be less personal (and, therefore, "easier") approaches, but they will also be far less effective. The natural selection process of the networking phenomenon is your assurance that water does indeed seek its own level—you will be matched up with companies and job opportunities in which there is a mutual fit.

Six Good Reasons to Network

Many people fear the networking process because they think they are "bothering" others with their own selfish demands. Nonsense! There are good reasons—six of them, at least—why the people on your networking list will be happy to help you:

▼

Why Should You Network?

- To unearth current information about the industry, company, and pertinent job functions. Remember: Your knowledge and understanding of broad industry trends, financial health, hiring opportunities, and the competitive picture are key.
- To investigate each company's hiring policies—who makes the decisions, who the key players are (personnel, staff managers), whether there's a hiring season, whether they prefer applicants going direct or through agentss, etc.
- To sell yourself—discuss your interests and research activities—and leave your calling card, your resume.
- To seek out advice on refining your job search process.
- To obtain the names of other persons (referrals) who can give you additional information on where the jobs are and what the market conditions are like.
- To develop a list of follow-up activities that will keep you visible to key contacts.

1. **Some day you will get to return the favor.** An ace insurance salesman built a successful business by offering low-cost coverage to first-year medical students. Ten years later, these now-successful practitioners remembered the company (and person) that helped them when they were just getting started. He gets new referrals every day.

2. **They, too, are seeking information.** An employer who has been out of school for several years might be interested in what the latest developments in the classroom are. He or she may be hoping to learn as much from you as you are from them, so be forthcoming in offering information. This desire for new information may be the reason he or she agreed to see you in the first place.

3. **Internal politics.** Some people will see you simply to make themselves appear powerful, implying to others in their organization that they have the authority to hire (they may or may not), an envied prerogative.

4. **They're "saving for a rainy day".** Executives know that it never hurts to look and that maintaining a backlog of qualified candidates is a big asset when the floodgates open and supervisors are forced to hire quickly.

5. **They're just plain nice.** Some people will see you simply because they feel it's the decent thing to do or because they just can't say "no."

6. **They are looking themselves.** Some people will see you because they are anxious to do a friend (whoever referred you) a favor. Or because they have another friend seeking new talent, in which case you represent a referral they can make (part of their own continuing network process). You see, networking never does stop—it helps them and it helps you.

Before you proceed to the next chapter, begin making your contact list. You may wish to keep a separate sheet of paper or note card on each person (especially the dozen or so you think are most important), even a separate telephone list to make your communications easier and more efficient. However you set up your list, be sure to keep it up to date—it won't be long before you'll be calling each and every name on the list.

CHAPTER NINETEEN

Preparing Your Resume

Your resume is a one-page summary of you—your education, skills, employment experience, and career objective(s). It is not a biography, but a "quick and dirty" way to identify and describe you to potential employers. Most importantly, its real purpose is to sell you to the company you want to work for. It must set you apart from all the other applicants (those competitors) out there.

So, as you sit down to formulate your resume, remember you're trying to present the pertinent information in a format and manner that will convince an executive to grant you an interview, the prelude to any job offer. All resumes must follow two basic rules—excellent visual presentation and honesty—but it's important to realize that different career markets require different resumes. The resume you are compiling for your career in performing arts is different than one you would prepare for a finance career. As more and more resume "training" services become available, employers are becoming increasingly choosy about the resumes they receive. They expect to view a professional presentation, one that sets a candidate apart from the crowd. Your resume has to be perfect and it has to be specialized—clearly demonstrating the relationship between your qualifications and the job you are applying for.

An Overview of Resume Preparation

- **Know what you're doing**—your resume is a personal billboard of accomplishments. It must communicate your worth to a prospective employer in specific terms.

- **Your language should be action-oriented,** full of "doing"-type words. And less is better than more—be concise and direct. Don't worry about using complete sentences.

- **Be persuasive.** In those sections that allow you the freedom to do so, don't hesitate to communicate your worth in the strongest language. This does not mean a numbing list of self-congratulatory superlatives; it does mean truthful claims about your abilities and the evidence (educational, experiential) that supports them.

- **Don't be cheap or gaudy.** Don't hesitate to spend the few extra dollars necessary to present a professional-looking resume. Do avoid outlandish (and generally ineffective) gimmicks like oversized or brightly-colored paper.

- **Find an editor.** Every good writer needs one, and you are writing your resume. At the very least, it will offer you a second set of eyes proofreading for embarrassing typos. But if you are fortunate enough to have a professional in the field—a recruiter or personnel executive—critique a draft, grab the opportunity and be immensely grateful.

- **If you're the next Michelangelo,** so multitalented that you can easily qualify for jobs in different career areas, don't hesitate to prepare two or more completely different resumes. This will enable you to change the emphasis on your education and skills according to the specific career objective on each resume, a necessary alteration that will correctly target each one.

- **Choose the proper format.** There are only three we recommend—chronological, functional, and targeted format—and it's important you use the one that's right for you.

Considerations in the Electronic Age

Like most other areas of everyday life, computers have left their mark in the resume business. There are the obvious changes—the increased number of personal computers has made it easier to produce a professional-looking resume at home—and the not so obvious changes, such as the development of resume databases.

There are two kinds of resume databases: 1) An internal file maintained by a large corporation to keep track of the flood of resumes it gets each day (*U.S. News and World Report* stated that Fortune 50 companies receive more than 1,000 unsolicited resumes a day and that four out of every five are thrown away after a quick review). 2) Commercial databases that solicit resumes from job-seekers around the United States and make them available to corporations, who pay a fee to search the database.

Internal Databases Mean Some of the Old Rules Don't Apply

The internal databases maintained by large companies are changing some of the time-honored traditions of resume preparation. In the past, it was acceptable, even desirable, to use italic type and other eye-catching formats to make a resume more visually appealing. Not so today. Most of the companies that have a database enter resumes into it by using an optical scanner that reads the resume character by character and automatically enters it into the database. While these scanners are becoming more and more sophisticated, there are still significant limits as to what they can recognize and interpret.

What does this mean to you? It means that in addition to the normal screening process that all resumes go through, there is now one more screening step that determines if the scanner will be able to read your resume. If it can't, chances are your resume is going to be one of the four that is thrown away, instead of the one that is kept. To enhance the chances of your resume making it past this scanner test, here are some simple guidelines you can follow:

- Use larger typefaces (nothing smaller than 12 point), and avoid all but the most basic typefaces. Among the most common are Times Roman and Helvetica.

- No italics or underlining, and definitely no graphic images or boxes.

- Do not send copies. Either print a fresh copy out on your own printer, or take the resume to a print shop and have it professionally copied onto high-quality paper. Avoid dot matrix printers.

- Use 8 1/2 x 11 paper, unfolded. Any words that end up in a crease will not be scannable.

- Use only white or beige paper. Any other color will lessen the contrast between the paper and the letters and make it harder for the scanner to read.

- Use only a single column format. Scanners read from right to left on a page, so two- or three-column formats lead to nonsensical information when the document is scanned.

- While it is still appropriate to use action words to detail your accomplishments (initiated, planned, implemented, etc.), it is also important to include precise technical terms whenever possible as well. That's because databases are searched by key words, and only resumes that match those key words will be looked at. For example, if a publishing company was seeking someone who was experienced in a desktop publishing, they might search the database for all occurrences of "PageMaker" or "Ventura," two common desktop publishing software packages. If your resume only said "Successfully implemented and oversaw in-house desktop publishing program," it would be overlooked, and you wouldn't get the job!

National Databases: Spreading Your Good Name Around

Commercial resume databases are also having an impact on the job search process in the 1990s, so much so that anyone about to enter the job market should seriously consider utilizing one of these services.

Most of these new services work this way: Job-seekers send the database company a copy of their resume, or they fill out a lengthy application provided by the company. The information is then loaded into the company's computer, along with hundreds of other resumes from other job-seekers. The cost of this listing is usually nominal—$20 to $50 for a six- to 12-month listing. Some colleges operate systems for their graduates that are free of charge, so check with your placement office before utilizing a commercial service.

Once in the system, the resumes are available for viewing by corporate clients who have openings to fill. This is where the database companies really make their money—depending on the skill-level of the listees and the professions covered, companies can pay thousands of dollars for annual subscriptions to the service or for custom searches of the database.

Worried that your current employer might just pull up *your* resume when it goes searching for new employees? No need to be—most services allow listees to designate companies that their resume should not be released to, thus allowing you to conduct a job search with the peace of mind that your boss won't find out!

One warning about these services—most of them are new, so do as much research as you can before paying to have your resume listed. If you hear about a database you think you might want to be listed in, call the company and ask some questions:

- How long have they been in business?
- What has their placement rate been?
- What fields do they specialize in? (In other words, will the right people even *see* your resume?)
- Can you block certain companies from seeing your resume?
- How many other resumes are listed in the database? How many in your specialty?
- Is your experience level similar to that of other listees in the database?

The right answers to these questions should let you know if you have found the right database for you.

To help you locate these resume databases, we have listed many of them in the **Career Resources** chapter of this book.

The Records You Need

Well, now that you've heard all the do's and don't's and rules about preparing a resume, it's time to put those rules to work. The resume-writing process begins with the assembly and organization of all the personal, educational, and employment data from which you will choose the pieces that actually end up on paper. If this information is properly organized, writing your resume will be a relatively easy task, essentially a simple process of just shifting data from a set of the worksheets to another, to your actual resume. At the end of this chapter, you'll find all the forms you need to prepare your resume, including worksheets, fill-in-the-blanks resume forms, and sample resumes.

As you will soon see, there is a great deal of information you'll need to keep track of. In order to avoid a fevered search for important information, take the time right now to designate a single location in which to store all your records. My recommendation is either a filing cabinet or an expandable pocket portfolio. The latter is less expensive, yet it will still enable you to sort your records into an unlimited number of more-manageable categories.

Losing important report cards, citations, letters, etc., is easy to do if your life's history is scattered throughout your room or, even worse, your house! While copies of many of these items may be obtainable, why put yourself through all that extra work? Making good organization a habit will ensure that all the records you need to prepare your resume will be right where you need them when you need them.

For each of the categories summarized below, designate a separate file folder in which pertinent records can be kept. Your own notes are important, but keeping actual report cards, award citations, letters, etc. is even more so. Here's what your record-keeping system should include:

Transcripts (Including GPA and Class Rank Information)

Transcripts are your school's official record of your academic history, usually available, on request, from your high school's guidance office or college registrar's office. Your college may charge you for copies and "on request" doesn't mean "whenever you want"—you may have to wait some time for your request to be processed (so **don't** wait until the last minute!).

Your school-calculated GPA (Grade Point Average) is on the transcript. Most schools calculate this by multiplying the credit hours assigned to each course times a numerical grade equivalent (e.g., "A" = 4.0, "B" = 3.0, etc.), then dividing by total credits/courses taken. Class rank is simply a listing of GPAs, from highest to lowest.

Employment Records

Details on every part-time or full-time job you've held, including:

• Each employer's name, address, and telephone number
• Name of supervisor
• Exact dates worked
• Approximate numbers of hours per week
• Specific duties and responsibilities
• Specific skills utilized and developed
• Accomplishments and honors
• Copies of awards and letters of recommendation

Volunteer Activities

Just because you weren't paid for a specific job—stuffing envelopes for the local Democratic candidate, running a car wash to raise money for the homeless, manning a drug hotline—doesn't mean that it wasn't significant or that you shouldn't include it on your resume.

So keep the same detailed notes on these volunteer activities as you have on the jobs you've held:

• Each organization's name, address, and telephone number
• Name of supervisor
• Exact dates worked
• Approximate numbers of hours worked per week
• Specific duties and responsibilities
• Specific skills utilized
• Accomplishments and honors
• Copies of awards and letters of recommendation

Extracurricular Activities

List all sports, clubs, or other activities in which you've participated, either inside or outside school. For each, you should include:

- Name of activity/club/group
- Office(s) held
- Purpose of club/activity
- Specific duties/responsibilities
- Achievements, accomplishments, awards

If you were a long-standing member of a group or club, also include the dates that you were a member. This could demonstrate a high-level of commitment that could be used as a selling point.

Honors and Awards

Even if some of these honors are previously listed, specific data on every honor or award you receive should be kept, including, of course, the award itself! Keep the following information in your awards folder:

- Award name
- Date and from whom received
- What it was for
- Any pertinent details

Military Records

Complete military history, if pertinent, including:

- Dates of service
- Final rank awarded
- Duties and responsibilities
- All citations and awards
- Details on specific training and/or special schooling
- Skills developed
- Specific accomplishments

At the end of this chapter are seven **Data Input Sheets**. The first five cover employment, volunteer work, education, activities, and awards and are essential to any resume. The last two—covering military service and language skills—are important if, of course, they apply to you. I've only included one copy of each but, if you need to, you can copy the forms you need or simply write up your own using these as models.

Here are some pointers on how to fill out these all-important Data Sheets:

Employment Data Input Sheet: You will need to record the basic information—employer's name, address, and phone number; dates of employment; and supervisor's name—for your own files anyway. It may be an important addition to your networking list and will be necessary should you be asked to supply a reference list.

Duties should be a series of brief action statements describing what you did on this job. For example, if you worked as a hostess in a restaurant, this section might read: "Responsible for the delivery of 250 meals at dinner time and the supervision of 20 waiters and busboys. Coordinated reservations. Responsible for check and payment verification."

Skills should enumerate specific capabilities either necessary for the job or developed through it.

If you achieved *specific results*—e.g., "developed new filing system," "collected over $5,000 in previously-assumed bad debt," "instituted award-winning art program," etc.—or *received any award, citation or other honor*—"named Employee of the Month three times," "received Mayor's Citation for Innovation," etc.—make sure you list these.

Prepare one employment data sheet for each of the last three positions you have held; this is a basic guideline, but you can include more if relevant. Do not include sheets for short-term jobs (i.e., those that lasted one month or less).

Volunteer Work Data Input Sheet: Treat any volunteer work, no matter how basic or short (one day counts!), as if it were a job and record the same information. In both cases, it is especially important to note specific duties and responsibilities, skills required or developed, and any accomplishments or achievements you can point to as evidence of your success.

Educational Data Input Sheet: If you're in college, omit details on high school. If you're a graduate student, list details on both graduate and undergraduate course work. If you have not yet graduated, list your anticipated date of graduation. If more than a year away, indicate the numbers of credits earned through the most recent semester to be completed.

Activities Data Input Sheet: List your participation in the Student Government, Winter Carnival Committee, Math Club, Ski Patrol, etc., plus sports teams and/or any participation in community or church groups. Make sure you indicate if you were elected to any positions in clubs, groups, or on teams.

Awards and Honors Data Input Sheet: List awards and honors from your school (prestigious high school awards can still be included here, even if you're in graduate school), community groups, church groups, clubs, etc.

Military Service Data Input Sheet: Many useful skills are learned in the armed forces. A military stint often hastens the maturation process, making you a more attractive candidate. So if you have served in the military, make sure you include details in your resume. Again, include any computer skills you gained while in the service.

Language Data Input Sheet: An extremely important section for those of you with a real proficiency in a second language. And do make sure you have at least conversational fluency in the language(s) you list. One year of college French doesn't count, but if you've studied abroad, you probably are fluent or proficient. Such a talent could be invaluable, especially in today's increasingly international business climate.

While you should use the **Data Input Sheets** to summarize all of the data you have collected, do not throw away any of the specific information—report cards, transcripts, citations, etc.—just because it is recorded on these sheets. Keep all records in your files; you'll never know when you'll need them again!

Creating Your First Resume

There are many options that you can include or leave out. In general, we suggest you always include the following data:

1. Your name, address, and telephone number
2. Pertinent educational history (grades, class rank, activities, etc.) Follow the grade point "rule of thumb"—mention it only if it is above 3.0.
3. Pertinent work history
4. Academic honors
5. Memberships in organizations
6. Military service history (if applicable)

You have the option of including the following:

1. Your career objective
2. Personal data
3. Hobbies
4. Summary of qualifications
5. Feelings about travel and relocation (Include this if you know in advance that the job you are applying for requires it. Often times, for future promotion, job seekers **must** be willing to relocate
6. Photographs or illustrations (of yourself or anything else) especially if they are required by your profession—e.g., actors' composites

And you should never include the following:

1. Why you left past jobs
2. References
3. Salary history or present salary objectives/requirements (if salary history is specifically requested in an ad, it may be included in your cover letter)

Special note: There is definitely a school of thought that discourages any mention of personal data—marital status, health, etc.—on a resume. While I am not vehemently opposed to including such information, I am not convinced it is particularly necessary, either.

As far as hobbies go, I would only include such information if it were in some way pertinent to the job/career you're targeting, or if it shows how well-rounded you are. Your love of reading is pertinent if, for example, you are applying for a part-time job at a library. But including details on the joys of "hiking, long walks with my dog, and Isaac Asimov short stories" is nothing but filler and should be left out.

Maximizing Form and Substance

Your resume should be limited to a single page if possible. A two-page resume should be used **only** if you have an extensive work background related to a future goal. When you're laying out the resume, try to leave a reasonable amount of "white space"—generous margins all around and spacing between entries. It should be typed or printed (not Xeroxed) on 8 1/2" x 11" white, cream, or ivory stock. The ink should be black. Don't scrimp on the paper quality—use the best bond you can afford. And since printing 100 or even 200 copies will cost only a little more than 50, if you do decide to print your resume, *over*estimate your needs and opt for the highest quantity you think you may need. Prices at various "quick print" shops are not exorbitant and the quality look printing affords will leave the impression you want.

Use Power Words for Impact

Be brief. Use phrases rather than complete sentences. Your resume is a summary of your talents, not a term paper. Choose your words carefully and use "power words" whenever possible. "Organized" is more powerful than "put together;" "supervised" better than "oversaw;" "formulated" better than "thought up." Strong words like these can make the most mundane clerical work sound like a series of responsible, professional positions. And, of course, they will tend to make your resume stand out. Here's a starter list of words that you may want to use in your resume:

accomplished	composed	formulated	organized
achieved	computed	gathered	overhauled
acted	conceptualized	gave	oversaw
adapted	conducted	generated	participated
addressed	consolidated	guided	planned
administered	contributed	implemented	prepared
advised	coordinated	improved	presented
allocated	critiqued	initiated	presided
analyzed	defined	installed	produced
applied	delegated	instituted	programmed
approved	delivered	instructed	promoted
arranged	demonstrated	introduced	proposed
assembled	designed	invented	publicized
assessed	determined	issued	ran
assigned	developed	launched	recommended
assisted	devised	learned	recruited
attained	directed	lectured	regulated
budgeted	discovered	led	remodeled
built	drafted	litigated	renovated
calculated	edited	lobbied	reorganized
chaired	established	made	researched
changed	estimated	managed	restored
classified	evaluated	marketed	reviewed
collected	executed	mediated	revised
communicated	expanded	negotiated	rewrote
compiled	fixed	obtained	saved
completed	forecast	operated	scheduled

selected	streamlined	taught	utilized
served	studied	tested	won
sold	suggested	trained	wrote
solved	supervised	updated	
started	systematized	upgraded	

Choose the Right Format

There is not much mystery here—your background will generally lead you to the right format. For an entry-level job applicant with limited work experience, the chronological format, which organizes your educational and employment history by date (most recent first) is the obvious choice. For older or more experienced applicants, the functional—which emphasizes the duties and responsibilities of all your jobs over the course of your career, may be more suitable. If you are applying for a specific position in one field, the targeted format is for you. While I have tended to emphasize the chronological format in this chapter, one of the other two may well be the right one for you.

A List of Do's and Don't's

In case we didn't stress them enough, here are some rules to follow:

- **Do** be brief and to the point—two pages if absolutely necessary, one page if at all possible. Never longer!
- **Don't** be fancy. Multicolored paper and all-italic type won't impress employers, just make your resume harder to read (and easier to discard). Use plain white or ivory paper, black ink, and an easy-to-read standard typeface.
- **Do** forget rules about sentences. Say what you need to say in the fewest words possible; use phrases, not drawn-out sentences.
- **Do** stick to the facts. Don't talk about your dog, vacation, etc.
- **Don't** ever send a resume blind. A cover letter should always accompany a resume and that letter should always be directed to a specific person.
- **Don't** have any typos. Your resume must be perfect—proofread everything as many times as necessary to catch any misspellings, grammatical errors, strange hyphenations, or typos.
- **Do** use the spell check feature on your personal computer to find errors, and also try reading the resume backwards—you'll be surprised at how errors jump out at you when you do this. Finally, have a friend proof your resume.
- **Do** use your resume as your sales tool. It is, in many cases, as close to you as an employer will ever get. Make sure it includes the information necessary to sell yourself the way you want to be sold!
- **Do** spend the money for good printing. Soiled, tattered, or poorly reproduced copies speak poorly of your own self-image. Spend the money and take the time to make sure your resume is the best presentation you've ever made.
- **Do** help the reader, by organizing your resume in a clear-cut manner so key points are easily gleaned.

- **Don't** have a cluttered resume. Leave plenty of white space, especially around headings and all four margins.
- **Do** use bullets, asterisks, or other symbols as "stop signs" that the reader's eye will be naturally drawn to.

On the following pages, I've included a "fill-in-the-blanks" resume form so you can construct your own resume right away, plus one example each of a chronological, functional, and targeted resume.

EMPLOYMENT DATA INPUT SHEET

Employer name: _____

Address: _____

Phone: _____ Dates of employment: _____

Hours per week: _____ Salary/Pay: _____

Supervisor's name and title: _____

Duties: _____

_____

_____

Skills utilized: _____

_____

_____

_____

Accomplishments/Honors/Awards: _____

_____

_____

_____

Other important information: _____

_____

_____

_____

_____

VOLUNTEER WORK DATA INPUT SHEET

Organization name: _____

Address: _____

Phone: _____ Dates of activity: _____

Hours per week: _____

Supervisor's name and title: _____

Duties: _____

_____

_____

Skills utilized: _____

_____

_____

_____

Accomplishments/Honors/Awards: _____

_____

_____

_____

Other important information: _____

_____

_____

_____

HIGH SCHOOL DATA INPUT SHEET

School name: _____

Address: _____

Phone: _____ Years attended:_____

Major studies: _____

GPA/Class rank: _____

Honors: _____

Important courses: _____

_____

_____

_____

_____

OTHER SCHOOL DATA INPUT SHEET

School name: _____

Address: _____

Phone: _____ Years attended:_____

Major studies: _____

GPA/Class rank: _____

Honors: _____

Important courses _____

_____

_____

_____

_____

COLLEGE DATA INPUT SHEET

College: _____

Address: _____

Phone: _____ Years attended: _____

Degrees earned: _____ Major: _____ Minor: _____

Honors: _____

Important courses: _____

_____

_____

_____

_____

GRADUATE SCHOOL DATA INPUT SHEET

College: _____

Address: _____

Phone: _____ Years attended: _____

Degrees earned: _____ Major: _____ Minor: _____

Honors: _____

Important courses: _____

_____

_____

_____

_____

MILITARY SERVICE DATA INPUT SHEET

Branch: _____

Rank (at discharge): _____

Dates of service: _____

Duties and responsibilities: _____

_____

_____

_____

Special training and/or school attended: _____

_____

_____

_____

Citations or awards: _____

_____

_____

_____

Specific accomplishments: _____

_____

_____

_____

_____

_____

ACTIVITIES DATA INPUT SHEET

Club/activity: _____Office(s) held: _____

Description of participation: _____

_____

_____

Duties/responsibilities: _____

_____

Club/activity: _____Office(s) held: _____

Description of participation: _____

_____

_____

Duties/responsibilities: _____

_____

Club/activity: _____Office(s) held: _____

Description of participation: _____

_____

_____

Duties/responsibilities: _____

_____

_____

_____

AWARDS AND HONORS DATA INPUT SHEET

Name of Award or Citation: _____

From Whom Received: _____ Date: _____

Significance: _____

_____

Other pertinent information: _____

_____

Name of Award or Citation: _____

From Whom Received: _____ Date: _____

Significance: _____

_____

Other pertinent information: _____

_____

Name of Award or Citation: _____

From Whom Received: _____ Date: _____

Significance: _____

_____

Other pertinent information: _____

_____

LANGUAGE DATA INPUT SHEET

Language: _____

___Read   ___Write   ___Converse

Background (number of years studied, travel, etc.) _____

_____

_____

_____

Language: _____

___Read   ___Write   ___Converse

Background (number of years studied, travel, etc.) _____

_____

_____

_____

Language: _____

___Read   ___Write   ___Converse

Background (number of years studied, travel, etc.) _____

_____

_____

_____

FILL-IN-THE-BLANKS RESUME OUTLINE

Name: _____

Address: _____

City, state, ZIP Code: _____

Telephone number: _____

OBJECTIVE: _____

_____

_____

_____

_____

SUMMARY OF QUALIFICATIONS: _____

_____

_____

_____

_____

EDUCATION

GRADUATE SCHOOL: _____

Address: _____

City, state, ZIP Code: _____

Expected graduation date:_____Grade Point Average: _____

Degree earned (expected):_____Class Rank: _____

Important classes, especially those related to your career: _____

_____

_____

_____

_____

_____

_____

_____

COLLEGE: _____

Address: _____

City, state, ZIP Code: _____

Expected graduation date:_____Grade Point Average: _____

Class rank:_____Major:_____Minor:_____

Important classes, especially those related to your career: _____

_____

_____

_____

_____

_____

_____

_____

_____

_____

_____

HIGH SCHOOL: _____

Address: _____

City, state, ZIP Code: _____

Expected graduation date: _____Grade Point Average: _____

Class rank: _____

Important classes, especially those related to your career: _____

_____

_____

_____

_____

_____

_____

_____

HOBBIES AND OTHER INTERESTS (OPTIONAL) _____

_____

_____

_____

_____

_____

_____

_____

_____

_____

EXTRACURRICULAR ACTIVITIES (Activity name, dates participated, duties and responsibilities, offices held, accomplishments): _____

_____

_____

_____

_____

_____

_____

_____

AWARDS AND HONORS (Award name, from whom and date received, significance of the award and any other pertinent details): _____

_____

_____

_____

_____

_____

_____

_____

_____

_____

WORK EXPERIENCE. Include job title, name of business, address and telephone number, dates of employment, supervisor's name and title, your major responsibilities, accomplishments, and any awards won. Include volunteer experience in this category. List your experiences with the most recent dates first, even if you later decide not to use a chronological format.

_____

_____

_____

_____

_____

_____

_____

_____

_____

_____

_____

_____

_____

_____

_____

_____

_____

_____

REFERENCES. Though you should *not* include references in your resume, you do need to prepare a separate list of at least three people who know you fairly well and will recommend you highly to prospective employers. For each, include job title, company name, address, and telephone number. Before you include anyone on this list, make sure you have their permission to use their name as a reference and confirm what they intend to say about you to a potential employer.

1. _____

_____

_____

2. _____

_____

_____

3. _____

_____

_____

4. _____

_____

_____

5. _____

_____

_____

Margaret E. Bimmer

Local
N. Quad # 367
Los Angeles, CA 90078
(415) 002-5940

Permanent
852 Erin Ct.
Novato, CA 94947
(415) 039-4930

GOAL Entry level position in **Fund Raising.**

EDUCATION Bachelor of Arts in **Public Relations**
University of Southern California Los Angeles, CA
May, 1995 **Cum Laude**

**PROFESSIONAL
EXPERIENCE**

Summer, 1994 Meadowbrook Theater Los Angeles, CA
Public Relations Intern
Organized monthly publications. Skilled in PageMaker
and CorelDraw.

Summer, 1993 American Lung Association Novato, CA
Special Events Intern
Monitored special events programming. Achieved record
turnout for annual fund raiser, "The Great Smoke-Out".

EMPLOYMENT

9/94 - Present Pier One Imports Los Angeles, CA
9/93 - 5/94 *Sales*
9/92 - 5/93 Assist customers in purchase selection. Arrange store
displays.
Commended by district manager for customer relations
technique.

5/90 - 8/92 Stacey's Art Supply Marin, CA
Counter/Cashier

HONORS PRSSA, Secretary
National Honor Society

ACTIVITIES Downhill skiing, camping, and rollerblading
Enjoy home computing

REFERENCES Furnished Upon Request

SAMPLE RESUME - FUNCTIONAL

MARTIN KRAMER

1424 Kent Ct.	Cleveland Heights, OH 34615	(216) 993-1017

OBJECTIVE   A Job in Theater Design.

THEATER DESIGN

A Christmas Carol	Set Designer/Construction	Blossom
Josh White Jr. University	Set Construction	John Carroll
Fantasia Review University	Technical Assistant	John Carroll
King Arthur	Set Design	Renaissance Festival

STAGE

Les Miserables	Stage Hand/Technical Assistant	Power Center
Foreigner	Property Master/Light Crew	The Attic Theater
The Effects of Gamma Rays on Man-in-the-Moon Marigolds	Lights/Sound Operator	Power Center

DESIGN TECHNICIAN

Grounds Coffee House	Load in/Load out	John Carroll University
Talent Show	Load In/Load out	Calihan Hall

EDUCATION

Bachelor of Arts Degree in Theater Arts   John Carroll University
Minor in English   Cleveland, OH
May, 1995

AWARDS/ACTIVITIES

Set Design of the Year   May, 1994
Woodworking Enthusiast

Portfolio and References available upon request

SAMPLE RESUME - TARGETED

MARIE HANDLEY
123 Herman Rd.
Detroit, MI 48221
(313) 793-1923

Age: 23	**Eyes:** Green-Blue
Height: 5'6"	**Voice:** Mezzo-Soprano
Weight 125	**Dress:** 6-8
Hair: Blonde	**Shoe:** 8M

STAGE

Bacchae	Lead Chorus	University of Chicago/Italy
Cantorial	Donna	Jewish Ensemble Theatre
Boy's Life	Maggie	University of Chicago
Two by Two	Goldie	University of Chicago
Chicago Zoo Boo	Girl Dancer	Chicago Zoo
Man of LaMancha	Antonia	Marysville College
Pirates of Penzance	Edith	Marysville College

TOURS
Italy 1994
Greece 1993

EDUCATION/TRAINING

MUSIC   Bachelor of Arts in Music   University of Chicago
May, 1995
Jim Turner, Caroline Rodgers, Barbara Youngerman, Glen Carlos

ACTING   Theater Minor   Marysville College
Consortium
Arthur Willis, Teresa Fleischer, David King, Mary Bremm
(Dynamics, Scene Study, Styles, Body Electrics, Movement)

DANCE   Tap, Jazz, Ballet, Ballroom, Modern
Iacob Lasco, Penny Goldberg, Mary Raymond, Vicki Parris, Gus
Sabin, Kathryn Horan, Donald Kelly, Susan Urban

**SPECIAL
SKILLS**   Singing, Dancing, Choreography, Piano

CHAPTER TWENTY

Writing Better Letters

Stop for a moment and review your resume draft. It is undoubtedly (by now) a near-perfect document that instantly tells the reader the kind of job you want and why you are qualified. But does it say anything personal about you? Any amplification of your talents? Any words that are ideally "you?" Any hint of the kind of person who stands behind that resume?

If you've prepared it properly, the answers should be a series of ringing "no's"—your resume should be a mere sketch of your life, a bare-bones summary of your skills, education, and experience.

To the general we must add the specific. That's what your letters must accomplish—adding the lines, colors, and shading that will help fill out your self-portrait. This chapter will cover the kinds of letters you will most often be called upon to prepare in your job search. There are essentially nine different types you will utilize again and again, based primarily on what each is trying to accomplish. One well-written example of each is included at the end of this chapter.

Answer these Questions

Before you put pencil to paper to compose any letter, there are five key questions you must ask yourself:

- **Why** are you writing it?
- To **Whom?**
- **What** are you trying to accomplish?
- **Which** lead will get the reader's attention?
- **How** do you organize the letter to best accomplish your objectives?

Why?

There should be a single, easily definable reason you are writing any letter. This reason will often dictate what and how you write—the tone and flavor of the letter—as well as what you include or leave out.

Have you been asked in an ad to amplify your qualifications for a job and provide a salary history and college transcripts? Then that (minimally) is your objective in writing. Limit yourself to following instructions and do a little personal selling—but very little. Including everything asked for and a simple, adequate cover letter is better than writing a "knock 'em, sock 'em" letter and omitting the one piece of information the ad specifically asked for.

If, however, you are on a networking search, the objective of your letter is to seek out contacts who will refer you for possible informational or job interviews. In this case, getting a name and address—a referral—is your stated purpose for writing. You have to be specific and ask for this action.

You will no doubt follow up with a phone call, but be certain the letter conveys what you are after. Being vague or oblique won't help you. You are after a definite yes or no when it comes to contact assistance. The recipient of your letter should know this. As they say in the world of selling, at some point you have to ask for the order.

Who?

Using the proper "tone" in a letter is as important as the content—you wouldn't write to the owner of the local meat market using the same words and style as you would employ in a letter to the director of personnel of a major company. Properly addressing the person or persons you are writing to is as important as what you say to them.

Always utilize the recipient's job title and level (correct title and spelling are a **must**). If you know what kind of person he/she is (based on your knowledge of the area of involvement) use that knowledge to your advantage as well. It also helps if you know his or her hiring clout, but even if you know the letter is going through a screening stage instead of to the actual person you need to contact, don't take the easy way out. You have to sell the person doing the screening just as convincingly as you would the actual contact, or else you might get passed over instead of passed along! Don't underestimate the power of the person doing the screening.

For example, it pays to sound technical with technical people—in other words, use the kinds of words and language that they use on the job. If you have had the opportunity to speak with them, it will be easy for you. If not, and you have formed some opinions as to their types then use these as the basis of the language you employ. The cardinal rule is to say it in words you think the recipient will be comfortable hearing, not in the words you might otherwise personally choose.

What?

What do you have to offer that company? What do you have to contribute to the job, process, or work situation that is unique and/or of particular benefit to the recipient of your letter.

For example, if you were applying for a sales position and recently ranked number one in a summer sales job, then conveying this benefit is logical and desirable. It is a factor you may have left off your resume. Even if it was listed in the skills/accomplishment section of the resume, you can underscore and call attention to it in your letter. Repetition, when it is properly focused, can be a good thing.

Which?

Of all the opening sentences you can compose, which will immediately get the reader's attention? If your opening sentence is dynamic, you are already 50 percent of the way to your end objective—having your entire letter read. Don't slide into it. Know the point you are trying to make and come right to it. One word of caution: your first sentence **must** make mention of what led you to write—was it an ad, someone at the company, a story you saw on television? Be sure to give this point of reference.

How?

While a good opening is essential, how do you organize your letter so that it is easy for the recipient to read in its entirety? This is a question of *flow*—the way the words and sentences naturally lead one to another, holding the reader's interest until he or she reaches your signature.

If you have your objective clearly in mind, this task is easier than it sounds: Simply convey your message(s) in a logical sequence. End your letter by stating what the next steps are—yours and/or the reader's.

One More Time

Pay attention to the small things. Neatness still counts. Have your letters typed. Spend a few extra dollars and have some personal stationery printed.

And most important, make certain that your correspondence goes out quickly. The general rule is to get a letter in the mail during the week in which the project comes to your attention or in which you have had some contact with the organization. I personally attempt to mail follow-up letters the same day as the contact; at worst, within 24 hours.

When to Write

- To answer an ad
- To prospect (many companies)
- To inquire about specific openings (single company)
- To obtain a referral
- To obtain an informational interview
- To obtain a job interview
- To say "thank you"
- To accept or reject a job offer
- To withdraw from consideration for a job

In some cases, the letter will accompany your resume; in others, it will need to stand alone. Each of the above circumstance is described in the pages that follow. I have included at least one sample of each type of letter at the end of this chapter.

Answering an Ad

Your eye catches an ad in the Positions Available section of the Sunday paper for an assistant stage manager. It tells you that the position is with a theatre production company and that, though some experience would be desirable, it is not required. Well, you possess *those* skills. The ad asks that you send a letter, resume, and an 8 x 10 glossy photograph, to a Post Office Box. No salary is indicated, no phone number given. You decide to reply.

Your purpose in writing—the objective (why?)—is to secure a job interview. Since no person is singled out for receipt of the ad, and since it is a large company, you assume it will be screened by Human Resources.

Adopt a professional, formal tone. You are answering a "blind" ad, so you have to play it safe. In your first sentence, refer to the ad, including the place and date of publication and the position outlined. (There is a chance that the company is running more than one ad on the same date and in the same paper, so you need to identify the one to which you are replying.) Tell the reader what (specifically) you have to offer that company. Include your resume, phone number, and the times it is easiest to reach you. Ask for the order—tell them you'd like to have an appointment.

Blanket Prospecting Letter

In June of this year you will graduate from a four-year college with a degree in theatre. You seek a position (internship or full-time employment) at a theatre production company. You have decided to write to 50 top companies, sending each a copy of your resume. You don't know which, if any, have job openings.

Such blanket mailings are effective given two circumstances: 1) You must have an exemplary record and a resume that reflects it; and 2) You must send out a goodly number of packages, since the response rate to such mailings is very low.

A blanket mailing doesn't mean an impersonal one—you should always be writing to a specific executive. If you have a referral, send a personalized letter to that person. If not, do not simply mail a package to the Human Resources department; identify the department head and *then* send a personalized letter. And make sure you get on the phone and follow up each letter within about 10 days. Don't just sit back and wait for everyone to call you. They won't.

Just Inquiring

The inquiry letter is a step above the blanket prospecting letter; it's a "cold-calling" device with a twist. You have earmarked a company (and a person) as a possibility in your job search based on something you have read about them. Your general research tells you that it is a good place to work. Although you are not aware of any specific openings, you know that they employ entry-level personnel with your credentials.

While ostensibly inquiring about any openings, you are really just "referring yourself" to them in order to place your resume in front of the right person. This is what I would call a "why not?" attempt at securing a job interview. Its effectiveness depends on their actually having been in the news. This, after all, is your "excuse" for writing.

Networking

It's time to get out that folder marked "Contacts" and prepare a draft networking letter. The lead sentence should be very specific, referring immediately to the friend, colleague, etc. "who suggested I write you about..." Remember: Your objective is to secure an informational interview, pave the way for a job interview, and/or get referred to still other contacts.

This type of letter should not place the recipient in a position where a decision is necessary; rather, the request should be couched in terms of "career advice." The second paragraph can then inform the reader of your level of experience. Finally, be specific about seeking an appointment.

Unless you have been specifically asked by the referring person to do so, you will probably not be including a resume with such letters. So the letter itself must highlight your credentials, enabling the reader to gauge your relative level of experience. For entry-level personnel, education, of course, will be most important.

For an Informational Interview

Though the objectives of this letter are similar to those of the networking letter, they are not as personal. These are "knowledge quests" on your part and the recipient will most likely not be someone you have been referred to. The idea is to convince the reader of the sincerity of your research effort. Whatever selling you do, if you do any at all, will arise as a consequence of the meeting, not beforehand. A positive response to this type of request is in itself a good step forward. It is, after all, exposure, and amazing things can develop when people in authority agree to see you.

Thank-You Letters

Although it may not always seem so, manners do count in the job world. But what counts even more are the simple gestures that show you actually care—like writing a thank-you letter. A well-executed, timely thank-you note tells more about your personality than anything else you may have sent, and it also demonstrates excellent follow-through skills. It says something about the way you were brought up—whatever else your resume tells them, you are, at least, polite, courteous, and thoughtful.

Thank-you letters may well become the beginning of an all-important dialogue that leads directly to a job. So be extra careful in composing them, and make certain that they are custom made for each occasion and person.

The following are the primary situations in which you will be called upon to write some variation of thank-you letter:

1. After a job interview
2. After an informational interview

3. Accepting a job offer

4. Responding to rejection: While optional, such a letter is appropriate if you have been among the finalists in a job search or were rejected due to limited experience. Remember: Some day you'll *have* enough experience; make the interviewer want to stay in touch.

5. Withdrawing from consideration: Used when you decide you are no longer interested in a particular position. (A variation is usable for declining an actual job offer.) Whatever the reason for writing such a letter, it's wise to do so and thus keep future lines of communication open.

10 E. 89th Street
New York, NY 10028
April 4, 1994

The *New York Times*
PO Box 7520
New York, NY 10128

Dear Sir or Madam:

This letter is in response to your advertisement for a performing arts education professor which appeared in the March 24th issue of the *New York Times*. I have the qualifications you are seeking. I graduated from Columbia University, Teachers College with a MFA in arts education. Prior to that, I earned a BFA in dance from the University of Maryland.

I worked as an intern for two summers at the Maryland Amphitheatre and as a volunteer for the Asia Society. For the past year, I have been employed as a teaching assistant at the St. Boniface School of Drama. I am also a member of the New York City Drama Guild.

My resume is enclosed. I would like to have the opportunity to meet with you personally to discuss your requirements for the position. I can be reached at (212) 785-1225 between 8:00 a.m. and 5:00 p.m. and at (212) 785-4221 after 5:00 p.m. I look forward to hearing from you.

Sincerely,

Karen Weber

Enclosure: Resume

PROSPECTING LETTER

Kim Kerr
8 Robutuck Hwy.
Hammond, IN 54054
555-875-2392
April 4, 1994

Mr. Fred Jones
Personnel Director
Chicago Philharmonic Orchestra
Chicago, Illinois 91221

Dear Mr. Jones:

The name of the Chicago Philharmonic Orchestra continually pops up in our classroom discussions of outstanding municipal symphonies. Given my interest in the performing arts as a career and cello accompaniment as a specialty, I've taken the liberty of enclosing my resume.

As you can see, I have just completed a very comprehensive educational program at Warren University, majoring in music with a minor in German. Though my resume does not indicate it, I will be graduating in the top 10% of my class, with honors.

I will be in the Chicago area on April 20th and will call your office to see when it is convenient to arrange an appointment.

Sincerely yours,

Kim Kerr

INQUIRY LETTER

42 7th Street
Ski City, Vermont 85722
April 4, 1994

Dr. Julie A. Pitti
Executive Director
Riverview Repertory Theatre
521 West Elm Street
Indianapolis, IN 83230

Dear Dr. Pitti:

I just completed reading the article in the March issue of Theater Week on your company's record-breaking season. Congratulations!

Your innovative approach to showcasing disabled actors is of particular interest to me because of my background in dance therapy and theatre.

I am interested in learning more about your work as well as the possibilities of joining your company. My qualifications include:

- BFA in Dance Therapy and Theatre
- Active member of the Association for Theatre and Disability
- Cultural Sensitivity Seminar participation (Univ. of Virginia)
- Lead and corps member performances in a number of shows, including *A Raisin in the Sun.*

I will be in Indianapolis during the week of April 18th and hope your schedule will permit us to meet briefly to discuss our mutual interests. I will call your office next week to see if such a meeting can be arranged.

I appreciate your consideration.

Sincerely yours,

Ronald W. Sommerville

Rochelle A. Starky
42 Bach St.,
Musical City, MO 20202
317-555-1515
April 4, 1994

Dr. Michelle Fleming
Company Director
Fulton Ballet Company
42 Jenkins Avenue
Fulton, Missouri 23232

Dear Dr. Fleming:

Sam Kinney suggested I write you. I am interested in dancing in the corps of a major ballet company. Sam felt it would be mutually beneficial for us to meet and talk.

I have a BFA from Musical City University in dance and an MFA from the Juilliard School. While working on my postgraduate degree, I volunteered with a nonprofit organization that encourages children with Down's syndrome to take an active interest in the performing arts. I also worked as an intern for a year at the Columbia Music Conservatory in Columbia, MO.

I know from Sam how similar our backgrounds are—the same training, the same interests. And, of course, I am aware of how successful you have become—a principal dancer in 2 years!

As I begin my job search during the next few months, I am certain your advice would help me. Would it be possible for us to meet briefly? My resume is enclosed.

I will call your office next week to see when your schedule would permit such a meeting.

Sincerely,

Rochelle A. Starky

TO OBTAIN AN INFORMATIONAL INTERVIEW

16 NW 128th Street
Raleigh, NC 75755
April 4, 1994

Ms. Jackie B. McClure
General Manager
Uncle Miltie's Comedy Club
484 Smithers Road
Awkmont, North Carolina 76857

Dear Ms. McClure:

I'm sure a good deal of the credit for your club's success last year is attributable to the highly-motivated and knowledgeable staff you have recruited during the last three years. I hope to obtain an entry-level management position with a club just as committed to growth.

I have two years of managerial experience, which I acquired while working as an intern at the Laughtrack Comedy Club. I graduated from Gresham University with a B.S. in marketing and a minor in theatre. I believe that my experience and education have properly prepared me for a career in entertainment management.

As I begin my job search, I am trying to gather as much information and advice as possible before applying for positions. Could I take a few minutes of your time next week to discuss my career plans? I will call your office on Monday, April 11, to see if such a meeting can be arranged.

I appreciate your consideration and look forward to meeting you.

Sincerely,

Karen R. Burns

Lazelle Wright
921 West Fourth Street
Steamboat, Colorado 72105
303-310-3303

April 4, 1994

Dr. James R. Payne
Managing Director
Ogden Drama Guild
241 Snowridge
Ogden, Utah 72108

Dear Dr. Payne:

Jinny Bastienelli was right when she said you would be most helpful in advising me on a career in costume design.

I appreciated your taking the time from your busy schedule to meet with me. Your advice was most helpful and I have incorporated your suggestions into my resume. I will send you a copy next week.

Again, thanks so much for your assistance. As you suggested, I will contact Joe Simmons at Salt Lake City Repertory Theatre next week in regard to a possible opening.

Sincerely,

Lazelle Wright

1497 Lilac Street
Old Adams, MA 01281
April 4, 1994

Mr. Rudy Delacort
Director of Personnel
East Coast Amusement Park
175 Boylston Avenue
Ribbit, Massachusetts 02857

Dear Mr. Delacort:

Thank you for the opportunity to interview yesterday for the director of development position. I enjoyed meeting with you and Dr. Cliff Stoudt and learning more about East Coast.

Your facility appears to be growing in a direction that parallels my interests and goals. The interview with you and your staff confirmed my initial positive impressions of East Coast, and I want to reiterate my strong interest in working for you.

I am convinced that my prior experience as an intern with the Fellowes Conservatory in Old Adams, BFA in theatre, and MBA from the University of Adams would enable me to progress steadily through your training program and become a productive member of your staff.

Again, thank you for your consideration. If you need any additional information from me, please feel free to call.

Yours truly,

Harold Beaumont

cc: Dr. Cliff Stoudt

1497 Lilac Street
Old Adams, MA 01281
April 4, 1994

Mr. Rudy Delacort
Director of Personnel
East Coast Amusement Park
175 Boylston Avenue
Ribbit, Massachusetts 01281

Dear Mr. Delacort:

I want to thank you and Dr. Cliff Stoudt for giving me the opportunity to work for East Coast. I am very pleased to accept the director of development position. The position entails exactly the kind of work I want to do, and I know that I will do a good job for you.

As we discussed, I shall begin work on May 23, 1994. In the interim, I shall complete all the necessary employment forms and locate housing.

I plan to be in Ribbit within the next two weeks and would like to deliver the paperwork to you personally. At that time, we could handle any remaining items pertaining to my employment. I'll call next week to schedule an appointment with you.

Sincerely yours,

Harold Beaumont

cc: Dr. Cliff Stoudt

1497 Lilac Street
Old Adams, MA 01281
April 4, 1994

Mr. Rudy Delacort
Director of Personnel
East Coast Amusement Park
175 Boylston Avenue
Ribbit, Massachusetts 01281

Dear Mr. Delacort:

It was indeed a pleasure meeting with you and Dr. Cliff Stoudt last week to discuss your needs for a director of development. Our time together was most enjoyable and informative.

As I discussed with you during our meetings, I believe one purpose of preliminary interviews is to explore areas of mutual interest and to assess the fit between the individual and the position. After careful consideration, I have decided to withdraw from consideration for the position.

I want to thank you for interviewing me and giving me the opportunity to learn about your needs. You have a fine staff and I would have enjoyed working with them.

Yours truly,

Harold Beaumont

cc: Dr. Cliff Stoudt

IN RESPONSE TO REJECTION

1497 Lilac Street
Old Adams, MA 01281
April 4, 1994

Mr. Rudy Delacort
Director of Personnel
East Coast Amusement Park
175 Boylston Avenue
Ribbit, Massachusetts 01281

Dear Mr. Delacort:

Thank you for giving me the opportunity to interview for the director of development position. I appreciate your consideration and interest in me.

Although I am disappointed in not being selected for your current vacancy, I want to you to know that I appreciated the courtesy and professionalism shown to me during the entire selection process. I enjoyed meeting you, Dr. Cliff Stoudt, and the other members of your staff. My meetings confirmed that East Coast would be an exciting place to work and build a career.

I want to reiterate my strong interest in working for you. Please keep me in mind if a similar position becomes available in the near future.

Again, thank you for the opportunity to interview and best wishes to you and your staff.

Sincerely yours,

Harold Beaumont

cc: Dr. Cliff Stoudt

CHAPTER TWENTY-ONE

Questions for You, Questions for Them

You've finished your exhaustive research, contacted everyone you've known since kindergarten, compiled a professional-looking and sounding resume, and written brilliant letters to the dozens of companies your research has revealed are perfect matches for your own strengths, interests, and abilities. Unfortunately, all of this preparatory work will be meaningless if you are unable to successfully convince one of those ensembles to hire you.

If you were able set up an initial meeting at one of these companies, your resume and cover letter obviously piqued someone's interest. Now you have to traverse the last minefield—the job interview itself. It's time to make all that preparation pay off.

This chapter will attempt to put the interview process in perspective, giving you the "inside story" on what to expect and how to handle the questions and circumstances that arise during the course of a normal interview—and even many of those that surface in the bizarre interview situations we have all experienced at some point.

Why Interviews Shouldn't Scare You

Interviews shouldn't scare you. The concept of two (or more) persons meeting to determine if they are right for each other is a relatively logical idea. As important as research, resumes, letters, and phone calls are, they are inherently impersonal. The interview is your chance to really see and feel the company firsthand, so think of it as a positive opportunity, your chance to succeed.

That said, many of you will still be put off by the inherently inquisitive nature of the process. Though many questions *will* be asked, interviews are essentially experiments in chemistry. Are you right for the company? Is the company right for you? Not just on paper—*in the flesh.*

If you decide the company is right for you, your purpose is simple and clear-cut—to convince the interviewer that you are the right person for the job, that you will fit in, and that you will be an asset to the company now and in the future. The interviewer's purpose is equally simple—to decide whether he or she should buy what you're selling.

This chapter will focus on the kinds of questions you are likely to be asked, how to answer them, and the questions you should be ready to ask of the interviewer. By removing the workings of the interview process from the "unknown" category, you will reduce the fear it engenders.

But all the preparation in the world won't completely eliminate your sweaty palms, unless you can convince yourself that the interview is an important, positive life experience from which you will benefit—even if you don't get the job. Approach it with enthusiasm, calm yourself, and let your personality do the rest. You will undoubtedly spend an interesting hour, one that will teach you more about yourself. It's just another step in the learning process you've undertaken.

What to Do First

Start by setting up a calendar on which you can enter and track all your scheduled appointments. When you schedule an interview with a company, ask them how much time you should allow for the appointment. Some require all new applicants to fill out numerous forms and/or complete a battery of intelligence or psychological tests—all before the first interview. If you've only allowed an hour for the interview—and scheduled another at a nearby firm 10 minutes later—the first time you confront a three-hour test series will effectively destroy any schedule.

Some companies, especially if the first interview is very positive, like to keep applicants around to talk to other executives. This process may be planned or, in a lot of cases, a spontaneous decision by an interviewer who likes you and wants you to meet some other key decision makers. Other companies will tend to schedule such a series of second interviews on a separate day. Find out, if you can, how the company you're planning to visit generally operates. Otherwise, a schedule that's too tight will fall apart in no time at all, especially if you've traveled to another city to interview with a number of firms in a short period of time.

If you need to travel out-of-state to interview with a company, be sure to ask if they will be paying some or all of your travel expenses. (It's generally expected that you'll be paying your own way to firms within your home state.) If they don't offer—and you don't ask—presume you're paying the freight.

Even if the company agrees to reimburse you, make sure you have enough money to pay all the expenses yourself. While some may reimburse you immediately, the majority of firms may take from a week to a month to send you an expense check.

Research, Research, and More Research

The research you did to find these companies is nothing compared to the research you need to do now that you're beginning to narrow your search. If you followed our detailed suggestions when you started targeting these firms in the first place, you've already amassed a great deal of information about them. If you didn't do the research *then,* you sure better decide to do it *now.* Study each company as if you were going to be tested on your detailed knowledge of their organization and operations. Here's a complete checklist of the facts you should try to know about each company you plan to visit for a job interview:

The Basics

1. The address of (and directions to) the office you're visiting
2. Headquarters location (if different)
3. Some idea of domestic branches
4. Relative size (compared to other similar companies)
5. Annual billings, sales, and/or income (last two years)
6. Subsidiary companies and/or specialized divisions
7. Departments (overall structure)

The Subtleties

1. History of the ensemble (specialties, honors, awards, famous names)
2. Names, titles, and backgrounds of top management
3. Existence (and type) of training program
4. Relocation policy
5. Relative salaries (compared to other companies in field or by size)
6. Recent developments concerning the company and its activities (from your trade magazine and newspaper reading)
7. Everything you can learn about the career, likes, and dislikes of the person(s) interviewing you

The amount of time and work necessary to be this well prepared for an interview is considerable. It will not be accomplished the day before the interview. You may even find some of the information you need is unavailable on short notice.

Is it really so important to do all this? Well, somebody out there is going to. And if you happen to be interviewing for the same job as that other, well-prepared, knowledgeable candidate, who do you think will impress the interviewer more?

As we've already discussed, if you give yourself enough time, most of this information is surprisingly easy to obtain. In addition to the reference sources covered in the **Career Resources** chapter, the company itself can probably supply you with a great deal of data. An ensemble's annual report—which all publicly-owned companies must publish yearly for their stockholders—is a virtual treasure trove of information. Write each company and request copies of their last two annual reports. A comparison of sales, income, and other data over this period may enable you to discover some interesting things about their overall financial health and growth potential. Many libraries also have collections of annual reports from major companies.

Attempting to learn about your interviewer is hard work, the importance of which is underestimated by most applicants (who then, of course, don't bother to do it). Being one of the exceptions may get you a job. Find out if he or she has written any articles that have appeared in the trade press or, even better, books on his or her area(s) of expertise. Referring to these writings during the course of an interview, without making it too obvious a compliment, can be very effective. We all have egos and we all like people to talk about us. The interviewer is no different from the rest of us. You might also check to see if any of your networking contacts worked with him or her at his current (or a previous) company and can help fill you in.

Selection vs. Screening Interviews

The process to which the majority of this chapter is devoted is the actual **selection interview,** usually conducted by the person to whom the new hire will be reporting. But there is another process—the **screening interview**—which many of you may have to survive first.

Screening interviews are usually conducted by a member of the human resources department. Though they may not be empowered to hire, they are in a position to screen out or eliminate those candidates they feel (based on the facts) are not qualified to handle the job. These decisions are not usually made on the basis of personality, appearance, eloquence, persuasiveness, or any other subjective criteria, but rather by clicking off yes or no answers against a checklist of skills. If you don't have the requisite number, you will be eliminated from further consideration. This may seem arbitrary, but it is a realistic and often necessary way for companies to minimize the time and dollars involved in filling even the lowest jobs on the career ladder.

Remember, screening personnel are not looking for reasons to *hire* you; they're trying to find ways to *eliminate* you from the job search pack. Resumes sent blindly to the personnel department will usually be subjected to such screening; you will be eliminated without any personal contact (an excellent reason to construct a superior resume and not send out blind mailings).

If you are contacted, it will most likely be by telephone. When you are responding to such a call, keep these four things in mind: 1) It is an interview, be on your guard; 2) Answer all questions honestly; 3) Be enthusiastic; and 4) Don't offer any more information than you are asked for. Remember, this is another screening step, so don't say anything that will get you screened out before you even get in. You will get the standard questions from the interviewer—his or her attempts to "flesh out" the information included on your resume and/or cover letter. Strictly speaking, they are seeking out any negatives that may exist. If your resume is honest and factual (and it should be), you have no reason to be anxious, because you have nothing to hide.

Don't be nervous—be glad you were called and remember your objective: to get past this screening phase so you can get on to the real interview.

The Day of the Interview

On the day of the interview, wear a conservative (not funereal) business suit—*not* a sports coat, *not* a "nice" blouse and skirt. Shoes should be shined, nails cleaned, hair cut and in place. And no low-cut or tight-fitting clothes.

It's not unusual for resumes and cover letters to head in different directions when a company starts passing them around to a number of executives. If you sent them, both may even be long gone. So bring along extra copies of your resume and your own copy of the cover letter that originally accompanied it.

Whether or not you make them available, we suggest you prepare a neatly-typed list of references (including the name, title, company, address, and phone number of each person). You may want to bring along a copy of your high school or college transcript, especially if it's something to brag about. (Once you get your first job, you'll probably never use it—or be asked for it—again, so enjoy it while you can!)

On Time Means 15 Minutes Early

Plan to arrive 15 minutes before your scheduled appointment. If you're in an unfamiliar city or have a long drive to their offices, allow extra time for the unexpected delays that seem to occur with mind-numbing regularity on important days.

Arriving early will give you some time to check your appearance, catch your breath, check in with the receptionist, learn how to correctly pronounce the interviewer's name, and get yourself organized and battle ready.

Arriving late does not make a sterling first impression. If you are only a few minutes late, it's probably best not to mention it or even excuse yourself. With a little luck, everybody else is behind schedule and no one will notice. However, if you're more than 15 minutes late, have an honest (or at least serviceable) explanation ready and offer it at your first opportunity. Then drop the subject as quickly as possible and move on to the interview.

> ### You Don't Have to Say a Word
>
> "Eighty percent of the initial impression you make is nonverbal," asserts Jennifer Maxwell Morris, a New York-based image consultant, quoting a University of Minnesota study. Some tips: walk tall, enter the room briskly while making eye contact with the person you're going to speak to, keep your head up, square your shoulders and keep your hand ready for a firm handshake that involves the whole hand but does not pump.
>
> Source: *Working Woman*

The Eyes Have It

When you meet the interviewer, shake hands firmly. People notice handshakes and often form a first impression based solely on them.

Try to maintain eye contact with the interviewer as you talk. This will indicate you're interested in what he or she has to say. Eye contact is important for another reason—it demonstrates to the interviewer that you are confident about yourself and your job skills. That's an important message to send.

Sit straight. Body language is also another important means of conveying confidence.

Should coffee or a soft drink be offered, you may accept (but should do so only if the interviewer is joining you).

Keep your voice at a comfortable level, and try to sound enthusiastic (without imitating Charleen Cheerleader). Be confident and poised and provide direct, accurate, and honest answers to the trickiest questions.

And, as you try to remember all this, just be yourself, and try to act like you're comfortable and almost enjoying this whole process!

Don't Name Drop . . . Conspicuously

A friendly relationship with other company employees may have provided you with valuable information prior to the interview, but don't flaunt such relationships. The interviewer is interested only in how you will relate to him or her and how well he or she surmises you will fit in with the rest of the staff. Name dropping may smack of favoritism. And you are in no position to know who the interviewer's favorite (or least favorite) people are.

On the other hand, if you have established a complex network of professionals through informational interviews, attending performances, reading trade magazines, etc., it is perfectly permissible to refer to these people, their companies, conversations you've had, whatever. It may even impress the interviewer with the extensiveness of your preparation.

Fork on the Left, Knife on the Right

Interviews are sometimes conducted over lunch, though this is not usually the case with entry-level people. If it does happen to you, though, try to order something in the middle price range, neither filet mignon nor a cheeseburger.

Do not order alcohol—ever! If your interviewer orders a carafe of wine, politely decline. You may meet another interviewer later who smells the alcohol on your breath, or your interviewer may have a drinking problem. It's just too big a risk to take after you've come so far. Just do your best to maintain your poise, and you'll do fine.

The Importance of Last Impressions

There are some things interviewers will always view with displeasure: street language, complete lack of eye contact, insufficient or vague explanations or answers, a noticeable lack of energy, poor interpersonal skills (i.e., not listening or the basic inability to carry on an intelligent conversation), and a demonstrable lack of motivation.

Every impression may count. And the very *last* impression an interviewer has may outweigh everything else. So, before you allow an interview to end, summarize why you want the job, why you are qualified, and what, in particular, you can offer their company.

Then, take some action. If the interviewer hasn't told you about the rest of the interview process and/or where you stand, ask him or her. Will you be seeing other people that day? If so, ask for some background on anyone else with whom you'll be interviewing. If there are no other meetings that day, what's the next step? When can you expect to hear from them about coming back?

Ask for a business card. This will make sure you get the person's name and title right when you write your follow-up letter. You can staple it to the company file for easy reference as you continue networking. When you return home, file all the business cards, copies of correspondence, and notes from the interview(s) with each company in the appropriate files. Finally, but most importantly, ask yourself which ensembles you really want to work for and which you are no longer interested in. This will quickly determine how far you want the process at each to develop before you politely tell them to stop considering you for the job.

Immediately send a thank-you letter to each executive you met. These should, of course, be neatly typed business letters, not handwritten notes (unless you are most friendly, indeed, with the interviewer and want to stress the "informal" nature of your note). If you are still interested in pursuing a position at their company, tell them in no uncertain terms. Reiterate why you feel you're the best candidate and tell each of the executives when you hope (expect?) to hear from them.

On the Eighth Day God Created Interviewers

Though most interviews will follow a relatively standard format, there will undoubtedly be a wide disparity in the skills of the interviewers you meet. Many of these executives (with the exception of the human resources staff) will most likely not have extensive interviewing experience, have limited knowledge of interviewing techniques, use them infrequently, be hurried by the other duties, or not even view your interview as critically important.

Rather than studying standardized test results or utilizing professional evaluation skills developed over many years of practice, these nonprofessionals react intuitively—their initial (first five minutes) impressions are often the lasting and over-riding factors they remember. So you must sell yourself—fast.

The best way to do this is to try to achieve a comfort level with your interviewer. Isn't establishing rapport—through words, gestures, appearance, common interests, etc.—what you try to do in *any* social situation? It's just trying to know one another better. Against this backdrop, the questions and answers will flow in a more natural way.

> A new style of interview called the "situational interview," or low-fidelity simulation, asks prospective employees what they would do in hypothetical situations, presenting illustrations that are important in the job opening. Recent research is encouraging employers to use this type of interview approach, because studies show that what people say they would do is pretty much what they will do when the real-life situation arises.
>
> Source: *Working Woman*

The Set Sequence

Irrespective of the competence levels of the interviewer, you can anticipate an interview sequence roughly as follows:

- Greetings
- Social niceties (small talk)
- Purpose of meeting (let's get down to business)
- Broad questions/answers
- Specific questions/ answers
- In-depth discussion of company, job, and opportunity
- Summarizing information given and received

• Possible salary probe (this should only be brought up at a second interview).

• Summary/indication as to next steps

When you look at this sequence closely, it is obvious that once you have gotten past the greeting, social niceties, and some explanation of the job (in the "getting down to business" section), the bulk of the interview will be questions—yours and the interviewer's. In this question and answer session, there are not necessarily any right or wrong answers, only good and bad ones.

Be forewarned, however. This sequence is not written in stone, and some interviewers will deliberately **not** follow it. Some interviewers will try to fluster you by asking off-the-wall questions, while others are just eccentric by nature. Be prepared for anything once the interview has started.

It's Time to Play Q & A

You can't control the "chemistry" between you and the interviewer—do you seem to "hit it off" right from the start or never connect at all? Since you can't control such a subjective problem, it pays to focus on what you *can* control—the questions you will be asked, your answers, and the questions you had better be prepared to ask.

Not surprisingly, many of the same questions pop up in interview after interview, regardless of company size, type, or location. I have chosen the 14 most common— along with appropriate hints and answers for each—for inclusion in this chapter. Remember: There are no right or wrong answers to these questions, only good and bad ones.

Substance counts more than speed when answering questions. Take your time and make sure that you listen to each question—there is nothing quite as disquieting as a lengthy, intelligent answer that is completely irrelevant to the question asked. You wind up looking like a programmed clone with stock answers to dozens of questions who has, unfortunately, pulled the wrong one out of the grab bag.

Once you have adequately answered a specific question, it is permissible to go beyond it and add more information if doing so adds something to the discussion and/or highlights a particular strength, skill, course, etc. But avoid making lengthy speeches just for the sake of sounding off. Even if the interviewer asks a question that is right up your "power alley", one you could talk about for weeks, keep your answers short. Under two minutes for any answer is a good rule of thumb.

Study the list of questions (and hints) that follow, and prepare at least one solid, concise answer for each. Practice with a friend until your answers to these most-asked questions sound intelligent, professional and, most importantly, unmemorized and unrehearsed.

"Why do you want to be in this field?"

Using your knowledge and understanding of the particular field, explain why you find the business exciting and where and what role you see yourself playing in it.

"Why do you think you will be successful in this business?"

Using the information from your self-evaluation and the research you did on that particular company, formulate an answer that marries your strengths to their's and to the characteristics of the position for which you're applying.

"Why did you choose our company?"

This is an excellent opportunity to explain the extensive process of education and research you've undertaken. Tell them about your strengths and how you match up with their firm. Emphasize specific things about their company that led you to seek an interview. Be a salesperson—be convincing.

"What can you do for us?"

Construct an answer that essentially lists your strengths, the experience you have that will contribute to your job performance, and any other unique qualifications that will place you at the head of the applicant pack. Use action-oriented words to tell exactly what you think you can do for the company—all your skills mean nothing if you can't use them to benefit the company you are interviewing with. Be careful: This is a question specifically designed to *eliminate* some of that pack. Sell yourself. Be one of the few called back for a second interview.

"What position here interests you?"

If you're interviewing for a specific position, answer accordingly. If you want to make sure you don't close the door on other opportunities of which you might be unaware, you can follow up with your own question: "I'm here to apply for your assistant stage manager opening. Is there another position open for which you feel I'm qualified?"

If you've arranged an interview with a company without knowing of any specific openings, use the answer to this question to describe the kind of work you'd like to do and why you're qualified to do it. Avoid a specific job title, since they will tend to vary from company to company.

If you're on a first interview with the human resources department, just answer the question. They only want to figure out where to send you.

"What jobs have you held and why did you leave them?"

Or the direct approach: "Have you ever been fired?" Take this opportunity to expand on your resume, rather than precisely answering the question by merely recapping your job experiences. In discussing each job, point out what you liked about it, what factors led to your leaving, and how the next job added to your continuing professional education. If you have been fired, say so. It's very easy to check.

"What are your strengths and weaknesses?"

Or **"What are your hobbies (or outside interests)?"** Both questions can be easily answered using the data you gathered to complete the self-evaluation process. Be wary of being too forthcoming about your glaring faults (nobody expects you to volunteer every weakness and mistake), but do not reply, "I don't have any." They won't believe you and, what's worse, you won't believe you. After all, you did the evaluation—you know it's a lie!

Good answers to these questions are those in which the interviewer can identify benefits for him or herself. For example: "I consider myself to be an excellent planner. I am seldom caught by surprise and I prize myself on being able to anticipate problems and schedule my time to be ahead of the game. I devote a prescribed number of hours each week to this activity. I've noticed that many people just react. If you plan ahead, you should be able to cut off most problems before they arise."

You may consider disarming the interviewer by admitting a weakness, but doing it in such a way as to make it relatively unimportant to the job function. For example: "Costume design has never been my strong suit. In this area, though, I haven't found this to be a liability."

"Do you think your extracurricular activities were worth the time you devoted to them?"

This is a question often asked of entry-level candidates. One possible answer: "Very definitely. As you see from my resume, I have been quite active in the Student Government and French Club. My language fluency allowed me to spend my junior year abroad as an exchange student, and working in a functioning government gave me firsthand knowledge of what can be accomplished with people in the real world. I suspect my marks would have been somewhat higher had I not taken on so many activities outside of school, but I feel the balance they gave me contributed significantly to my overall growth as a person."

"What are your career goals?"

Interviewers are always seeking to probe the motivations of prospective employees. Nowhere is this more apparent than when the area of ambition is discussed. The key answer to this question might be: "Given hard work, company growth, and personal initiative, I'd look forward to being in a top executive position by the time I'm 35. I believe in effort and the risk/reward system—my research on this company has shown me that it operates on the same principles. I would hope it would select its future leaders from those people who displaying such characteristics."

"At some future date would you be willing to relocate?"

Pulling up one's roots is not the easiest thing in the world to do, but it is often a fact of life in the world of performing arts. If you're serious about your career (and such a move often represents a step up the career ladder), you will probably not mind such a move. Tell the interviewer. If you really *don't* want to move, you may want to say so, too—though I would find out how probable or frequent such relocations would be before closing the door while still in the interview stage.

Keep in mind that as you get older, establish ties in a particular community, marry, have children, etc., you will inevitably feel less jubilation at the thought of moving once a year or even "being out on the road." So take the opportunity to experience new places and experiences while you're young. If you don't, you may never get the chance.

"How did you get along with your last supervisor?"

This question is designed to understand your relationship with (and reaction to) authority. Remember: Companies look for team players, people who will fit in with their hierarchy, their rules, their ways of doing things. An answer might be: "I prefer to work with smart, strong people who know what they want and can express themselves. I learned in the military that in order to accomplish the mission, someone has to be the leader and that person has to be given the authority to lead. Someday I aim to be that leader. I hope then my subordinates will follow me as much and as competently as I'm ready to follow now."

"What are your salary requirements?"

If they are at all interested in you, this question will probably come up, though it is more likely at a second interview. The danger, of course, is that you may price yourself too low or, even worse, right out of a job you want. Since you will have a general idea of industry figures for that position (and may even have an idea of what that company tends to pay new people for the position), why not refer to a range of salaries, such as $25,000 - $30,000?

If the interviewer doesn't bring up salary at all, it's doubtful you're being seriously considered, so you probably don't need to even bring the subject up. (If you know you aren't getting the job or aren't interested in it if offered, you may try to nail down a salary figure in order to be better prepared for the next interview.)

"Tell me about yourself"

Watch out for this one! It's often one of the first questions asked. If you falter here, the rest of the interview could quickly become a downward slide to nowhere. Be prepared, and consider it an opportunity to combine your answers to many of the previous questions into one concise description of who you are, what you want to be, and why that company should take a chance on you. Summarize your resume—briefly—and expand on particular courses or experiences relevant to the firm or position. Do not go on about your hobbies or personal life, where you spent your summer vacation, or anything that is not relevant to securing that job. You may explain how that particular job fits in with your long-range career goals and talk specifically about what attracted you to their company in the first place.

Your Turn to Ask the Questions

1. What will my typical day be like?
2. What happened to the last person who had this job?
3. Given my attitude and qualifications, how would you estimate my chances for career advancement at your company?
4. Why did you come to work here? What keeps you here?
5. If you were I, would you start here again?
6. How would you characterize the management philosophy of your company?
7. What characteristics do the successful employees at your company have in common?
8. What's the best (and worst) thing about working here?

"Do you have any questions?"

It's the last fatal question on our list, often the last one an interviewer throws at you after an hour or two of grilling. Even if the interview has been very long and unusually thorough, you *should* have questions—about the job, the company, even the industry. Unfortunately, by the time this question off-handedly hits the floor, you are already looking forward to leaving and may have absolutely nothing to say.

Preparing yourself for an interview means more than having answers for some of the questions an interviewer may ask. It means having your own set of questions—at least five or six—for the interviewer. The interviewer is trying to find the right person for the job. You're trying to find the right job. So you should be just as curious about him or her and the company as he or she is about you. Be careful with any list of questions prepared ahead of time. Some of them were probably answered during the course of the interview, so to ask that same question at this stage would demonstrate poor listening skills. Listening well is becoming a lost art, and its importance cannot be stressed enough. (See the box on this page for a short list of questions you may consider asking on any interview).

The Not-So-Obvious Questions

Every interviewer is different and, unfortunately, there are no rules saying he or she has to use all or any of the "basic" questions covered above. But we think the odds are against his or her avoiding all of them. Whichever of these he or she includes, be assured most interviewers do like to come up with questions that are "uniquely theirs." It may be just one or a whole series—questions developed over the years that he or she feels help separate the wheat from the chaff.

You can't exactly prepare yourself for questions like, "What would you do if...(fill in the blank with some obscure occurrence)?," "What do you remember about kindergarten?," or "What's your favorite ice cream flavor?" Every interviewer we know has his or her favorites and all of these questions seem to come out of left field. Just stay relaxed, grit your teeth (quietly), and take a few seconds to frame a reasonably intelligent reply.

The Downright Illegal Questions

Some questions are more than inappropriate—they are illegal. The Civil Rights Act of 1964 makes it illegal for a company to discriminate in its hiring on the basis of race, color, religion, sex, or national origin. It also means that any interview questions covering these topics are strictly off-limits. In addition to questions about race and color, what other types of questions can't be asked? Some might surprise you:

- Any questions about marital status, number and ages of dependents, or marriage or child-bearing plans.
- Any questions about your relatives, their addresses, or their place of origin.
- Any questions about your arrest record. If security clearance is required, it can be done after hiring but before you start the job.

A Quick Quiz to Test Your Instincts

After reading the above paragraphs, read through the 10 questions below. Which ones do you think would be legal to ask at a job interview? Answers provided below.

1. Confidentially, what is your race?

2. What kind of work does your spouse do?

3. Are you single, married, or divorced?

4. What is your native language?

5. Who should we notify in case of an emergency?

6. What clubs, societies, or organizations do you belong to?

7. Do you plan to have a family?

8. Do you have any disability?

9. Do you have a good credit record?

10. What is your height and weight?

The answer? Not a single question out of the 10 is legal at a job interview, because all could lead to a discrimination suit. Some of the questions would become legal once you were hired (obviously a company would need to know who to notify in an emergency), but none belong at an interview.

Now that you know what an interviewer can't ask you, what if he or she does? Well, don't lose your cool, and don't point out that the question may be outside the law—the nonprofessional interviewer may not realize such questions are illegal, and such a response might confuse, even anger, him or her. Also, actors should be aware that physical type *is* often a factor when roles are cast.

Instead, whenever any questions are raised that you feel are outside legal boundaries, politely state that you don't understand how the question has bearing on the job opening and ask the interviewer to clarify his or herself. If the interviewer persists, you may be forced to state that you do not feel comfortable answering questions of that nature. Bring up the legal issue as a last resort, but if things reach that stage, you probably don't want to work for that company after all.

Testing and Applications, and Auditions

Though not part of the selection interview itself, job applications, skill tests, psychological testing, and auditions are often part of the pre-interview process. You should know something about them.

The job application is essentially a record-keeping exercise—simply the transfer of work experience and educational data from your resume to a printed application forms. Though taking the time to recopy data may seem like a waste of time, some companies simply want the information in a particular order on a standard form. One difference: Applications often require the listing of references and salary levels achieved. Be sure to bring your list of references with you to any interview (so you can transfer the pertinent information), and don't lie about salary history; it's easily checked.

Many companies now use a variety of psychological tests as additional mechanisms to screen out undesirable candidates. Although their accuracy is subject to question, the companies that use them obviously believe they are effective at identifying applicants whose personality makeups would preclude their participating positively in a given work situation, especially those at the extreme ends of the behavior spectrum.

Their usefulness in predicting job accomplishment is considered limited. If you are normal (like the rest of us), you'll have no trouble with these tests and may even find them amusing. Just don't try to outsmart them—you'll just wind up outsmarting yourself.

Auditioning is an unavoidable process in landing a role in a performing arts production. However, it is important to enter an audition in the right frame of mind— you shouldn't feel desperate or needy. Your ego should not be wrapped up in one job.

Upon entering the reception area, sign in. The casting director will call performers into the studio based on the sign-up sheet, and those who don't sign in risk being passed over.

After signing in, if you are an actor, take a script and start going over the lines. Become familiar with it, but don't over-rehearse—try to maintain spontaneity and freshness. For other types of work, simply take a seat and be prepared when the casting director calls *next*.

Once called into the auditioning room, the audition begins. A team of at least eight people decide on which performer gets the job. If you are selected among the finalists for the role, you will receive a *callback*. At the callback, the director's role becomes more visible, since the director needs to see with whom he/she might ultimately be working. Based on your talent and some fortuitous coincidences, you'll land the part!

Stand Up and Be Counted

Your interview is over. Breathe a sigh of relief. Make your notes—you'll want to keep a file on the important things covered for use in your next interview. Some people consider one out of 10 (one job offer for every 10 interviews) a good score—if you're keeping score. We suggest you don't. It's virtually impossible to judge how others are judging you. Just go on to the next interview. Sooner than you think, you'll be hired. For the right job.

JOB
OPPORTUNITIES
DATABANK

CHAPTER TWENTY-TWO

Job Opportunities Databank

T he Job Opportunities Databank contains listings for more than 360 commercial and nonprofit performing arts centers, companies, and festivals; Broadway, off-Broadway, regional, and community theatres; opera companies; music ensembles; dance companies and troupes; and theatre production companies that offer entry-level hiring and/or internships. It is divided into two sections: Entry-Level Job and Internships Listings, which provides full descriptive entries for companies and theatres in the United States; and Additional Companies, which includes name, address, and telephone information for companies that did not respond to our inquiries or theatres that only rent out their space for performance purposes. For complete details on the information provided in this chapter, please consult "How to Use the Job Opportunities Databank" at the front of this directory.

Entry-Level Job and Internship Listings

13th Street Repertory Company
50 W. 13th St.
New York, NY 10011
Phone: (212)675-6677

Business Description: A resident, non-Equity theatre established in 1972, the 13th Street Repertory Company performs original full-length plays, one-acts, and children's shows. The company has a resident director's unit, acting company, and playwright's workshop.

Employees: 100.

Human Resources: Rita Williams, Gen. Mgr.

▶ **Internships**

Contact: Edith O'Hara, Artistic Dir.

Type: Offers unpaid theater internships for high school seniors and graduates, college students, and graduates. Provides college credit, placement assistance, and letters of recommendation. Offers opportunities to attend seminars and workshops.

Duties: Duties include participation in such aspects of theatre as developing plays, auditioning, understudying, performing, and assisting directors, and lighting and sound technicians.

161

The Acting Company-Group I Acting Company, Inc.

420 W. 42nd St.
PO Box 898
Times Square Sta.
New York, NY 10108
Phone: (212)564-3510
Fax: (212)714-2643

Business Description: A primarily classical repertory company of young American actors that tours the country about 30 weeks each year.

Application Procedures: Send resume and photo to the attention of the casting director.

▶ Internships

Contact: John Miller, Assoc. Producer.

Type: Offers administration and stage management internships with a $50/week stipend. College credit is available.

Application Procedure: Address inquiries to John Miller.

Action Entertainment Talent Agency Speakers Bureau

PO Box 40886
Cincinnati, OH 45246
Phone: (513)742-9000

Opportunities: Offers opportunities for clowns, magicians, and sketch performers.

Application Procedures: Send materials to Bob Croskey, Sr. Talent Coord.

▶ Internships

Type: The company does not offer an internship program.

Affiliated Models Inc.

The Affiliated Bldg.
1680 Crooks Rd.
Troy, MI 48084
Phone: (313)244-8770

Business Description: Talent agency.

Opportunities: Hires models and on-camera talent.

Human Resources: Linda Hack, Pres.

Application Procedures: Send resume listing experience and detailing all physical characteristics including height, weight, and hair color. Include four candid photographs (two head shots/two full-length). Enclose a self-addressed, stamped envelope for reply. Send to the attention of the New Talent Department.

▶ Internships

Type: The company does not offer an internship program.

Agency for the Performing Arts

9000 Sunset Blvd.
Los Angeles, CA 90069
Phone: (310)273-0744

Application Procedures: Send resume and cover letter.

▶ Internships

Type: The company does not offer an internship program.

Alabama Shakespeare Festival

1 Festival Dr.
Montgomery, AL 36117-4605
Phone: (205)271-5300

Business Description: Alabama's state theatre, the company presents year-round productions.

Human Resources: Nicki Starkey, Business Office.

Application Procedures: Actors should send resume, cover letter, and head shot to the attention of Bob Vardamon; production staff should send resume and cover letter to the attention of Terry Cermak; those interested in the MFA program should send resume and cover letter to the attention of Jared Sakaren; administration staff should send resume and cover letter to the attention of Beau Williams.

▶ Internships

Contact: Jared Sakaren, Dir. of PHT/MFA Program.

Type: Offers internships for college credit to graduate students. Stipends available. **Number Available Annually:** 5-10.

Alice Tully Hall

Lincoln Center
65th St. & Broadway
New York, NY 10023
Phone: (212)875-5050

Business Description: The Hall is home of the Chamber Music Society and the New York Film Festival. Presents many international instrumental and vocal artists.

Opportunities: Hires entry-level administrative

staff to assist with performances. Requirements include a college degree.

Benefits: Benefits include medical insurance, life insurance, dental insurance, savings plan, and profit sharing.

Human Resources: Jackie Galletta, Asst. Human Resources Dir.

Application Procedures: Send resume with cover letter to Jay D. Spivack, Human Resources Dir.

▶ **Internships**

Type: Offers paid summer internships to college students. **Number Available Annually:** 2-3.

Application Procedure: Send resume and cover letter to Jay Spivack.

American Ballet Theatre
890 Broadway, 3rd Fl.
New York, NY 10003
Phone: (212)477-3030

Business Description: Performs a repertory of ballets, including premieres, revivals, and classics.

Benefits: Benefits include medical insurance and dental insurance.

Application Procedures: Apply in person as positions are posted.

▶ **Internships**

Contact: Leslie Schoof, Gen. Mgr.

Type: Offers unpaid summer internships to college students. College credit is available.

American Conservatory Theater
450 Geary St.
San Francisco, CA 94102
Phone: (415)749-2200

Business Description: Performs both classical and modern theatre.

Benefits: Benefits include medical insurance, dental insurance, and optional life insurance.

Application Procedures: Auditions are held once a year in May. Those interested should send resume and photograph to Meryl Shaw, Casting Dir. 30 Grand Ave., 6th Fl., San Francisco, CA 94108.

▶ **Internships**

Contact: Christopher Downing, Co. Mgr.

Type: Offers paid internships to college students. **Number Available Annually:** 10-13 between Sept. and April.

Application Procedure: Send resume and personal statement to Christopher Downing.

American Heritage Dance Company
West Side Dance Project
309 W. 107th St.
New York, NY 10025
Phone: (212)865-0854

Business Description: Features new and reconstructed works by Isadora Duncan.

Opportunities: Hires only volunteer technical workers.

Application Procedures: Send resume to Maria Boscaino, Artistic Dir.

▶ **Internships**

Type: The company does not offer an internship program.

Women will represent over half of all entrants into the labor force during the 1990s. While accounting for 39 percent of the labor force in 1972 and 41 percent of the labor force in 1976, women in the year 2005 will constitute over 47 percent of the labor force. By the year 2005, 4 out of 5 women between the ages of 25 and 54 will be in the labor force.

Source: *Discover the Best Jobs for You!*

American Jewish Theatre
Susan Bloch Theatre
307 W. 26th St.
New York, NY 10001
Phone: (212)633-9797

Business Description: Presents plays dealing with Jewish themes.

Human Resources: Ellen Rusconi, Managing Dir.

Application Procedures: Send resume to Ellen Rusconi, Managing Dir.

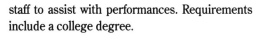

The American Place Theatre

111 W. 46th St.
New York, NY 10036
Phone: (212)840-2960
Fax: (212)391-4019

Business Description: A not-for-profit company that was founded for educational and developmental purposes. The American Place Theatre presents new works representing all cultures.

Human Resources: Tricia Kiley, Exec. Dir.; Derek Todd, Art. Dir.

Application Procedures: Audition workshops for performers are held twice a year; associate members are chosen from them. Send resume and cover letter.

▶ Internships

Type: Offers unpaid internships in production. **Number Available Annually:** 3-4.

American Repertory Theatre

64 Brattle St.
Cambridge, MA 02138
Phone: (617)495-2668
Fax: (617)495-1705

Business Description: Presents classics, revivals, and new American works. The theatre consists of actors, directors, playwrights, designers, and administrators.

Application Procedures: Send resume to Jan Geidt, Artistic Admin.

▶ Internships

Contact: Rebecca Hayden, Intern. Coord.

Type: Offers unpaid internships. College credit is available. **Number Available Annually:** 10.

Application Procedure: Write to the internship director. An interview is required.

American Stage

11 3rd St.
PO Box 1560
St. Petersburg, FL 33731
Phone: (813)823-1600

Business Description: As St. Petersburg's resident professional theatre, American Stage produces and presents classic and contemporary works. The ensemble includes such diverse programming as theatre for young audiences, a free outdoor theatre festival, and a summer re-run production.

Benefits: Benefits include medical insurance and dental insurance.

Application Procedures: Open auditions are held twice a year. Performers should send resume and photograph to Tom Block, Co. Mgr.

▶ Internships

Contact: Richard Crowell, Prod. Mgr.

Type: Offers full-time, paid internships in technical and administrative areas to those with a background in performing arts. Housing is provided. **Number Available Annually:** 4.

Application Procedure: Send resume, cover letter, and references to company manager. June is the best time to apply.

Amphitheater Entertainment Corp.

301 N. Biscayne Blvd.
Miami, FL 33132
Phone: (305)358-7550

Application Procedures: Hiring is done through an employment agency.

▶ Internships

Type: Offers a paid internship program. **Number Available Annually:** 2.

Application Procedure: Call for information.

Arena Stage

6th & Maine Ave. SW
Washington, DC 20024
Phone: (202)554-9066

Business Description: Arena Stage features everything from classic and new American plays, revivals, and foreign works. The company also runs a social outreach program that entertains children, the elderly, handicapped, and the incarcerated.

Application Procedures: Openings are posted in *Back Stage* and the *Washington Post*. The best time to request auditions is in the spring; open calls are in late June. To arrange an audition, contact by phone or mail (include resume, cover letter, and head shot) the assisant casting director, Tony Angelini, or Jerry Manning, Casting Dir.

▶ Internships

Type: Offers paid internships in stage management and in the literary and drama departments. **Number Available Annually:** 10.

Application Procedure: Contact the

internship coordinator or Jerry Manning, Casting Dir., or Tony Angelini, Asst. Casting Dir.

Ariza Talent & Modeling Agency, Inc.

909 E. Semoran Blvd.
Casselberry, FL 32707
Phone: (407)332-0011

Opportunities: Hires acting and modeling talent.

Human Resources: Jeff Callender, Agent.

Application Procedures: Send resume with photograph or contact by phone.

▶ Internships

Type: The company does not offer an internship program.

Arizona Theatre Company

PO Box 1631
Tucson, AZ 85702
Phone: (602)884-8210

Business Description: A nonprofit company that offers both classic and contemporary plays and musicals.

Human Resources: Robert Alpaugh, Mng. Dir.

Application Procedures: Those interested in performing positions should send resume and head shot to David Ira Goldstein, Artistic Dir.

▶ Internships

Contact: Matthew Wiener, Asst. Artistic Dir.

Type: Offers full-time internship positions in acting, props, management, and technical areas. College credit is available.

Application Procedure: Send cover letter, resume, and photographs to Matthew Wiener.

Arts at St. Ann's

Church of St. Ann & The Holy Trinity
157 Montague St.
Brooklyn, NY 11201
Phone: (718)858-2424

Business Description: Arts at St. Ann's presents American music concerts, new classical, and new music theatre.

Opportunities: Hires entry-level production staff.

Benefits: Benefits include medical insurance and dental insurance.

Application Procedures: Send resume and cover letter to Bill Bradford, Tech. Dir.

▶ Internships

Type: Offers unpaid internships to those interested in the arts.

Application Procedure: Send resume and cover letter to Bill Bradford.

Atlanta Ballet

477 Peachtree St.
Atlanta, GA 30308
Phone: (404)873-5811
Fax: (404)874-7905

Business Description: Established in 1929, the Atlanta Ballet performs five major ballets a year.

Employees: 20.

Benefits: Benefits include medical insurance.

Application Procedures: Send resume (include ballet-related courses/training) to the director of human resources; call to arrange an interview.

▶ Internships

Contact: Sara duBignon, Assoc. Dir. of Development.

Type: Offers unpaid internships to high school seniors and college students. Accepts international applicants. Housing assistance is available. **Applications Received:** 25.

Application Procedure: Send letter or call to arrange an interview with Sarah duBignon, Associate Director of Development at (404)873-5811.

Atlantic Theatre Company

336 W. 20th St.
New York, NY 10011
Phone: (212)645-8015

Business Description: The theatre bases its work on Mamet's philosophy of practical aesthetics. It runs a school in New York City and a workshop in Burlington, Vermont.

Opportunities: Offers acting opportunities for individuals that have attended a two-year acting program.

Application Procedures: Send resume and cover letter or contact by phone Matthew Silver, Prod. Mgr.

▶ Internships

Type: Offers unpaid internships in production and theatre management to college students 18-years or older. College credit is available. **Number Available Annually:** 6.

Application Procedure: Contact Matthew Silver to arrange an interview.

Avery Fisher Hall

Lincoln Center
65th St. & Broadway
New York, NY 10023
Phone: (212)875-5030

Business Description: Avery Fisher Hall is the home of the New York Philharmonic and the Mostly Mozart Festival. Hosts many other music events annually.

Benefits: Benefits include medical insurance and dental insurance.

Human Resources: Jackie Galletta, Asst. Human Resources Dir.

Application Procedures: Send resume and cover letter to Jay D. Spivack, Human Resources Dir. 70 Lincoln Center Plaza, 9th Fl., New York, NY 10023-6585.

▶ Internships

Type: Offers paid and unpaid internships to college students. **Number Available Annually:** 2.

Application Procedure: Send resume and cover letter to Jay D. Spivack.

Ballet Hispanico of New York

167 W. 89th St.
New York, NY 10024
Phone: (212)362-6710

Business Description: Presents ballet, modern, and Spanish dance productions.

Opportunities: Hires dancers and production staff. Dancers should currently be involved in a dance group, while production personnel are required to have a college degree.

Benefits: Benefits include medical insurance, life insurance, and dental insurance, through several healthcare plans.

Human Resources: Linda Shelpon, Exec. Prod.

Application Procedures: Dance groups should send video of their work. Production staff should send resume.

▶ Internships

Type: Offers unpaid internships for college credit; monetary compensation is negotiable.

Application Procedure: Send resume to Linda Shelphon.

Battery Dance Company

380 Broadway, 5th Fl.
New York, NY 10013
Phone: (212)219-3910

Business Description: Touring internationally, the company works extensively in the public school system.

Employees: 8.

Application Procedures: Send resume and cover letter in care of the administrative assistant or call to arrange interview.

▶ Internships

Contact: Robin Hastings, Office Mgr.

Type: Offers three-month unpaid internships to college students. College credit and placement assistance are available. International applicants accepted. Internships may lead to full-time employment. **Number Available Annually:** 3.

Application Procedure: Send letter or resume or call Robin Hastings, Office Manager at (212)219-3910.

Beach Associates

370 S. Washington St., Ste. 400
Falls Church, VA 22046
Phone: (703)536-0444
Fax: (703)536-2353

Employees: 8.

▶ Internships

Contact: Kay Leonard, Exec. VP/Gen. Mgr.

Type: Offers unpaid internships for production and marketing assistants to college juniors and seniors. College credit is available. Placement and housing assistance provided. **Number Available Annually:** 2. **Applications Received:** 12.

Duties: Production assistant interns answer phones, work with tapes and scripts, run errands, dub, type, and make travel arrangements. Marketing assistant interns research potential clients, assist with specialized campaigns, and perform various clerical tasks.

Application Procedure: Contact Kay Leonard, Exec. VP/Gen. Mgr.

Berkeley Repertory Theatre

2025 Addison St.
Berkeley, CA 94704
Phone: (510)204-8901
Fax: (510)841-7711

Business Description: Established in 1968, the theatre presents classic and contemporary works.

Opportunities: Hires candidates for entry-level positions with a background in theatre arts.

Benefits: Benefits include medical insurance and housing.

Application Procedures: Open calls for performers are held in late spring and early summer. Check newspaper advertisements for openings. Does not accept unsolicited resumes.

▶ Internships

Type: Offers full-time, paid internships to those with a strong background in theatre arts. College credit is available. **Number Available Annually:** 9-15.

Application Procedure: Check newspaper advertisements for openings.

Berkshire Public Theatre

30 Union St.
PO Box 860
Pittsfield, MA 01202
Phone: (413)445-4680

Business Description: Established in 1976, the theatre's repertoire encompasses classical and contemporary drama, comedy, musicals, revues, and experimental and original works.

Employees: 8.

Benefits: Benefits include workers' compensation.

Application Procedures: Send resume to the managing director for administrative positions. For artistic positions, send resume to Frank Bessell, Artistic Director.

▶ Internships

Contact: Michael Lichtenstein.

Type: Offers unpaid internships to high school and college students and to individuals between high school and college.

Application Procedure: Send inquiries or resumes to Michael Lichtenstein.

Bilingual Foundation of the Arts

421 North Ave. 19
Los Angeles, CA 90031
Phone: (213)225-4044
Fax: (213)225-1250

Business Description: Produces and presents professional theatre in Spanish and English, seeking to advance the Hispanic culture. The center also presents a series of theatre productions, traveling to local schools.

Benefits: Health coverage offered to administrative personnel.

Human Resources: Jim Payne, Managing Dir.

Application Procedures: Advertises in *Drama-logue*, a Los Angeles weekly theater publication.

▶ Internships

Type: Offers unpaid internships for college students. College credit is available. **Number Available Annually:** 2.

Application Procedure: Contact the internship coordinator in your college's theater department.

Birch Creek Music Center

Box 230
Egg Harbor, WI 54209
Phone: (312)828-0036

Business Description: Birch Creek provides professional training for young musicians in big band, classical, and jazz.

Officers: James Dutton, Pres.

Employees: 6.

Benefits: Benefits include tuition assistance.

Application Procedures: Apply in person (by appointment) or call or send tape and resume with letter to James Dutton, Pres.

▶ **Internships**

Contact: James Dutton, Pres. or Francis Dutton.

Type: Offers three-month paid internships to college students of junior status. College credit and placement assistance are available. Housing is provided at no cost. **Number Available Annually:** 6.

Application Procedure: Send resume and letter to James or Francis Dutton, President, 505 Lake Shore Dr., Chicago, IL 60611 from September to May. From June to August, send materials to Box 230, Egg Harbor, WI 54209.

Application Deadline: January 15.

Bloomsburg Theatre Ensemble

226 Center St.
Bloomsburg, PA 17815
Phone: (717)784-5530

Business Description: This resident company performs year-round in its own theatre in rural Pennsylvania. Performs a six-play season and develops two new projects a year that tour elementary schools.

Benefits: Benefits include medical insurance and life insurance. Pension plan is available through employee deductions.

Application Procedures: For administrative positions, send resume to Steven Bevans, administrative director; for production/technical positions, send resume to the production manager; for acting positons, send resume and photo to the casting coordinator.

▶ **Internships**

Type: Offers unpaid administrative and production internships for college students.

Acting internships require an audition and include a stipend.

Application Procedure: For acting internships, contact the ensemble intern advisor. For administrative and production internships, contact Steve Bevan, Admin. Dir.

The Body Politic Theatre

2261 N. Lincoln
Chicago, IL 60614
Phone: (312)348-7901

Business Description: Chicago's oldest off-loop theatre produces classic and contemporary literature and has developed an ensemble of over 20 professional theatre artists.

Employees: 1.

Opportunities: Offers entry-level administrative opportunities to individuals with previous experience and some college course work.

Application Procedures: Send resume to the attention of the human resources department; check for advertisements in the newspaper.

▶ **Internships**

Type: Offers unpaid internships to college students.

Bonneville Broadcasting System Bonneville International Corporation Inc.

2211 5th Ave.
Seattle, WA 98121
Phone: (708)291-0110
Toll-free: 800-426-9082

Opportunities: Hires on-air talent.

Human Resources: Becky Brenner, Program Director.

Application Procedures: Send resume to Becky Brenner, Program Dir.

▶ **Internships**

Type: The company does not offer an internship program.

Boston Ballet

19 Clarendon St.
Boston, MA 02116
Phone: (617)695-6950
Fax: (617)695-6995

Employees: 70.

Benefits: Benefits include medical insurance and tuition assistance.

Application Procedures: Send resume with cover letter or call to arrange an interview. Contact the executive director.

▶ **Internships**

Contact: Steve Scheller, Public Relations Asst.

Type: Offers unpaid internships to college and international students. Interns receive placement assistance, free performances, and free dance classes. **Number Available Annually:** 12.

Application Procedure: Send resume and letter or call Steve Scheller, Public Relations Asst.

Brooklyn Academy of Music (BAM)

30 Lafayette Ave.
Brooklyn, NY 11217
Phone: (718)636-4100

Business Description: The Academy presents baroque and contemporary opera, theatre, classical and new music, African and new dance events, and family programming.

Benefits: Benefits include medical insurance and dental insurance.

Human Resources: Liz Sharp, Dir. of Personnel.

Application Procedures: Mail or fax resume with cover letter to Liz Sharp, Dir. of Personnel.

▶ **Internships**

Type: Offers paid internships for credit to college students. **Number Available Annually:** 2.

Application Procedure: Fax or mail resume with cover letter to Liz Sharp.

Brooklyn Center for the Performing Arts

Whitman Hall/Gershwin Theatre
Campus Rd. & Hillel Pl.
Brooklyn, NY 11210
Phone: (718)951-4500

Business Description: The Center presents a music and dance series as well as many ethnic, community, and student events.

Opportunities: Hires entry-level, nonperformance staff in ticket sales and subscriptions.

Human Resources: John Vetter, Dir. of Ticket Sales.

Application Procedures: Contact the theater department of Brooklyn College of the City University of New York.

▶ **Internships**

Type: Offers internships for credit to students at Brooklyn College of the City University of New York.

Brooklyn Conservatory of Music

Recital Hall
58 7th Ave.
Brooklyn, NY 11217
Phone: (718)622-3300

Business Description: Presents concerts and classes.

Opportunities: Hires performers and production staff.

Human Resources: Dexter Hinton, Dir.

Application Procedures: Send resume and portfolio.

▶ **Internships**

Type: The company does not offer an internship program.

Buddy Lee Attractions Inc.

38 Music Sq. E.
Nashville, TN 37203
Phone: (615)244-4336

Opportunities: Hires performers that have a recording out on a major label.

Benefits: Benefits include medical insurance, dental insurance, vision insurance, and savings plan.

Human Resources: Tony Conway, Pres.

Application Procedures: Send resume to Tony Conway, Pres.

▶ **Internships**

Type: Offers internships for college credit. Students must be enrolled in music business study programs and be at least at the junior level.

Application Procedure: Apply through Middle Tennessee State University in Murfreesboro, TN, or Belmont College in Nashville, TN.

Caribbean Cultural Center
408 W. 58th St.
New York, NY 10019
Phone: (212)307-7420

Business Description: Focusing on African diasporo cultures, the Center presents music, poetry, dance, and visual art.

Opportunities: Hires performers and production staff.

Human Resources: Laura Noreno, Contact.

Application Procedures: Send resume and portfolio to Martha Vega, Exec. Dir.

▶ **Internships**

Type: The company does not offer an internship program.

New occupations for the 1990s and beyond will center around information, energy, high-tech, healthcare, and financial industries. They promise to create a new occupational structure and vocabulary relating to computers, robotics, biotechnology, lasers, and fiber optics. And as these fields begin to apply new technologies to developing new innovations, they in turn will generate other new occupations in the 21st century.

Source: *Discover the Best Jobs for You!*

Carnegie Hall
154 W. 57th St.
New York, NY 10019
Phone: (212)247-7800

Business Description: Promotes musical excellence by hosting performances by talented artists from around the world.

Opportunities: Hires artistic talent and administrative staff.

Human Resources: Kimo Gerald, House Mgr.

Application Procedures: For administrative positions, send resume and cover letter to Lauren Scott, Director of Human Resources. For artistic talent positions, have manager forward portfolio to Katherine Gevers, Music Administrator.

▶ **Internships**

Type: The company does not offer an internship program.

Cathedral Arts
Cathedral of St. John the Divine
112 St. & Amsterdam Ave.
New York, NY 10025
Phone: (212)662-2133

Business Description: Cathedral Arts presents a variety of performing arts events.

Opportunities: Hires free-lance performers. Prefers those with a college degree and/or experience in the field.

Human Resources: Karen DeFrancis, Contact.

▶ **Internships**

Type: The company does not offer an internship program.

CD Enterprises, Inc.
300 I St., NE
Washington, DC 20002
Phone: (202)347-0001

Application Procedures: Send cassette recording or video tape, photograph, and resume to Gerald Scott, Prod. Mgr.

▶ **Internships**

Type: The company does not offer an internship program.

Center Stage
700 N. Calvert St.
Baltimore, MD 21202
Phone: (410)685-3200

Business Description: Center Stage produces classic and contemporary works.

Opportunities: Offers performing and technical opportunities.

Benefits: Benefits include medical insurance, life insurance, dental insurance, savings plan, and tuition assistance.

Application Procedures: For technical positions, send resume and cover letter to J.R. Conklin, audio engineer (for sound technician positions) or Jeff Harris, electrical engineer (for electrical positions). For performing positions, open calls are held twice a year; contact Dell Risbeerg, Assoc. Artistic Dir.

▶ **Internships**

Type: Offers full-time, paid internships to college students and college graduates. Housing is provided. College credit is available. **Number Available Annually:** 15.

Application Procedure: Call for information.

Chamber Music America

545 8th Ave.
New York, NY 10018
Phone: (212)244-2772
Fax: (212)244-2776

Employees: 10.

Opportunities: Opportunities are available to experienced candidates.

Benefits: Benefits include medical insurance.

Application Procedures: Send resume and cover letter to Dean K. Stein, Exec. Dir. Phone: (212)244-2772.

▶ **Internships**

Contact: Dean K. Stein, Exec. Dir.

Type: Offers internships for college credit to high school seniors. Placement assistance provided. Full-time employment possible. **Number Available Annually:** 4.

Charas/El Bohio Cultural and Community Center

605 E. 9th St.
New York, NY 10009
Phone: (212)533-6835

Business Description: A grassroots community center that presents dance, music, and theatre events year round. The center also provides youth programs, art exhibits, and media workshops.

Application Procedures: Send resume and head shot to Armando Perez, Chm. of the Board of Dir.

▶ **Internships**

Application Procedure: Those interested in internships should contact Armando Perez.

Cheng & Dancers

Mulberry Street Theatre
70 Mulberry St.
New York, NY 10013
Phone: (212)349-0126

Business Description: An Asian-American dance company that combines modern dance with traditional Asian themes.

Application Procedures: Attend open auditions in the spring or send resume and cover letter to David Cheng.

▶ **Internships**

Type: Offers unpaid internships.

Cherry Lane Theatre

38 Commerce St.
New York, NY 10014
Phone: (212)719-3090

Business Description: Cherry Lane presents new contemporary plays and musicals.

Human Resources: Pam Bernhardt.

Application Procedures: Those interested in entry-level production or performing positions should send resume, cover letter, and head shot (if applicable) to Carol Prugh, Theater Mgr.

▶ **Internships**

Type: Offers unpaid internships to those interested in theatre. **Number Available Annually:** 1.

Application Procedure: Send resume and cover letter to Carol Prugh.

Chicago City Limits

George Todisco Improvisational Theatre
351 E. 74th St.
New York, NY 10021
Phone: (212)772-8707

Business Description: Chicago City Limits is a long-running comedy revue featuring improvisational comedy with social and political satire. The company produces its own comedy news show on the USA cable network and has appeared on such television programs as *PM Magazine, Entertainment Tonight,* and PBS's *Reading Rainbow* series.

Opportunities: Offers a variety of opportunities for local individuals with previous theatre experience.

Application Procedures: Send resume and cover letter to Paul Zuckerman, Producer.

▶ **Internships**

Contact: David Miner, Producer.

Type: Offers unpaid internships for college credit and free acting classes.

Application Procedure: Send resume and cover letter to the attention of David Miner, Producer.

The Children's Theatre Company
2400 3rd Ave. S.
Minneapolis, MN 55404
Phone: (612)874-0500
Fax: (612)874-8119

Business Description: This company's entire repertoire is drawn from children's classics, folk tales, fantasies, and original plays. The theatre annually produces a seven-play mainstage series in Minneapolis.

Benefits: Benefits include medical insurance, life insurance, dental insurance, vision insurance, vacation days and sick leave.

Application Procedures: Send resume to the general manager.

▶ Internships

Type: Offers internships.

Application Procedure: Send resume to the general manager.

In 1992, women experienced their highest labor-force participation rate of all time—57.8 percent. They also accounted for 60 percent of total growth between 1982 and 1992.

Source: *Working Woman*

Child's Play Touring Theatre
2650 W. Belden Ave.
Chicago, IL 60647
Phone: (312)235-8911
Fax: (312)235-5478

Business Description: The theatre's mission is to share, encourage, and validate the creative writing of children. A typical performance runs 45 minutes and contains 7 to 10 original pieces.

Opportunities: Entry-level opportunities are available in the public relations, clerical, and administrative areas. Some college course work is required.

Benefits: Benefits include medical insurance, life insurance, dental insurance, and vision insurance.

Application Procedures: Send resume with cover letter to June Podagrosi, Exec. Dir.

▶ Internships

Contact: June Podagrosi, Exec. Dir.

Type: Offers unpaid internships in administration, public relations, and production. Also provides $5/day for lunch and transportation costs.

Application Procedure: Send resume and cover letter to June Podagrosi.

Cincinnati Opera
1241 Elm St.
Cincinnati, OH 45210
Phone: (513)621-1919

Employees: 200.

Opportunities: Opportunities are available for individuals with training in the field.

Benefits: Benefits include medical insurance and tuition assistance for related classes only.

Application Procedures: Call for an application or send resume with cover letter to Anne Schmidt, Admin. Asst.

▶ Internships

Contact: Anne Schmidt, Admin. Asst.

Type: Offers paid summer internships. International applicants accepted. Interns receive formal training, opportunities to attend seminars/workshops, and reimbursement for travel expenses. **Applications Received:** 400.

Application Procedure: Send cover letter and resume to Anne Schmidt. Application deadline for the "Young American Artist Program" only is October 15.

Application Deadline: March 1.

Cincinnati Playhouse in the Park
Box 6537
Cincinnati, OH 45206
Phone: (513)345-2242

Business Description: Founded in 1960, the Playhouse's audiences have grown from 12,000 people in its first year to more than 250,000 people attending 1992 productions.

Opportunities: Offers entry-level opportunities in public relations, administration, and production to individuals with previous experience and some college course work.

Application Procedures: Send resume with cover letter to the attention of Gail Lawrence.

▶ **Internships**

Contact: Gail Lawrence.

Type: Offers unpaid internships to college students.

Application Procedure: Send resume with cover letter to the attention of Gail Lawrence.

Circa '21 Dinner Playhouse

1828 3rd Ave.
Rock Island, IL 61201
Phone: (309)786-2667
Fax: (309)786-4119

Business Description: Full-time, year-round professional theatre housed in a renovated 1921 vaudeville theatre.

Opportunities: Administrative and production opportunities are available for individuals with previous experience and some college course work.

Benefits: Benefits include medical insurance and dental insurance. Free passes to productions are provided.

Application Procedures: Send resume with a cover letter that identifies area of interest to Gene Hitchcock, Mgr.

▶ **Internships**

Type: Offers unpaid internships to college students.

Application Procedure: Send resume and a cover letter indicating interest in an internship.

Circle in the Square Theatre

1633 Broadway
New York, NY 10019-6795
Phone: (212)307-2732

Opportunities: Administrative opportunities are available to college graduates.

Benefits: Benefits include medical insurance, dental insurance, and vision insurance.

Application Procedures: Send resume to human resources department.

▶ **Internships**

Type: Offers unpaid administrative internships to college students.

Application Procedure: Send a resume and a cover letter indicating interest in an internship.

Circle Repertory Company

99 7th Ave. S.
New York, NY 10013
Phone: (212)505-6010

Business Description: Founded in 1969, Circle Repertory Company is made up of over 200 theatre artists dedicated to presenting new American plays.

Opportunities: Hires performers and production staff.

Benefits: Benefits include medical insurance, life insurance, and dental insurance.

Human Resources: Trevor Brown, Asst. to the Prod. Mgr.

Application Procedures: Send resume with cover letter and head shot (if applicable) to Jodi Boese, Prod. Mgr.

▶ **Internships**

Contact: Niclas Nigler, Intern. Coord.

Type: Offers paid office and production internships to college students. College credit is available. **Number Available Annually:** 15-20.

Application Procedure: Send resume and cover letter to Niclas Nigler. Auditions and interviews are typically held in late spring.

Circuit Playhouse-Playhouse on the Square

51 S. Cooper
Memphis, TN 38104
Phone: (901)725-0776

Business Description: Established over 20 years ago, Circuit Playhouse is a member of the Theatre Communications Group, the national organization for nonprofit, professional theatre.

Employees: 30.

Opportunities: Offers opportunities in the areas of technical assistance, production, administration, and performing.

Human Resources: Jackie Nichols, Exec. Dir.

Application Procedures: Send resume to contact. Applicants must audition at regional try-outs or by video.

▶ **Internships**

Type: Offers paid technical, administrative, and performance internships to postgraduates or individuals with an MFA. Interns receive

$75/day in addition to housing. **Number Available Annually:** 6.

Duties: Interns work on assignments consistent with theatre needs. Acting interns typically perform in four to five productions if they work at the theatre for one year. Interns have the opportunity work on off-hours workshops.

Application Procedure: Call or write for information.

City Center
55 Street Theatre Foundation, Inc.
130 W. 56th St.
New York, NY 10019
Phone: (212)581-1212

Business Description: The City Center is the home to seven American dance companies.

Benefits: Benefits include medical insurance.

Human Resources: Ditas Samson, Office Mgr.

Application Procedures: Call or send resume and cover letter to Art Davies, Prod. Mgr.

▶ **Internships**

Contact: Ditas Samson, Office Mgr.

Type: Offers unpaid internships for credit to college students and high school seniors. **Number Available Annually:** 3-4.

Application Procedure: Send resume, cover letter, and letter of recommendation to Ditas Samson, Office Mgr.

Clarence Brown Theatre Company
PO Box 8450
Knoxville, TN 37996-4800
Phone: (615)974-6011

Business Description: Founded in 1974, the Clarence Brown Theatre Company is the professional theatre company in residence at the University of Tennessee, Knoxville.

Application Procedures: Audition by appointment. Contact Thomas Cervone, Company Mgr.

▶ **Internships**

Type: Offers internships to college students for credit at the University of Tennessee. **Number Available Annually:** 8-10.

The Cleveland Play House
8500 Euclid Ave.
Cleveland, OH 44106
Phone: (216)795-7010

Business Description: The house presents new and classical American plays.

Employees: 60. Employees number 170-180 during the performance season.

Opportunities: Hires entry-level clerical staff and performers.

▶ **Internships**

Contact: David Eliet, Dir. of Education.

Type: Offers internships to college seniors, graduates, graduate students, and others. Production assistant, assistant director, and literary, marketing, development, business, and shop interns are unpaid. Directing fellows, playwright fellows, and playwright interns earn $200/week. Educational credit is available. Placement and housing assistance provided. Full-time employment possible. **Number Available Annually:** 29. **Applications Received:** 100.

Duties: Production assistants help stage managers during rehearsals and performances. Assistant directors aid directors during rehearsals. Directing fellows assist directors, direct lab company, teach, and direct stage readings. Playwright fellows are responsible for writing workshops, touring show, and dramaturg. Playwright interns assist the literary manager. Literary interns read and evaluate scripts and assist dramaturg. Marketing interns assist in all aspects of marketing. Development interns write grants and are involved in telemarketing and fundraising. Business interns assist in the business office. Shop interns work with costumes, sets, lights, and sound.

Application Procedure: Contact David Eliet, Dir. of Education.

Application Deadline: April 30.

Coconut Grove Playhouse
Box 607
Coconut Grove, FL 33133
Phone: (305)442-2662

Business Description: Built as a movie house, the Coconut Grove Playhouse became a legitimate playhouse in 1956. The company produces six plays a year, as well as an intimate cabaret theatre, and an educational program for both adults and young people.

Benefits: Benefits include medical insurance, life insurance, and dental insurance.

Application Procedures: For production positions, send resume to E.R. Hughes, prod. mgr. Performers may audition each fall. For designing and acting positions, send resume to Lynne Peyser, Assoc. Prod.

▶ **Internships**

Contact: E.R. Hughes, Prod. Mgr. or Peg McCue, Assoc. Prod.

Type: Offers paid apprenticeships for college graduates. **Number Available Annually:** 9.

Application Procedure: Contact E.R. Hughes for production positions and Peg McCue for acting positons.

Colden Center for the Performing Arts
Colden Auditorium, Queens College
6530 Kissena Blvd.
Flushing, NY 11367
Phone: (718)793-8080

Business Description: A multi-disciplinary performing arts center that presents dance concerts, children's theatre, classical and jazz music, and solo artists.

Opportunities: Hires entry-level production staff.

Application Procedures: Phone (718)544-2996 or send resume to Vivian Charlop, Exec. Dir.

▶ **Internships**

Type: The company does not offer an internship program.

College Light Opera Company
Falmouth on Cape Cod
Falmouth, MA 02541
Phone: (216)774-8485

Business Description: Summer stock music theatre.

▶ **Internships**

Contact: Robert A. Haslun, Producer.

Type: Offers unpaid internships to singers,

actors, orchestra musicians, stage crew, costume crew, in the box office, and publicity. Open to high school seniors and graduates, college students and graduates, and graduate school students. College credit is available. **Number Available Annually:** 60. **Applications Received:** 400-500.

Duties: Singers, actors, and orchestra musicians participate in musicals; stage crew help with the creation of scenery and sets; and costume interns assist in making costumes.

Application Procedure: Contact Robert A. Haslun, Producer, 162 S. Cedar St., Oberlin, OH 44024.

Female managers currently represent 41 percent of all professional and managerial occupations. Also, women are more likely to move into management positions in areas where they are already concentrated: medicine, human resources, labor relations, and education.

Source: *Working Woman*

Connecticut Opera Association, Inc.
226 Farmington Ave.
Hartford, CT 06105
Phone: (203)527-0713
Fax: (203)293-1715

Employees: 8.

Benefits: Benefits include medical insurance.

Application Procedures: Call for application or to arrange interview, apply in person, or send resume. Contact the executive director of the personnel/human resources department.

▶ **Internships**

Contact: Betty Hughes, Dir. of Mktg. and Development.

Type: Offers unpaid internships to high school graduates. College credit is available. Interns receive on-the-job training and formal training. **Number Available Annually:** 4.

Application Procedure: Send letter and resume to Betty Hughes.

Cortland Repertory Theatre, Inc.
37 Franklin St.
Cortland, NY 13045
Phone: (607)753-6161

Business Description: Cortland Repertory Theatre is a professional summer theatre.

Employees: 20.

Opportunities: Advertises in art magazines for clerical and administrative positions and posts notices for open auditions.

▶ Internships

Type: Offers paid internships in acting, production, box office, house management, and publicity. Interns earn between $500 and $700 for 12 to 13 weeks. Educational credit is available. Housing is provided at no cost. **Number Available Annually:** 7-9. **Applications Received:** 25.

Duties: Acting interns perform in productions. Production interns work on props, scenery, costumes, lighting, and sound as well as run crews. Box office interns work as cashiers, do phone work, work in the box office, and sell tickets. House management interns train and supervise ushers, clean, and handle seating problems. Publicity interns coordinate media, write press releases, and develop media kits.

Application Procedure: Contact the managing director at PO Box 783, Cortland, NY 13045.

Application Deadline: February 15.

The Costume Collection
1501 Broadway, Ste. 2110
New York, NY 10036
Phone: (212)989-5855

Business Description: The Costume Collection, established in 1967, provides theatrical costumes to nonprofit performing arts and educational organizations.

Employees: 10.

Opportunities: Hires entry-level clerical personnel.

Application Procedures: Inquiries should be sent to Kenneth Yount. 601 W. 26th St., 17th Fl., New York, NY 10001.

▶ Internships

Type: Offers internships to college juniors, seniors, graduates, and graduate students. Interns are paid $4.25/hour and receive formal training, the opportunities to attend workshops and seminars, and placement assistance. **Number Available Annually:** 8. **Applications Received:** 15.

Application Procedure: Call for information.

Application Deadline: March 31.

Council of Performing Arts for Children
345 State St. SE, Ste. 26A
Grand Rapids, MI 49503
Phone: (616)774-9922

Business Description: The Council is involved in performing arts programs for children in the Grand Rapids area.

Employees: 2.

Human Resources: Sarah Keranen, Exec. Dir.

▶ Internships

Type: Offers an unpaid internship in general arts administration to college students, college graduates, and graduate students. Placement assistance is provided. **Number Available Annually:** 1. **Applications Received:** 5.

Application Procedure: Send resume and cover letter to Sarah Keranen, Exec. Dir.

Creede Repertory Theatre
Main St.
Creede, CO 81130
Phone: (719)658-2541
Fax: (719)658-2343

Business Description: A nonprofit theatre established in 1966.

Employees: 36. Number reflects both in-season and off-season employees.

▶ Internships

Contact: Richard Baxter, Producing/Artistic Dir.

Type: Offers paid summer internships in business and shop/set at $90/week and in stage management, costume, and light/sound at $75/week. Interns receive college credit, placement assistance, and housing. High school graduates, college students and graduates, graduate students, and others are eligible. **Number Available Annually:** 9. **Applications Received:** 200.

Application Procedure: Contact Richard

Baxter, Producing/Artistic Dir., at PO Box 269, Creede, CO 81130.

Application Deadline: March 1.

Cromarty and Company

110 W. 40th St., Ste. 405
New York, NY 10018
Phone: (212)944-8191

Business Description: Cromarty and Company is a theatrical press agency that is responsible for the publicity for many Broadway, off-Broadway, and dance and music clients.

Employees: 5.

▶ Internships

Contact: Lynne McCreary, Internship Coord.

Type: Offers unpaid internships to college students, college graduates, graduate students, and career changers. General office skills required. Interns are reimbursed for travel expenses and for lunch on work days. Placement assistance provided. Full-time employment possible. **Number Available Annually:** 2. **Applications Received:** 20.

Application Procedure: Write to Ms. Lynne McCreary, Internship Coord.

CSC Repertory, Ltd. (Classic Stage Company)

136 E. 13th St.
New York, NY 10003
Phone: (212)677-4210
Fax: (212)477-7504

Business Description: An off-Broadway, not-for-profit theatre that features adaptions of the classics. The company also has an educational outreach program for students from Manhattan.

Employees: 30.

▶ Internships

Contact: Patricia Taylor, Managing Dir.

Type: Offers unpaid technical, developmental, marketing/administrative, and literary/dramaturg internships. Open to high school graduates, college students, college graduates, and graduate students. Interns receive placement assistance. College credit is available and full-time employment is possible. **Number Available Annually:** 8. **Applications Received:** 30.

Application Procedure: Contact Patricia Taylor, Managing Dir.

Dance Theater Workshop

Bessie Schonberg Theater
219 W. 19th St.
New York, NY 10011-4079
Phone: (212)924-0077

Benefits: Benefits include medical insurance.

Application Procedures: Resume of work-related experience required. To set up an interview, contact Gail Goldstein, Assoc. Producer.

▶ Internships

Contact: Gail Goldstein, Assoc. Producer.

Type: Offers internships for college credit to high school students. Full-time employment possible. Placement assistance and housing assistance available. **Number Available Annually:** 6.

> **T**he business of managing the arts requires a special love and dedication that goes beyong mere competence in various job skills. If art is the record of civilization and artists our true historians, then the mission of arts management must include a far-reaching sense of obligation. It must also include a sense of joy and fascination with the arts—this is an important aspect of the compensation you will receive for working in this field.
>
> Source: *Jobs in Arts & Media Management*

Dance Theatre of Harlem

247 W. 30th St.
New York, NY 10001
Phone: (212)967-3470
Fax: (212)594-2783

Employees: 8.

Benefits: Benefits include medical insurance.

Application Procedures: Send resume or call to arrange appointment for interview. Contact the personnel director.

▶ Internships

Contact: Donna Walker-Collins, Assoc. Dir. of Mktg.

Type: Offers unpaid internships to college students. Graduate students preferred. Placement assistance, reimbursement of travel expenses, and complimentary tickets to performances provided. Full-time employment possible. **Number Available Annually:** 4.

Application Procedure: Send resume and cover letter to Donna Walker-Collins.

DanceCleveland

1148 Euclid Ave., Ste. 311
Cleveland, OH 44115
Phone: (216)861-2213
Fax: (216)781-8124

Employees: 5.

Benefits: Benefits include medical insurance.

Application Procedures: Apply in person, call, or send resume with cover letter to the director of personnel.

▶ **Internships**

Contact: Stephanie Brown, Dir.

Type: Offers unpaid internships for college credit to college students. Foreign applicants accepted. Full-time employment possible. Placement and housing assistance available. Offers workshops and seminars for interns. **Number Available Annually:** 3.

Application Procedure: Send cover letter with resume to Stephanie Brown or call to arrange an interview.

Danse Mirage Theatre

153 Mercer St., 2nd Fl.
New York, NY 10012
Phone: (212)226-5767
Fax: (212)219-0601

Business Description: Presents emerging, experimental, and minority artists in dance, theatre, and music events.

Application Procedures: Part-time opportunities available. Send resume to Elinor Coleman, Art. Dir.

▶ **Internships**

Type: Offers unpaid internships to those interested in dance.

Application Procedure: Send resume with cover letter to Elinor Coleman.

Denver Center Theatre Company

1245 Champa
Denver, CO 80204
Phone: (303)893-4000
Fax: (303)825-2117

Employees: 470. Includes full-time and seasonal/part-time employees.

Application Procedures: Send resume with cover letter expressing area of interest. Performance positions require auditions.

▶ **Internships**

Contact: Barbara Sellers, Producing Dir.

Type: Offers internships for scenic artists, draftsmen, costume assistants, prop artisans, lighting assistants, design assistants, administrative assistants, carpenters, stage management assistants, production assistants, literary assistants, and publicity assistants. Full-time employment possible. Placement assistance provided. **Number Available Annually:** 14. **Applications Received:** 40.

Application Procedure: Write to Barbara Sellers.

Application Deadline: August 1.

The Director's Company, Inc.

Space 603
311 W. 43rd St.
New York, NY 10036
Phone: (212)246-5877

Business Description: Committed to the development and presentation of directional talent, the Director's Company offers production opportunities, programs, and workshops.

Opportunities: Offers opportunities for actors and directors.

Application Procedures: Directors should send resume with cover letter; actors should send head shot and resume to the attention of Victoria Chesshire, Artistic Managing Dir. or to Michael Parva, Artistic Producing Dir.

▶ **Internships**

Contact: Matt Beres, Intern Coord.

Type: Offers unpaid full- or part-time internships to college students. College credit is available. **Number Available Annually:** 10.

Application Procedure: Send resume and cover letter to Matt Beres, Intern Coord.

Dixon Place

258 Bowery
New York, NY 10012
Phone: (212)219-3088
Fax: (212)274-9114

Business Description: A small, alternative, artist-run theatre, Dixon Place features emerging and established artists. Programming includes performance art, music, dance, and poetry. With seven to nine diverse performances and readings per week, Dixon Place encourages experimental and interdisciplinary work.

Officers: Ellie Covan, Dir.

Employees: 5.

Opportunities: Offers opportunities for individuals with a college degree, previous experience, and/or some college course work.

Application Procedures: Send resume to Ellie Covan, Dir.

▶ Internships

Type: Offers paid (stipend) internships to college students. Positions available include assistant arts administrator and stage manager internships. A background in office management or theatrical production is preferred. Minimum length of interships is three months. **Number Available Annually:** 2-5.

Duties: Assistant arts administrator interns assist in the preparation of monthly calendars, press listings, and targeted press releases. Other duties include scheduling artists' rehearsals and volunteer work, opening the theatre and collecting ticket fees, working in the cafe, and clerical duties. Stage manager interns schedule artists rehearsals, provide technical assistance for performers, prepare and tidy the performance space, stock the cafe, help with press and calendar mailings, open the theatre and collect ticket fees, schedule volunteers, and perform clerical duties.

Application Procedure: Send cover letter and resume to Ellie Covan, Dir.

Douglas Fairbanks Theatre

432 W. 42nd St.
New York, NY 10036
Phone: (212)239-4321

Business Description: Performs the long-running musical *Nunsense*.

Employees: 4.

Opportunities: Hires production staff. Requirements include some college coursework or previous experience.

Benefits: Benefits include medical insurance.

Human Resources: Eric Knebs, Theatrical Mgr.

Application Procedures: Send resume to Paul Moore, Contact.

▶ Internships

Contact: Eric Krebs, Theatrical Mgr.

Type: Offers unpaid internships for college credit. **Number Available Annually:** 2-3.

Application Procedure: Send resume and cover letter.

Edith Stephen Electric Current Dance Company

Dance Connection
55 Bethune St., 630A
New York, NY 10014
Phone: (212)989-2250
Fax: (212)645-7495

Business Description: A multi-media company combining dance, film, visuals, sculpture, and poetry.

Application Procedures: Send resume or application to Edith Stephen, Owner.

▶ Internships

Type: Offers paid internships to college students. **Number Available Annually:** 2.

Application Procedure: Send resume to Edith Stephen.

Elinor Coleman Dance Studio/Danse Mirage Inc.

153 Mercer St., 2nd Fl.
New York, NY 10012
Phone: (212)226-5767

Business Description: Collaborating with sculptors, musicians, and puppet makers, the Elinor Coleman Dance Ensemble is a multi-ethnic modern dance company.

Employees: 2.

Opportunities: Offers performance opportunities to college graduates.

Application Procedures: Holds open auditions. Send resume and samples or apply in person to Lady Matasovsky, Admin. Dir.

▶ **Internships**

Type: Offers unpaid internships to college students with an interest in performing arts. Excellent communication and computer skills, and theatre technical experience required. College credit is available. **Number Available Annually:** 1.

Application Procedure: Send resume and cover letter to Lady Matasovsky.

The restructuring of the American work force will mean that this country's best businesses will be giving their workers—in particular, women—more responsibility, pushing that responsibility downward, making use of frontline workers, and achieving a greater degree of flexibility. It will mean relying on the motivation and loyalty of workers as their key competitive strategy. It will be what makes them unique and capable of delivering a better product, a higher quality product—and a bigger profit for themselves, their shareholders, and their workers.

Source: Working Woman

Elisa Monte Dance Company
39 Great Jones St.
New York, NY 10012
Phone: (212)533-2226
Fax: (212)254-4071

Officers: Bernard Schmidt, Managing Dir.

Employees: 2.

Benefits: Benefits include medical insurance.

Application Procedures: Send resume with cover letter to Bernard Schmidt, Managing Dir.

▶ **Internships**

Contact: Bernard Schmidt, Managing Dir.

Type: Offers paid internships to college graduates. College credit is available. Housing assistance is provided. Full-time employment possible. **Number Available Annually:** 1.

Ensemble Theatre of Cincinnati
1127 Vine St.
Cincinnati, OH 45210
Phone: (513)421-3556

Business Description: The company features one-acts, new plays, workshops, and readings.

Employees: 50.

▶ **Internships**

Contact: Mark Mocahbee, Intern Dir.

Type: Offers unpaid acting, directing, administrative, stage management, and technical internships to college graduates and graduate students. Placement and housing assistance provided. Full-time employment possible. Interns receive formal training and the opportunity to attend workshops and seminars. **Number Available Annually:** 22. **Applications Received:** 100.

Application Procedure: Contact Mark Mocahbee, Intern Director. Administrative and technical applicants will be interviewed. Others must audition.

Application Deadline: April 1.

Fargo-Moorehead Community Theatre
PO Box 644
Fargo, ND 58107

Business Description: Regional theatre presenting children's shows, senior vaudeville, a biennial playwrights' contest and mainstage productions.

Employees: 12.

Application Procedures: All openings are posted. Does not accept unsolicited resumes.

▶ **Internships**

Contact: Bruce Tinker, Artistic Dir.

Type: Offers unpaid internships in scenery and lighting, costumes, children's theater, marketing, box office, and general administration. Open to high school students and graduates, college students and graduates, and graduate students. **Number Available Annually:** 8.

Application Procedure: 20 received each year.

Application Deadline: 4-8 weeks prior to the start of the internship.

Feld Ballets/NY
Joyce Theatre
19th St./890 Broadway, 8th Fl.
New York, NY 10003
Phone: (212)777-7710

Business Description: Choreographer Eliot

Feld has created over 70 ballets over 27 years for the company.

Benefits: Benefits include medical insurance, life insurance, dental insurance, and vision insurance.

Application Procedures: For production positions, send resume and cover letter to Pat Thomas, Production Mgr. Dancers should send resumes to Elliot Feld, Artistic Dir.

▶ **Internships**

Type: The company does not offer an internship program.

Flat Rock Playhouse
PO Box 310
Flat Rock, NC 28731
Phone: (704)693-0731

▶ **Internships**

Contact: Robin Farquhar, Exec. Dir.

Type: Offers internships in the following areas: acting, technical, public relations, and general management. Housing and placement assistance provided. Internships pay $50 to $175 per week. Available to college students, college graduates, and graduate students. Full-time employment possible. Previous experience required for some of the internships. **Number Available Annually:** 4. **Applications Received:** 350.

Application Procedure: Write to Robin Farquhar. In-person interview required.

Application Deadline: April 30.

Florello Dance Festivals
La Guardia High School
100 Amsterdam Ave.
New York, NY 10023
Phone: (212)877-1361

Business Description: Holds summer and winter dance festivals presented by the high school of performing art's dance department.

Opportunities: Offers opportunities for technical consultants and dance instructors with at least six years of experience with a major dance company.

Application Procedures: For technical positions, send resume to Ron McIntyre, theatre manager. For dance instructor positions, send resume with cover letter to Michelle Mathesius,

Chm. of Dance Dept. 65 Court St., Brooklyn, NY 11201.

▶ **Internships**

Type: Offers unpaid dance, technical, management, and public relations internships to college students. College credit is available. **Number Available Annually:** 4.

Application Procedure: Call La Guardia High School at (212)496-0700 for information.

Florida Shakespeare Festival
2121 Ponce de Leon Blvd., No. 550
Coral Gables, FL 33134
Phone: (305)441-9149
Fax: (305)445-8645

▶ **Internships**

Contact: Rose McVeigh, Artistic Dir.

Type: Offers paid acting, technical, production, management, and public affairs internships. Open to college graduates and graduate students. College credit is available. **Number Available Annually:** 10. **Applications Received:** 50-100.

Application Procedure: Write to Rose McVeigh, Artistic Director.

Florida Studio Theatre
1241 N. Palm Ave.
Sarasota, FL 34236
Phone: (813)366-9017
Fax: (813)955-4137

Business Description: A contemporary, nonprofit theatre, the Florida Studio Theatre develops new plays and playwrights, conducts theatre workshops, and caters to the well-educated retirees living in the area.

Human Resources: Jayne Dowd, Gen. Mgr.

▶ **Internships**

Type: Offers paid internships in such areas as production, administration, and children's education. Open to college students and graduates. Benefits include college credit and free use of YMCA pool and facilities. **Number Available Annually:** 12. **Applications Received:** 50.

Application Procedure: Contact the intern coordinator for further information.

Fools Company Inc.

358 W. 44th St., No. 3
New York, NY 10036-5426
Phone: (212)307-6000

Business Description: Established in 1970, this not-for-profit company produces and presents nontraditional works and workshops in all areas of the performing arts.

Employees: 6.

▶ Internships

Contact: Ms. Jill Russell, Exec. Dir.

Type: Offers unpaid internships to high school students. International applicants accepted. Internships available in administration and production areas. Production interns should have knowledge of video production or theatre arts. Placement assistance and job counseling are available. **Number Available Annually:** 6. **Applications Received:** 10-20.

Duties: Administration interns work in funding, publicity, public relations, and at the annual theatre festival. Production interns assist with festival and related video production.

Foundation for the Joffrey Ballet

130 W. 56th St.
New York, NY 10019
Phone: (212)265-7300

Employees: 150.

Benefits: Benefits include medical insurance and tuition assistance.

Application Procedures: Call to arrange an interview. For an application, write to the attention of Robert Bulger, Dir. of Finance and Admin.

▶ Internships

Type: Offers unpaid internships to high school graduates and college and international students. College credit and placement assistance are available. Full-time employment is possible. **Number Available Annually:** 7.

Application Procedure: Write for an application or call to arrange an interview with Robert Bulger.

Franklin Furnace

New School of Social Research
112 Franklin St.
New York, NY 10013-2980
Phone: (212)925-4671

Business Description: Presents music and multi-media works by emerging artists.

Employees: 9.

Opportunities: Not hiring at this time.

Benefits: Offers basic benefits package.

Human Resources: Anita Chad, Personnel Contact.

▶ Internships

Type: Offers unpaid co-op positions in administrative and archives maintenance to high school and college students. Must have interest in contemporary art.

Application Procedure: Send resume to Personnel.

Geva Theatre
Genessee Valley Arts Foundation Inc.

75 Woodbury Blvd.
Rochester, NY 14607
Phone: (716)232-1366
Fax: (716)232-4031

Employees: 45.

Application Procedures: Those interested in entry-level positions should send resume, cover letter, and head shot (if applicable) to Timothy Shields, Personnel.

▶ Internships

Contact: Vicki Duval, Dir. of Education.

Type: Offers paid internships in state management, electrics, education, and festivals to college graduates and career changers with theatre experience. **Applications Received:** 50-75 each year.

Application Procedure: Write to Vicki Duval.

Glimmerglass Opera Inc.

Rte. 80 & Allen Lake Rd.
Cooperstown, NY 13326
Phone: (607)547-5704
Fax: (607)547-6030

Business Description: Founded in 1975, the company is interested in attracting young

American opera professionals and a new audience to musical theatre.

Employees: 11.

▶ **Internships**

Contact: Jeryl Dropp, Admin. Asst.

Type: Offers paid internships to high school graduates, college students, college graduates, graduate students, and others. Internships are available in such areas as public relations/marketing, box office, finance, management, music, production, and the costume shop. Placement assistance and housing provided. **Number Available Annually:** 20. **Applications Received:** 200.

Application Procedure: Contact Jeryl Dropp, Administrative Assistant.

Application Deadline: February 28.

Goliard Concerts
21-65 41st St.
Astoria, NY 11105
Phone: (718)728-8927

Employees: 2.

Benefits: Benefits include medical insurance.

Application Procedures: Send resume and cover letter to Ms. Limor Tomer, Exec. Dir.

▶ **Internships**

Type: Offers three-month paid management internship ($150/week) to college juniors or college graduates. College credit, placement assistance, and free seminars are available. Housing is provided; due to housing situation, intern must be male. **Number Available Annually:** 1.

Application Procedure: Send resume and cover letter to Ms. Limor Tomer.

Goodman Theatre/Chicago Theatre Group, Inc.
200 S. Columbus Dr.
Chicago, IL 60603
Phone: (312)443-3811

Business Description: Founded in 1925 as part of the Art Institute of Chicago, the Goodman Theatre produces a variety of plays, special events, and educational programs. The Chicago Theatre Group, founded in 1977, is the financial arm of the Goodman Theatre.

Opportunities: Offers opportunities in box office work, ticket service, and production. Previous experience is required. Professional positions are primarily jobbed in. Openings are advertised in *ArtSEARCH*.

Benefits: Benefits include medical insurance, life insurance, dental insurance, and savings plan.

Application Procedures: Open calls for performers are held in July and August; request audition in May or June. For all positions, send resume to Kendall Marlowe, Company Mgr.

▶ **Internships**

Contact: Steve Scott, Artistic Assoc.

Type: Offers production, management, and administrative internships for college credit. Interviews are required. **Number Available Annually:** 4.

Today new technology, in such forms as robot welders on auto assembly lines, is wiping out jobs. But economic historians point out that new technology in the long run has always created more jobs than it has destroyed, and should do so again.

Source: *Time*

Goodspeed Opera House
PO Box A
East Haddam, CT 06423
Phone: (203)873-8377

Business Description: Dedicated to the development, heritage, and preservation of the musical theatre, Goodspeed produces classic and contemporary musicals. Many of its productions have gone to Broadway, including *Annie* and *Man of La Mancha*, and over a dozen have won Tony Awards.

Human Resources: Michael Price, Exec. Dir.; Warren Pincus, Cast. Dir.

Application Procedures: Company posts job openings in *ArtSEARCH* magazine.

▶ **Internships**

Contact: Todd Little, Prod. Coord.

Type: Offers paid internships in carpentry, props, wardrobe, scenic art, stage management, and the administrative department. Open to high school graduates and college and graduate school students. Benefits include free housing and job placement assistance. College credit is available and full-time employment is possible. **Number Available Annually:** 7. **Applications Received:** 500.

Application Procedure: Send resume and cover letter to the production coordinator.

Gowanus Arts Exchange

295 Douglass St.
Brooklyn, NY 11217
Phone: (718)596-5250

Business Description: Presents new dance and performance works and an all-children's series.

Employees: 5.

Opportunities: Hires staff for technical positions. Must have college degree.

Human Resources: Marya Warshaw-Chu, Contact.

Application Procedures: Send resume and cover letter to Marya Warshaw-Chu, Contact.

▶ **Internships**

Type: Offers unpaid internships to high school and college students.

Application Procedure: Apply through school.

The Great American Children's Theatre Company

PO Box 92123
Milwaukee, WI 53202
Phone: (414)276-4230

Business Description: Traveling to 17 cities annually, the theatre is a professional company that presents full-scale productions for young audiences.

Benefits: Benefits include medical insurance, life insurance, and dental insurance.

Application Procedures: Check audition notices in newspapers, apply in person, or send resume and samples to Diane Kolosvsky.

▶ **Internships**

Type: In the process of developing an internship program.

Application Procedure: Send resumes to Diane Kolosvsky.

Great Lakes Theatre Festival

1501 Euclid Ave., Ste. 423
Cleveland, OH 44115
Phone: (216)241-5490

Business Description: A professional company founded in 1961, the Great Lakes Theatre Festival features classical repertoire. Performing in the Ohio Theatre, it is part of the Playhouse Square redevelopment in downtown Cleveland.

Opportunities: Hires performers and production staff.

Benefits: Benefits include medical insurance, life insurance, and dental insurance.

Human Resources: Tony Forman, Prod. Mgr.

Application Procedures: Send resume, cover letter, and head shot (if applicable) to Tony Forman, Prod. Mgr.

▶ **Internships**

Type: The company does not offer an internship program.

Greater Miami Opera Association

1200 Coral Way
Miami, FL 33145
Phone: (305)854-1643
Fax: (305)856-1042

Employees: 25.

Opportunities: Offers opportunities to individuals with previous training or experience in professional or educational theatre.

Benefits: Benefits include medical insurance.

Application Procedures: Send resume or call to arrange an interview with Willie Anthony Waters, Artistic Dir.

▶ **Internships**

Contact: Paul Lapinski, Dir. of Production.

Type: Offers paid internships ($125-$150/week) to college students. College credit, reimbursement of travel expenses, and housing available. Full-time employment possible. Production and music internships available. Vocal audition required for music interns. **Number Available Annually:** 10. **Applications Received:** 100.

Application Deadline: August 31.

Gus Giordano Jazz Dance Chicago

614 Davis St.
Evanston, IL 60201
Phone: (708)866-6779

Employees: 12.

Application Procedures: Send resume with cover letter or call to arrange an interview with Nan Giordano, Assoc. Dir.

▶ **Internships**

Type: Offers unpaid internships to high school graduates. Reimbursement for travel expenses and placement assistance are available. **Number Available Annually:** 4.

Application Procedure: Send letter and resume to Nan Giordano.

The Guthrie Theater

725 Vineland Pl.
Minneapolis, MN 55403
Phone: (612)347-1100
Fax: (612)347-1188

Business Description: Founded in 1963, the Guthrie Theatre presents both classic and contemporary drama.

Employees: 300.

Human Resources: Edward A. Martenson, Exec. Dir.

Application Procedures: Creative and technical staff openings are posted in *ArtSEARCH*. Casting notices for performers are listed with Actors Equity. Call company to set up an interview or audition.

▶ **Internships**

Contact: Julie Mandery, Admin. Asst.

Type: Offers unpaid internships to high school graduates. Internships are available in such areas as directing, literary/dramaturg, publicity/press, stage management, costuming, technical, administrative, communications/ marketing, and education. **Number Available Annually:** 50. **Applications Received:** 120.

Application Procedure: Fax or write Julie Mandery, Administrative Assistant.

Application Deadline: April 1.

The Hartford Stage Company

50 Church St.
Hartford, CT 06103
Phone: (203)525-5601

Business Description: Presents new works and reinterpretations of classics. Established in 1964, the company has an extensive community outreach program.

Employees: 50.

Human Resources: David Hawkanson, Mng. Dir.

Application Procedures: Those interested in management or technical positions should apply in the spring by sending resume and cover letter to the production manager. Performers are cast show by show; those interested should send materials to the casting office.

▶ **Internships**

Type: Offers unpaid internships in administration and production. Open to college graduates, and graduate students. Benefits include college credit, opportunities for full-time employment, and job placement assistance. Applicants should have experience in the field of interest. **Applications Received:** 100.

Application Procedure: Send resume and cover letter to the production office.

The big corporation of the future will consist of a relatively small core of central employees and a mass of smaller firms working for it under contract. And even within the central core, there will be much shifting around, more hiring of people for specific, temporary assignments.

Source: *Time*

Herbert H. Breslin Inc.

119 W. 57th St.
New York, NY 10019
Phone: (212)246-5480

▶ **Internships**

Contact: Marc Wilkins.

Type: Offers paid clerical internships to anyone.

Application Procedure: Send resume and cover letter to Marc Wilkins.

HOME for Contemporary Theatre and Art

44 Walker St.
New York, NY 10013
Phone: (212)431-7434

Business Description: Produces traditional and experimental works, plays, musicals, dance, and performance art by emerging artists. The company, founded in 1986, is dedicated to an open and positive environment in which artists can work and grow.

Employees: 4.

▶ Internships

Contact: Randy Rollison, Artistic Dir.

Type: Offers unpaid arts management, technical, and art internships to high school students, college and graduate students, and others. Applicants must be experienced in theatre education. Placement and housing assistance provided. Full-time employment possible. **Number Available Annually:** 3. **Applications Received:** 20.

Application Procedure: Call Randy Rollison, Artistic Dir., to arrange an interview.

Horse Cave Theatre

Box 215
Horse Cave, KY 42749
Phone: (502)786-1200

Business Description: A nonprofit repertory theatre that is involved in educational programs and workshops.

▶ Internships

Contact: Debbie Lindsey, Exec. Asst.

Type: Offers paid internships to those who want to further their professional careers or students who want to gain professional experience. **Number Available Annually:** 5.

Application Procedure: Contact Debbie Lindsey, Exec. Asst.

Application Deadline: May 15.

Hoyt's Greater Radio

200 W. Mercer St., Ste. 400
Seattle, WA 98119
Phone: (206)283-5333

Opportunities: Offers opportunities for radio voice-over actors.

Application Procedures: Send demo tape to Beth Smith, Office Mgr.

▶ Internships

Type: Offers unpaid internships to college students of junior or senior status with advertising or communication majors. **Number Available Annually:** 2.

Application Procedure: Check postings on department bulletin boards, contact by phone. Applicants will be screened and interviewed.

Huntington Theatre Company

252 Huntington Ave.
Boston, MA 02115
Phone: (617)266-7900

Business Description: Founded in 1982, the Company is the professional theatre in residence at Boston University. With a subscriber base of more than 16,000, it presents both classic works and contemporary plays.

Opportunities: Offers opportunities to individuals with previous experience.

Application Procedures: The best time to apply is mid-March. Send resume and cover letter to Mary Kiely, Controller, or Ron Meeker, Production Dir.

▶ Internships

Contact: Jayme Cozyn.

Type: Offers unpaid internships to high school graduates in technical capacities, props, management, public relations, development, dramaturgy, box office, and marketing areas.

Application Procedure: Send resume and letter of application to Jayme Cozyn.

Ichiban/Sky Records Inc.

PO Box 724677
Atlanta, GA 31139
Phone: (404)419-1414

Application Procedures: Send demo tape, allowing 6 to 8 weeks for review, to John Abbey, A & R Dept., Ichiban Records.

▶ Internships

Contact: Michelle Rosch.

Type: Offers unpaid internships to college students. College credit is available. **Number Available Annually:** 6.

Indiana Repertory Theatre
140 W. Washington St.
Indianapolis, IN 46204
Phone: (317)635-5277
Fax: (317)236-0767

Business Description: Located in the historic Indiana Theatre, the company is a resident professional theatre presenting classic and new works on three separate stages.

Employees: 80.

▶ Internships

Contact: Jane Robison, Artistic Admin.

Type: Offers paid internships in scenic painting, development, marketing, props, electrics, the scene shop, and sound. College credit is available. Placement and housing assistance provided. Full-time employment possible. College seniors, college graduates, those with professional experience, and international applicants are eligible. **Number Available Annually:** 5. **Applications Received:** 20.

Application Procedure: Contact Jane Robison, Artistic Admin.

Application Deadline: July 15.

Indianapolis Ballet Theatre
502 N. Capital, Ste. B
Indianapolis, IN 46204
Phone: (317)637-8979

Officers: Kathy Stephenson, Exec. Dir.

Employees: 32.

Opportunities: Offers associate staff and apprentice positions to college graduates.

Benefits: Benefits include medical insurance.

Application Procedures: Send resume and samples to area of interest.

▶ Internships

Contact: Kathy Stephenson, Exec. Dir.

Type: Offers unpaid internships to college students. **Number Available Annually:** 4.

Application Procedure: Send resume to Kathy Stephenson.

Irish Arts Center
553 W. 51st St.
New York, NY 10019
Phone: (212)757-3318

Business Description: A showcase for Irish drama in America, the Center presents works by new and established Irish playwrights and has occasional guest production from Ireland.

Benefits: Benefits include medical insurance and life insurance.

Application Procedures: Those interested in positions should send resume to the attention of the artistic director.

▶ Internships

Type: Offers internships for college credit to juniors and seniors. **Number Available Annually:** 1.

Application Procedure: Send resume and cover letter to the attention of the artistic director.

Look to small and medium-size companies. They have been the traditional engines of job creation even during the era of supposed domination by the corporate elephants, and though they have been lagging in hiring lately, many experts expect that to change.

Source: *Time*

Irish Repertory Theatre
163 W. 17th St.
New York, NY 10011
Phone: (212)255-0270

Business Description: Presents new Irish works and classics.

Benefits: Benefits include medical insurance.

Application Procedures: Apply through trade newspaper advertisements. No resumes accepted.

▶ Internships

Type: The company does not offer an internship program.

Isadora Duncan Foundation for Contemporary Dance
141 W. 26th St.
New York, NY 10001
Phone: (212)691-5040

Benefits: Benefits include tuition assistance.

Application Procedures: Apply in person or

send resume and samples to Lori Belilove, Artistic Dir.

▶ Internships

Type: Offers paid and unpaid internships to college students of junior or senior status. College credit is available. **Number Available Annually:** 3.

Application Procedure: Send letter of application.

Get as much education as possible. Never mind the tales of college graduates working as bellboys—even though such stories are true. On no opinion are the experts so unanimous as that the future belongs to the knowledge worker, master of his PC, fiber-optics whatsit, E-mail gizmo, and whatever takes its place.

Source: *Time*

Jack Rouse Associates

430 Reading Rd.
Cincinnati, OH 45202
Phone: (513)381-0055

Business Description: Provides theatrical production services.

Application Procedures: Send resume and head shot to Scott Moening, Prod. or Jean Deskins, Dir.

▶ Internships

Type: The company does not offer an internship program.

Jacob's Pillow Dance Festival, Inc.

PO Box 287
Lee, MA 01238
Phone: (413)637-1322
Fax: (413)243-4744

Officers: John MacClaren, Business Mgr.

Employees: 15.

Opportunities: Entry-level opportunities available for college graduates or those with previous experience.

Benefits: Benefits include medical insurance.

Application Procedures: Send resume to the general manager.

▶ Internships

Contact: Jackie Ketchen, Resource Mgr.

Type: Offers internships for college credit; includes room and board and a small stipend. **Number Available Annually:** 15.

Application Procedure: Send resume and three references to Jackie Ketchen.

JAM Creative Productions Inc.

5454 Parkdale Dr.
Dallas, TX 75227
Phone: (214)388-5454

Opportunities: Hires creative talent and technical staff.

Benefits: Benefits include medical insurance.

Human Resources: Mary Lynn Wolfert.

Application Procedures: Send resume and demo of work to Chris Kershaw, Vice President (for creative talent positions) or Mark Holland, Vice President, Corporate Development (for technical positions).

▶ Internships

Type: Offers internship positions as needed.

Jam Productions Ltd.

207 W. Goethe
Chicago, IL 60610
Phone: (312)266-6262

Business Description: Jam Productions Ltd. handles such services as concert promoting, corporate party and event managing, and advertising for radio stations.

Application Procedures: Interested candidates should send resume and cover letter.

▶ Internships

Type: The company does not offer an internship program.

Japan Society

Lila Acheson Wallace Auditorium
333 E. 47th St.
New York, NY 10017
Phone: (212)752-3015

Business Description: Presents traditional and contemporary performing arts from Japan.

Employees: 50.

Opportunities: Hires administrators, coordinators, and directors. Positions require knowledge of East Asian art forms.

Benefits: Benefits include medical insurance, life insurance, and dental insurance.

Human Resources: Iris Harris, Contact.

Application Procedures: Send resume.

▶ Internships

Type: Offers unpaid internships as needed. **Number Available Annually:** 1.

Jennifer Muller/The Works

131 W. 24th St.
New York, NY 10011
Phone: (212)691-3803

Employees: 11.

Opportunities: Opportunities available for individuals with previous experience.

Application Procedures: Apply in person to Jennifer Muller.

▶ Internships

Type: The company does not offer an internship program.

John Drew Theater of Guild Hall

158 Main St.
East Hampton, NY 11937
Phone: (516)324-4051
Fax: (516)324-2722

Business Description: A division of Guild Hall of East Hampton, the John Drew Theatre was established in 1931 and is associated with an art museum.

Employees: 30.

Application Procedures: Those interested in performing or production positions should send in resume, cover letter, and head shot (if applicable).

▶ Internships

Contact: Brigitte Blanchere, Program Coord.

Type: Offers publicity, production management, and technical internships to high school graduates. Interns are paid $70/week. College credit is available. Placement assistance is provided. **Number Available Annually:** 4. **Applications Received:** 50.

Application Procedure: Contact Brigitte Blanchere, Program Coord.

The John F. Kennedy Center for the Performing Arts

2700 F St. SW
Washington, DC 20566
Phone: (202)416-8800
Fax: (202)416-8802

▶ Internships

Contact: Darrell Ayers, Internship Program Mgr.

Type: Offers the following internships: Alliance for Arts Education; American College Theatre; National Symphony Orchestra; Theater for Young People; advertising; education; cultural diversity affairs; programming; development, Friends of Center; subscriptions; and marketing. Interns are paid $500/month. College graduates, graduate students, and art teachers are eligible. **Applications Received:** 200.

Application Procedure: Send letter, resume, transcript, and three letters of recommendation to Darrell Ayers, Internship Program Mgr.

Application Deadline: June 1 for fall; November 1 for winter/spring; March 1 for summer.

John Houseman Theatre

450 W. 42nd St.
New York, NY 10036
Phone: (212)967-9077

Application Procedures: Call or send resume with cover letter and head shot (if applicable) to the attention of Eric Krebs, Owner. 450 W. 42nd St., New York, NY 10036. Phone: (212)967-7079.

▶ Internships

Contact: Eric Krebs.

Type: Offers unpaid internships to college students.

Application Procedure: Send resume or contact Eric Krebs Theatrical Management.

Joseph Papp Public Theatre

425 Lafayette St.
New York, NY 10003
Phone: (212)598-7150

Business Description: Home of the New York Shakespeare Festival.

Opportunities: Hires performers and technical staff.

Human Resources: Ann Tanaka, Gen. Mgmt. Asst.

Application Procedures: Performance applicants should send resume and photograph to the attention of the Casting Director. Technical staff applicants should send resume to the attention of the Production Department.

▶ **Internships**

Type: Offers work-study programs for college credit on an as-needed basis.

Application Procedure: Send cover letter and resume to the attention of the General Management Office.

Juilliard School

60 Lincoln Center Plaza
New York, NY 10023
Phone: (212)799-5000

Benefits: Benefits include medical insurance.

Application Procedures: Send resume to the production department.

▶ **Internships**

Contact: Helen Taynton, Intern Dir.

Type: Offers internships for technical and administrative postions.

Application Procedure: Send resume to Helen Taynton.

Jujamcyn Theatre

246 W. 44th St.
New York, NY 10030
Phone: (212)840-8181

Opportunities: Hires entry-level production staff.

Application Procedures: Send resume and cover letter to the director of operations.

Kidskits Inc.

601 S. Broadway
Denver, CO 80209
Phone: (303)733-2852

Business Description: Theatrical agency engaged in live production and theatrical training.

Opportunities: Hires teachers in voice, dance, and acting.

Application Procedures: Send resume specifying area of interest to Maggie Nolan.

▶ **Internships**

Contact: Maggie Nolan, Contact.

Type: Occasionally offers paid and unpaid internships.

Application Procedure: Send resume.

The Kitchen: Center for Video, Music, Dance, Performance, Film and Literature

512 W. 19th St.
New York, NY 10011
Phone: (212)255-5793
Fax: (212)645-4258

Business Description: Presents performances by emerging artists in dance, music, video and film works, and performance art.

Employees: 16.

▶ **Internships**

Contact: Josie Caporuscio, Dir. of Development.

Type: Offers unpaid curatorial, technical, publicity, fundraising, and management/adminstration internships to college students and graduates. Interns receive formaltraining, exposure to artists, opportunity to attend seminars/workshops, college credit, job counseling, and housing assistance. Full-time employment possible. **Number Available Annually:** 5. **Applications Received:** 200.

Application Procedure: Contact Josie Caporuscio, Dir. of Development.

Kraine Arts Center

85 E. 4th St.
New York, NY 10003
Phone: (212)460-0982

Business Description: A nonprofit, multi-faceted center that runs a theatre, art gallery, and cabaret acts.

Employees: 3. The Center has 48 members.

Opportunities: Offers performing opportunities in such areas as farce, experimental, and realism theatre, singing, cabaret, etc. Offers full range of production opportunities including technical work.

Application Procedures: Send resume and cover letter to the attention of Jennifer Pias.

► Internships

Contact: Jennifer Pias.

Type: Offers unpaid internships.

Application Procedure: Write to the attention of Jennifer Pias.

La Guardia Performing Arts Center

La Guardia Community College
31-10 Thomson Ave.
Long Island City, NY 11101
Phone: (718)482-5151

Employees: 4.

Opportunities: Offers opportunities at all levels, from ushers to technicians.

Human Resources: Barbara Carson.

► Internships

Type: Offers an unpaid internship program. **Number Available Annually:** 2.

Application Procedure: Send resume and cover letter to contact.

La Jolla Chamber Music Society

Box 2168
La Jolla, CA 92038
Phone: (619)459-3724

Employees: 6.

Opportunities: Opportunities available for college graduates.

Benefits: Benefits include medical insurance and dental insurance.

Application Procedures: Send resume to Neal Perl, Dir.

► Internships

Type: The company does not offer an internship program.

Lamb's Theatre Company, Ltd.

130 W. 44th St.
New York, NY 10036
Phone: (212)997-0210

Business Description: Owned by the Manhattan Church of the Nazarene, the company presents plays and musicals geared to a family audience.

Employees: 8.

► Internships

Contact: Carl Jaynes, Internship Coord.

Type: Offers production, administrative, literary, business development, box office, and management internships. Interns are paid $75-$150/week. College credit is available and full-time employment is possible. Placement assistance and housing provided. College graduates, graduate students, and candidates with one year experience in the field are eligible. **Number Available Annually:** 6. **Applications Received:** 75.

Application Procedure: Send resume and recommendations to Carl Jaynes, Internship Coord.

To keep up with fast-changing technology and workplace requirements, some analysts say, workers can expect to change careers—not just jobs, careers—three or four times during their working lives. That may be extreme, but experts say a high-tech worker must be ready to go back to school and learn new skills, in his or her own if an employer will not finance it, at a minimum of every five to 10 years.

Be prepared to work in small groups or on your own. Even on assembly lines, work teams rather than masses of undifferentiated laborers are the order of the day. The trend is likely to go much further among knowledge workers.

Source: *Time*

Latin American Theatre Ensemble

172 E. 104th St.
New York, NY 10101
Phone: (212)246-7478

Business Description: A nonprofit theater involved in the development and exposure of Hispanic performing art forms.

Officers: Margarita Toirac, Exec. dir.

Limon Dance Foundation

622 Broadway
New York, NY 100012
Phone: (212)777-3353

Business Description: A modern repertory dance ensemble.

Benefits: Benefits include medical insurance.

Human Resources: Mark Jones, Contact.

Application Procedures: Dancers should submit resume and cover letter to Carla Maxwell, Artistic Director for opportunities to audition. Technical and production personnel should send resume to the attention of Michael Osso, Gen. Mgr.

▶ **Internships**

Contact: Carla Maxwell, Artistic Dir. or Michael Osso, Gen. Mgr.

Type: Offers paid and unpaid internships to students for college credit. **Number Available Annually:** 2.

Application Procedure: Dancers should send application and resume to Carla Maxwell. Technicians and production staff should send application and resume to Michael Osso.

Long Beach Civic Light Opera
Box 20280
Long Beach, CA 90801
Phone: (310)435-7605

Business Description: A professional music theatre company producing four shows and an operetta per year.

Human Resources: Peggy Logefeil, Exec. Dir.; Donald Hill, Prod. Mgr.

Application Procedures: Send resume and head shot to the attention of the casting department.

▶ **Internships**

Type: Offers internships in public relations to college students.

Application Procedure: Call Peggy Logefeil for information.

Louis Abrons Arts Center
Henry Street Settlement
466 Grand St.
New York, NY 10002
Phone: (212)598-0400

Business Description: A community-based center that hosts many multi-cultural, multi-art events.

Benefits: Benefits include medical insurance, life insurance, and dental insurance.

Application Procedures: Send resume and head shot to Jonathan Ward, Prog. Assoc.

▶ **Internships**

Type: Offers paid internships for credit to college students.

Application Procedure: Contact Jonathan Ward.

Lyric Opera of Chicago
20 N. Wacker Dr., Ste. 860
Chicago, IL 60606
Phone: (312)332-2244
Fax: (312)419-8345

Employees: 800.

Benefits: Benefits include medical insurance, life insurance, dental insurance, and short-term and long-term disability.

Application Procedures: Full-time administration staff send resume and cover letter to the attention of Larry Alario. Performers must audition; solo performers must also send resume and cover letter; chorus performers must contact Human Resources for further information. Advertises in *International Musician* for orchestra openings.

▶ **Internships**

Type: Sponsors the Lyric Opera Apprenticeship Program for singers. This is a paid program.

Application Procedure: The program conducts a series of auditions around the country. Call Lyric Opera of Chicago for information.

Maine State Music Theatre
PO Box 656
Brunswick, ME 04011
Phone: (207)725-8769
Fax: (207)725-1199

Business Description: Established in 1959, the company trains young theatre professionals.

Employees: 80.

▶ **Internships**

Contact: Billings LaPierre, Mgr.

Type: Offers paid internships to performers and technicians. Performers earn $25/week and have the opportunity to join professional equity theatre; technicians earn $50/week. College credit is available. Placement assistance, houisng, and meals are provided. Anyone 18 years or older is eligible. **Number Available Annually:** 28. **Applications Received:** 100.

Application Procedure: Contact Billings LaPierre, Mgr.

Application Deadline: March 31.

Manhattan Class Company

120 W. 28th St.
New York, NY 10014
Phone: (212)727-7765

Business Description: Presents a variety of studio productions and new American one-acts and full-length plays.

Human Resources: Donna Morea-Cupp, Dir. of Development.

Application Procedures: Apply in person or send resume and head shot to Donna Morea-Cupp, Dir. of Development.

▶ Internships

Type: Has no formal internship program but does accept volunteer workers.

Application Procedure: Contact the company.

Manhattan Theatre Club

453 W. 16th St.
New York, NY 10011
Phone: (212)645-5590
Fax: (212)691-9106

Business Description: Functioning as a performing arts center, the Manhattan Theatre Club presents a variety of musicals, plays, poetry, and readings.

Employees: 40.

Opportunities: All hiring is done at the union scale. Openings are listed in *ArtSEARCH* and the *Village Voice*.

▶ Internships

Contact: Monica Spencer, Internship Coord.

Type: Offers paid internships to college graduates and graduate students. Full-time interns earn $100/week. Interns receive formal training, the opportunity to attend seminars/workshops, college credit, placement assistance, and housing assistance. **Number Available Annually:** 30-40. **Applications Received:** 300.

Application Procedure: Contact Monica Spencer, Internship Coord.

Mannes College of Music

150 W. 85th St.
New York, NY 10024
Phone: (212)580-0210

Business Description: Presents orchestra, chamber music, and opera productions.

Employees: 25.

Opportunities: Hires entry-level staff for administrative positions.

Benefits: Benefits include medical insurance, life insurance, dental insurance, and vision insurance.

Application Procedures: Send resume to Janet Treadaway, Contact.

▶ Internships

Type: The company does not offer an internship program.

There are many people in both the artistic and managerial areas of the arts world who do not belong to an arts union or professional association but who maintain a high level of professionalism. These include many educators, people producing the arts for rehabilitation programs of various kinds, and countless others working on the community or grass-roots level. A large number earn their livings from such activities, which is the most widely accepted definition of a professional. But if one is ambitious for wide recognition, high position, and maximum income, it is unlikely that joining an arts-related union or professional association can be avoided for long.

Source: *Jobs in Arts & Media Management*

Mark Taper Forum

135 N. Grand Ave.
Los Angeles, CA 90012
Phone: (213)972-7353

Opportunities: Hires union actors and production personnel.

Benefits: Benefits include medical insurance, life insurance, dental insurance, child-care programs, and a pension plan.

Human Resources: Brad Lentz, Human Resources Dir.

Application Procedures: Actors should apply for positions posted in the Metwork Forum. Union actors and production staff can send resume to Brad Lentz, Human Resources Dir.

▶ **Internships**

Contact: Michael Solomon, Asst. to Gen. Mgr.

Type: Offers unpaid internships for college credit.

Application Procedure: Contact Michael Solomon.

Mary Anthony Dance Studio & Theatre

736 Broadway
New York, NY 10003
Phone: (212)674-8191

Application Procedures: Apply in person or send resume and samples to Mary Anthony, Owner.

▶ **Internships**

Type: Offers unpaid internships to college students. College credit is available. **Number Available Annually:** 3.

Application Procedure: Send resume and samples to Mary Anthony.

McCarter Theatre-Center for the Performing Arts

91 University Pl.
Princeton, NJ 08540
Phone: (609)683-9100
Fax: (609)497-0369

Business Description: Established in 1963, the McCarter Theatre presents nearly 400 presentations per year by contemporary, classical, and emerging playwrights. Features include works in modern dance and ballet; classical, pop, and jazz music; and many special events, including a summer cinema film series.

Employees: 130.

Opportunities: Most personnel are jobbed in. Hires for openings in management and technical capacities.

Human Resources: Jeff Woodward, Managing Dir.; Emily Mann, Artistic Dir.

▶ **Internships**

Contact: Timothy J. Shields, Gen. Mgr.

Type: Offers internships in: administration, marketing, development, the artistic director's office, stage management, sales, costumes, technical direction, and scene shop. Interns are paid $50/week. College credit and free workshops/seminars are available. Housing is provided. **Number Available Annually:** 10.

Application Procedure: Send resume of theatre experience and two recommendations to Timothy J. Schields, Gen. Mgr.

McConnell and Borow Inc.

210 Elizabeth St.
New York, NY 10012
Phone: (212)941-9550

Benefits: Benefits include medical insurance, dental insurance, and vision insurance.

Application Procedures: Those interested in free-lance positions making models/sets/props for advertising, photographic, and theatrical purposes should contact Steven Borow. A portfolio will be required.

▶ **Internships**

Type: Offers paid internships to college students and unpaid internships to high school students. **Number Available Annually:** 2.

Application Procedure: Send in application.

Meadow Brook Theatre

Oakland University
Rochester, MI 48309-4401
Phone: (313)370-3310

Business Description: An intimate theatre where national actors perform classic and modern drama.

Benefits: Benefits include medical coverage.

Application Procedures: Production staff applicants should send resume to Dan Jaffi, Production Manager. Those interested in acting positions should send resume and headshot to Jeff Bloomfield.

▶ **Internships**

Type: The company does not offer an internship program.

Medicine Show Theatre Ensemble

81 E. 2nd St.
New York, NY 10003
Phone: (212)254-3566

Business Description: Presents group works

and revivals of musicals and classics with a humorous approach.

Human Resources: Jim Barbosa, Mgr.

Application Procedures: Send resume and photograph to Jim Barbosa, Mgr. PO Box 20240, New York, NY 10025.

▶ **Internships**

Type: Offers unpaid internships for college credit. **Number Available Annually:** 1-2 per year.

Application Procedure: Send resume to Jim Barbosa.

Merce Cunningham Studio

55 Bethune St.
New York, NY 10041
Phone: (212)691-9751

Business Description: Home of the Merce Cunningham Dance Company, the studio acts as a space for emerging and established choreographers.

Employees: 15.

Opportunities: Hires dance performers and administrative staff.

Benefits: Benefits include medical insurance, dental insurance, and vision insurance.

Human Resources: Mark Feldman, Contact.

Application Procedures: For administrative positions, call or send resume. For dance performers, individuals must have or be working toward a four-year college degree to be eligible to audition. Teaching positions are only given to dance company members.

▶ **Internships**

Type: Offers paid understudy positions to those already accepted by the dance company. **Number Available Annually:** 6.

Merrimack Repertory Theatre

50 E. Merrimack St.
Lowell, MA 01852
Phone: (508)454-6324

Business Description: A professional theatre featuring classical and new plays and musicals.

Employees: 20.

Application Procedures: Performers and professional staff should send materials with a self-addressed stamped envelope to David Kent, Artistic Dir.

▶ **Internships**

Contact: Lynne Garboski, Admin. Mgr.

Type: Offers full-time, unpaid administrative and production internships to high school graduates. College credit is available. **Number Available Annually:** 5. **Applications Received:** 30.

Application Procedure: Contact Lynne Garboski, Admin. Mgr. at PO Box 228, Lowell, MA 01853.

Metropolitan Opera Association

Lincoln Center
New York, NY 10023
Phone: (212)799-3100

Business Description: Home of New York's Metropolitan Opera Company and American Ballet Theatre, the association hosts international dance and music events.

Benefits: Benefits include medical insurance, dental insurance, and vision insurance. For futher information on benefits, call (212) 265-3687.

Human Resources: Marianne Martini.

Application Procedures: Open auditions are held every Thursday between 3:00-6:00 p.m. during MET-New York Season (usually from September through May). Performers must provide their own accompanyist. Call for further information or send resume and photo.

▶ **Internships**

Type: The company does not offer an internship program.

Michigan Opera Theatre

6519 2nd Ave.
Detroit, MI 48202
Phone: (313)874-7850
Fax: (313)871-7213

Employees: 25.

Benefits: Benefits include medical insurance. Also offers dental insurance at employee expense.

Application Procedures: Send resume to the director of human resources.

▶ **Internships**

Type: Offers paid and unpaid internships to college students. **Number Available Annually:** 2.

Application Procedure: Send resume to the director of human resources.

To recent college grad with No Work Experience: Look back on your college career. Were you active in student government? How about other campus organizations? What did you do for these organizations? For example, did you coordinate events, prepare budgets, or lead an organization?

Next, look at the papers you wrote, projects, and case studies. What research and analytical skills were required? You should be able to develop a list of skills to base your resume on.

Source: *Detroit Free Press*

Mills/James Productions Inc.
3545 Fishinger Blvd.
Hilliard, OH 43026
Phone: (614)777-9933

Benefits: Benefits include medical insurance, life insurance, dental insurance, and 401(k).

Application Procedures: Send resume, call, or apply in person. Performers are almost exclusively hired through talent agencies. Those interested in production positions should apply in person or send resume and cover letter.

▶ **Internships**

Type: Offers unpaid internships to college students with a strong interest or major in the field.

Application Procedure: Contact Scott Lanum for facilities internships; Bruce Feid for video/film production internships; or Laura Fullen for business theatre internships.

Milwaukee Repertory Theatre
108 E. Wells
Milwaukee, WI 53202
Phone: (414)224-1761
Fax: (414)224-9097

Business Description: Features classical, contemporary, and new plays.

Employees: 150.

Human Resources: Joseph Hanreddy, Artistic Dir.; Sara O'Connor, Managing Dir.

▶ **Internships**

Contact: Fred Weiss, Internship Coord.

Type: Offers full-time, unpaid directing and acting internships. Interns receive formal training, the opportunity to attend seminars/workshops, college credit, placement assistance, job counseling, and housing assistance. College graduates are eligible. Full-time employment possible. **Number Available Annually:** 20-26. **Applications Received:** 100.

Application Procedure: Contact Fred Weiss, Internship Coord.

Minor Latham Playhouse
Barnard College Campus
3009 Broadway
New York, NY 10027
Phone: (212)854-5638

Business Description: Students of Barnard and Columbia University theatre departments present three major theatre and dance productions each year.

Human Resources: Shari Dross, Benefits Mgr.

▶ **Internships**

Type: Offers paid and unpaid internships to students that attend Barnard College.

Application Procedure: Contact Barnard College Career Services Internship Coordinator.

Missouri Repertory Theatre
4949 Cherry St.
Kansas City, MO 64110
Phone: (816)235-2727

Business Description: The Missouri Repertory Theatre was founded in 1964 at the University of Missouri-Kansas City. It is committed to contemporary works, the classics, and innovative dramaturgy.

Benefits: Benefits include medical insurance, life insurance, and dental insurance.

Application Procedures: Applicants may audition in mid-March (preferred) or send resume to George Keathley, Artistic Dir.

▶ **Internships**

Contact: Ron Schaeffer, Production Mgr.

Type: Offers paid and unpaid internships to graduate students with experience.

Application Procedure: Contact Ron Schaeffer, Production Mgr. at (816)235-2783. Audition is required for acting interns.

Movement Theatre International

3700 Chestnut St.
Philadelphia, PA 19104
Phone: (215)382-0600
Fax: (215)382-0627

Business Description: Presents dance, movement theatre, and performing art. Holds a biennial festival and training conference.

▶ **Internships**

Contact: Michael Pedre Hi, Artistic Dir.

Type: Offers unpaid internships in fiscal/ financial management, technical theatre, marketing/adverstising, fundraising/development, and festival work. Interns receive college credit and complimentary tickets to all events. College graduates, graduate students, and career changers are eligible. Applicants must speak and write English. **Number Available Annually:** 11. **Applications Received:** 25.

Application Procedure: Contact Michael Pedre Hi, Artistic Dir.

Application Deadline: August 1 for fall; May 1 for summer; January 1 for spring.

Music-Theatre Group

29 Bethune St.
New York, NY 10014
Phone: (212)924-3108

Business Description: Founded in 1970, the Music-Theatre Group presents innovative new music-theatre nationally and internationally.

Benefits: Benefits include medical insurance and life insurance.

Human Resources: Diane Wondisford, Gen. Dir.

Application Procedures: Send cover letter and resume to Diane Wondisford, Gen. Dir.

▶ **Internships**

Type: Offers paid internships. **Number Available Annually:** 2-3.

Application Procedure: Send cover letter and resume to Diane Wondisford.

Musical Theatre Works

440 Lafayette St., 4th Fl.
New York, NY 10003
Phone: (212)677-0040
Fax: (212)598-0105

Business Description: A not-for-profit organization, Musical Theatre Works is solely dedicated to the American musical. Founded in 1983, the company has developed nearly 100 new musicals. There is also a children's academy and a studio company for non-Equity performers.

Employees: 10.

Application Procedures: Professional (directors and managers) staff should send resume and cover letter to Literary Dept.; performers should send materials to Casting Dept.

▶ **Internships**

Contact: Marilyn Stimac, Gen. Mgr.

Type: Offers unpaid production office, literary/casting, conservatory/dance center, and adminstrative internships to high school seniors and graduates, college students and graduates, and graduate students. Interns receive formal training, the opportunity to attend seminars/workshops, college credit, and placement assistance. **Number Available Annually:** 6. **Applications Received:** 20.

Application Procedure: Contact Marilyn Stimac, Gen. Mgr.

Musical Touring Company Inc.

311 W. 43rd St., No. 700
New York, NY 10036
Phone: (212)713-1636
Fax: (212)307-7179

Business Description: Established in 1990, the company produces commercial theatre productions.

Employees: 6.

▶ **Internships**

Contact: David Coffman, Gen. Mgr.

Type: Offers a paid assistantship. Assistant will earn $10-$50/week and can receive college credit, placement assistance, job counseling, and housing assistance. Full-time employment possible. High school graduates, college students and graduates, graduate students, and others are eligible. **Number Available Annually:** 1. **Applications Received:** 3.

Application Procedure: Contact David Coffman, Gen. Mgr.

I f you truly want to accomplish things, part of your job is to identify the people with power and influence and identify what areas they control. Even if you are powerful, say a department head, you will not be able to accomplish your agenda if other key power people are not working with you, or if they are actively working against you.

Source: *Detroit Free Press*

National Endowment for the Arts (NEA)
1100 Pennsylvania Ave. NW
Washington, DC 20506
Phone: (202)682-5786
Fax: (202)682-5610

Business Description: A federal agency that supports the arts by offering competitive grants.

Application Procedures: Job hotline available for entry-level employees (202) 682-5799.

▶ **Internships**

Contact: Anya Nykyforiak, Internship Coordinator.

Type: Offers unpaid internships to high school and college students for college credit. Also offers paid arts administration fellowships to persons with a bachelor of arts degree, three years of professional experience, and/or graduate studies. Benefits include placement assistance and opportunities for full-time employment.

Duties: Duties for interns include reviewing applications and data entry. Arts administration fellows assist with overview of NEA operations and observe panel meetings.

Application Procedure: Interns should submit a resume, cover letter, and college transcripts. Fellowship applicants must contact the company for further information.

National Shakespeare Conservatory
Conservatory Theatre
591 Broadway
New York, NY 10012
Phone: (212)219-9874

Business Description: Performance space and rehearsal studio that hosts an actor's training program.

Opportunities: Hires actors and acting, dance/movement, and speech teachers.

Human Resources: Todd Pieper, Adm. Dir.

Application Procedures: Call 800-472-6667 for application. Return completed application, resume, and photo.

▶ **Internships**

Type: The company does not offer an internship program.

National Theatre of the Performing Arts/Biggs Rosati Productions, Inc.
250 W. 54th St., Ste. 702A
New York, NY 10019
Phone: (212)315-3788

Opportunities: Hires performers and production staff.

Human Resources: Jaz Dorsey, Prod. Coord.

Application Procedures: Performers can respond to calls placed in *Backstage Magazine*. Open auditions will then be followed by callbacks. Production staff send resume to Jaz Dorsey, Prod. Coord.

▶ **Internships**

Type: The company does not offer an internship program.

Nederlander Organization Inc.
810 7th Ave.
New York, NY 10019
Phone: (212)262-2400

Business Description: Theatre production company.

Application Procedures: Performers are hired through agents. Resumes also accepted.

▶ **Internships**

Type: The company does not offer an internship program.

Neil Simon Theatre

250 W. 52nd St.
New York, NY 10019
Phone: (212)757-8646

Business Description: A professional Broadway theatre.

Opportunities: Hires entry-level staff with previous experience.

Benefits: Benefits include medical insurance, life insurance, and a savings plan.

Human Resources: Kathleen Wraitt, Personnel Dir.

Application Procedures: Company suggests that applicants contact the production staff of each particular show. The *Theatrical Index*, (212)586-6343, maintains up-to-date listings of production managers. Applicants may also send resume with cover letter to Kathleen Wraitt, Personnel Dir.

▶ **Internships**

Type: Offers internships for credit to college juniors and seniors. **Number Available Annually:** 1-2.

Application Procedure: Send resume with cover letter to Kathleen Wraitt.

The New Conservatory Children's Theatre Company

25 Van Ness
San Francisco, CA 94102

Business Description: A nonprofit school and performing arts company for children.

Employees: 20.

▶ **Internships**

Contact: Carol Majewski, Exec. Asst.

Type: Offers unpaid internships in touring, marketing and promotion, and development. Also offers teaching assistantships. Interns/ assistants receive opportunity to attend seminars/workshops, placement assistance, and housing assistance. Full-time employment possible for teaching assistants. **Applications Received:** 25.

Application Procedure: Write to Carol Majewski, Exec. Asst.

New Dance Alliance

182 Duane St.
New York, NY 10013
Phone: (212)226-7624

Business Description: Features experimental multi-media works including music, dance, and performance art.

Application Procedures: Call or send resume and cover letter to Karen Bernard, Exec. Dir.

▶ **Internships**

Type: Offers unpaid internships to college students interested in the administration and production of performing arts organizations. College credit is available.

Application Procedure: Call for information.

New Dramatists

424 W. 44th St.
New York, NY 10036
Phone: (212)757-6960

Business Description: Founded in 1949 to encourage American playwrighting talent, New Dramatists has become a national organization/workshop for developing writers. The company offers writers workshops, studios, a national script distribution service, a theatre library, a loan fund, and more.

Employees: 5.

Application Procedures: Management openings are listed in *ArtSEARCH*. Performers are jobbed in for each reading/workshop. Send materials to Peggy Adler, Program Assoc.

▶ **Internships**

Type: Offers internships in public relations/ special events, literary management, development, and stage management/casting. Salary is $25 per week. Benefits include complimentary tickets to Broadway and off-Broadway performances and college credit. Interns must work at least three days per week.

Duties: Public relations/special events interns write newspaper articles and press releases, are involved in fundraising events, and design communications materials. Literary management interns are involved in ScriptShare and International Playwrights Exchange Program. Development/administrative interns assist with fundraisers, grant proposal writing, and bookeeping. Stage management/casting interns assist in stage management, auditions, rehearsals, and regulating behind-the-scenes activities.

Application Procedure: Send resume and cover letter to the attention of the Internship Coordinator.

New Federal Theatre, Inc.
466 Grand St.
New York, NY 10002
Phone: (212)598-0400

Business Description: In its 22nd season, the New Federal Theatre specializes in minority drama.

Employees: 7.

▶ Internships

Contact: Linda Herring, Managing Dir.

Type: Offers unpaid internships in administration, production, costume and wardrobe, lighting and sound operations, and properties for college credit. Open to high school seniors and graduates, college graduates, graduate school students, and others. Benefits include job placement and housing location assistance.

Application Procedure: Write to Linda Herring. In-person interview recommended.

New Georges/Theatre Labrador
Samuel Becket Theatre
410 W. 42nd St.
New York, NY 10036
Phone: (212)967-2718

Business Description: Features contemporary works by women playwrights.

Application Procedures: Send resume and cover letter to Susan Bernfield, Artistic Dir. 550 W. 43rd St., New York, NY 10036.

▶ Internships

Type: Offers unpaid internships for college students majoring in women's studies, liberal arts, or performing arts. **Number Available Annually:** 2.

Application Procedure: Send resume and letter of interest to Susan Bernfield.

New Jersey Shakespeare Festival
Drew University
Madison, NJ 07940
Phone: (201)408-3278

Business Description: A professional Equity theatre.

Employees: 200.

▶ Internships

Contact: Joe Discher, Asst. to the Artistic Dir.

Type: Offers unpaid internships in the following areas: box office, costume design, set design, stage management, theater administration, lighting and sound design, props, production, technical production, directing, and house management. Open to anyone with experience. Benefits include college credit, placement assistance, low-cost housing, formal training, and seminars/workshops.

Application Procedure: Send resume, cover letter, and head shot to the assistant to the artistic director.

Application Deadline: April 1.

New Mexico Repertory Theatre
PO Box 9279
Santa Fe, NM 87504-9279
Phone: (505)983-2382

Benefits: Benefits include medical insurance and dental insurance.

Application Procedures: Send resume to Drew Martorella, Producing Dir. or to Bob MacDonald, Managing Dir.

▶ Internships

Type: The company does not offer an internship program.

New Stage Theatre
1100 Carlisle St.
Jackson, MS 39202
Phone: (601)948-3533

Business Description: The New Stage performs everything from classical to contemporary plays.

Employees: 6.

Application Procedures: Those interested in performing, directing, or technical positions should send materials with a self-addressed stamped envelope to Jan Engelhardt, Mng. Dir.

▶ Internships

Contact: Francine Thomas, Education Dir.

Type: Offers paid acting and technical/management internships for college credit.

Open to college graduates and professionals. Benefits include formal training, opportunities to attend seminars and workshops, possible full-time employment, placement and housing location assistance, reimbursement of travel expenses, and letters of recommendation.

Duties: Acting interns participate in performances and in arts-in-education tour to high schools. Technical/management interns assist the theater designers.

Application Procedure: Send resume, cover letter, and a head shot to the education director. Requires in-person interview.

Application Deadline: May 15.

New Tuners Theatre

Theater Bldg.
1225 W. Belmont Ave.
Chicago, IL 60657
Phone: (312)929-7367
Fax: (312)327-1404

Business Description: The New Tuners Theatre develops and produces new American musicals.

Employees: 75.

▶ Internships

Contact: Ruth E. Higgins, Exec. Producer.

Type: Offers paid internships including: public relations/marketing assistant, production assistant, orchestrator, assistant dramaturg; assistant music director, technician, and administrative assistant. Interns earn $500/month. Educational credit is available, and full-time employment is possible. Formal training, placement assistance, and housing assistance provided. **Number Available Annually:** 12-13. **Applications Received:** 175.

Duties: Public relations/marketing assistants work with audience development. Production assistants help with production, rehearsal, and performance schedule. Orchestrator interns produce orchestrations for world premier musicals. Assistant dramaturg interns work with dramaturg and workshop directors. Assistant music director interns work with the music director on production and direction. Technicians work on building maintenance and work with a local lighting company. Administrative assistants help the building manager and perform box office duties.

Application Procedure: Send resume to Ruth E. Higgins, Exec. Producer.

New York Children's Theatre

Lincoln Square Neighborhood Center
250 W. 65th St.
New York, NY 10023
Phone: (212)496-8009

Business Description: Presents new one-act musicals for children. Encourages audience participation.

Human Resources: Tom Shaker, Marketing Dir.

Application Procedures: Apply in person, call, or send resume, head shot, script, or other credentials to Tom Shaker, Marketing Dir.

▶ Internships

Type: Offers unpaid internships.

Application Procedure: Call to arrange a personal interview with Tom Shaker.

"When would be the best month to send my resume?" a reader asks. The best time is right now. Much more important is following up with a polite but persistent phone call, about a week after your resume arrives.

Source: *Detroit Free Press*

New York City Ballet

New York State Theatre
Lincoln Center
65 St. & Broadway
New York, NY 10023
Phone: (212)870-5690

Business Description: Performs neo-classical and contemporary ballet works.

Benefits: Benefits include medical insurance, life insurance, and dental insurance.

Application Procedures: Those interested in production positions should send resume to Mark Mongold, Asst. Production Mgr. Those interested in performance opportunities should call Richard Dryden, Regisseur at (212)870-5669.

▶ **Internships**

Contact: Perry Silvey, Prod. Stage Mgr.

Type: Offers internships for college credit.
Number Available Annually: 1-2.

Application Procedure: Send resume to Perry
Silvey.

New York State Theatre Institute
PAC 266, 1400 Washington Ave.
Albany, NY 12222
Phone: (518)274-3200

Business Description: A professional,
educational theatre producing family theatre and
the development of new works.

Application Procedures: Performers are cast
show by show. Applicants should send materials
with a self-addressed stamped envelope to
Renee Hariton. Directors, designers, and
technical staff openings are posted in
ArtSEARCH. Send resume and cover letter to
Patricia B. Snyder, Prod. Dir.

▶ **Internships**

Contact: Arlene Leff, Intern Prog. Admin.

Type: Offers unpaid internships for college
credit. Open to high school seniors and
graduates and nontraditional interns of all ages.
Provides placement assistance, letters of
recommendation, housing location assistance,
and job counseling. **Number Available
Annually:** 20.

Duties: Interns participate in various aspects of
the theater including administration, education,
performance, promotion, and production.

Application Procedure: Contact the Intern
Program Administrator. An interview is
required.

New York Theatre Workshop
220 W. 42nd St.
New York, NY 10036
Phone: (212)302-6989

Business Description: Devoted to the
production of innovative new theatre by
American and international artists. Presents a
season of new plays, directorial debuts, and the
works of solo performers.

Benefits: Benefits include medical insurance,
life insurance, and dental insurance.

Human Resources: Esther Cohen, Gen. Mgr.

Application Procedures: Interested
performers should contact their agents; those
interested in production positions should send
resume and cover letter to Esther Cohen, Gen.
Mgr.

▶ **Internships**

Type: Offers a full-time, paid (stipend)
internship program in such areas as production
and management. College credit is available.
Number Available Annually: 4.

Application Procedure: Send resume and
cover letter to the general manager.

The Next Stage
The Studio
145 W. 46th St.
New York, NY 10036
Phone: (212)354-6121

Business Description: The Next Stage
presents original works in dance, music, drama,
and the visual arts.

Human Resources: Rebecca Ashley, Res.
Choreographer & Gen. Adm.

Application Procedures: Those interested in
artistic positions should contact the specific
department of interest. Those interested in
production positions should apply in person or
send resume to Rebecca Ashley, Res.
Choreographer & Gen. Admin.

▶ **Internships**

Contact: Gus Reyes, Artistic Dir.

Type: Offers unpaid internships, sometimes for
college credit. **Number Available Annually:** 2.

Application Procedure: Send resume and/or
application to Gus Reyes.

North Carolina Dance Theatre
800 N. College St.
Charlotte, NC 28202
Phone: (704)372-0101
Fax: (704)375-0260

Application Procedures: Send a performance
tape and resume to the artistic director.

▶ **Internships**

Type: Offers paid apprentice program. College
credit is available.

Application Procedure: Send inquiries to the
artistic director.

North Carolina Theatre

1 E. South St.
Raleigh, NC 27601
Phone: (919)831-6944

Business Description: A nonprofit theatre that produces five broadway-scale musicals a year.

Human Resources: William Jones, Gen. Mgr.

Application Procedures: Those interested in production or performing positions should send a resume, cover letter, and head shot (if applicable) to William Jones, Gen. Mgr.

▶ Internships

Type: The company does not offer an internship program.

North Shore Music Theatre

62 Dunham Rd.
Beverly, MA 01915-0062
Phone: (508)922-8220
Fax: (508)921-0793

Business Description: Dedicated to the American musical, the North Shore Music Theatre is a professional company providing programs for young audiences.

Employees: 38.

Opportunities: Hires entry-level staff in management, design, and technical areas. Posts openings in *ArtSEARCH*. Performers are cast show by show. Notices appear in *Backstage* and *Variety*. Open calls are in February and March.

▶ Internships

Contact: Beth Hays, Prog. Admin.

Type: Offers unpaid internships in such areas as carpentry, scenic art, wardrobe, sound, stage management, company management, production assistance, marketing and public relations. Open to high school graduates, college students, college graduates, graduate students, and others. Offers college credit to students.

Application Procedure: For further information, write to: Internships, PO Box 62, Beverly, MA, 01915-0062.

Application Deadline: March 30.

The Ogunquit Playhouse

PO Box 915
Ogunquit, ME 03907
Phone: (207)646-2402

Business Description: The Playhouse is a summer theatre.

Employees: 25.

▶ Internships

Contact: John Lane, Prod.

Type: Offers paid technical theatre summer internships for a minimum of 12 weeks for $225 per week. Open to high school graduates, college graduates, graduate school students, and others. Benefits include formal training, low-cost housing, and opportunities for full-time employment.

Application Procedure: Send resume and cover letter to the producer. Requires in-person interview. Phone calls not accepted.

Application Deadline: January-March.

Talk to the experts. Informational interviews are not just for students. Find out who is succeeding at what you do and request an interview. A few conversations with established professionals can compress an education into a few hours.

Source: *Detroit Free Press*

Ohio Ballet

354 E. Market St.
Akron, OH 44325
Phone: (216)972-7900
Fax: (216)972-7902

Officers: Jack Lemon, Gen. Mgr.

Opportunities: Offers entry-level administrative and dance positions.

Benefits: Benefits include medical insurance and dental insurance.

Application Procedures: Dancers are required to take the company dance course. All applicants should send resume to Jack Lemon, Gen. Mgr.

▶ Internships

Type: Offers paid internships to college students. College credit is available. **Number Available Annually:** 2.

Application Procedure: Send inquiries to Jack Lemon.

Ohio Theatre

66 Wooster St.
New York, NY 10012
Phone: (212)966-4844

Business Description: Presents experimental and political theatre, dance events, and performance art.

Opportunities: Hires technical staff and creative talent. Creative talent must have come in with one of the shows.

Human Resources: Robert Lyons, Exec. Dir.

Application Procedures: For technical positions, send letter of interest and follow-up with phone call. For creative talent positions, send resume and photograph and follow-up with phone call.

▶ Internships

Contact: Robert Lyons, Exec. Dir.

Type: Offers unpaid internships for college credit. Students must be of junior or senior status. **Number Available Annually:** 1.

Application Procedure: Contact Robert Lyons for interview and then contact attending college or university.

Omaha Magic Theatre

1417 Farnam St.
Omaha, NE 68102
Phone: (402)346-1227

Business Description: Established in 1968, the company produces and presents four new American works per year.

Employees: 7.

Application Procedures: Those interested in experimental, avante garde, or new performance work should send resume, cover letter, and head shot (if applicable) to Jo Anne Schmidman, Artistic Dir.

▶ Internships

Type: Offers unpaid internships in various areas of theatre. Benefits include college credit and the opportunity for full-time employment and to attend seminars and workshops. Provides placement and housing location assistance. Open to high school students and graduates, college and graduate students, and others. **Applications Received:** 12.

Duties: Duties include participation in such areas of the theatre as set construction, theater maintenance, performance, and correspondence.

Application Procedure: Send resume and personal letter to the artistic director. Phone calls not accepted.

On Stage Productions

Hartley House Theatre
413 W. 46th St.
New York, NY 10025
Phone: (212)666-1716

Business Description: A multi-ethnic theatre company.

Benefits: Benefits include liability insurance.

Application Procedures: Performers and production personnel with previous experience may audition. Send resume and work samples to Lee Frank, Artistic Dir.

▶ Internships

Type: The company does not offer an internship program.

The Open Eye: NEW STAGINGS

The Open Eye Theatre
270 W. 89th St.
New York, NY 10024
Phone: (212)769-4143

Business Description: Produces and presents original works and classics, many of which are based on folklore and ancient myths.

Opportunities: Theatre is currently in a hiring freeze.

Human Resources: Amie Brockway, Artistic Dir.

Application Procedures: Send resume and cover letter to Amie Brockway, Artistic Dir.

▶ Internships

Type: Offers unpaid internships to college students. College credit is available. **Number Available Annually:** 3.

Application Procedure: Send application listing qualifications and experience to Amie Brockway.

Oregon Shakespeare Festival

PO Box 158
Ashland, OR 97520
Phone: (503)482-2111

Business Description: A nonprofit theatre that

operates a season of rotating repertory. Four vastly different theatres exist: the Elizabethan stage, the Angus Bowmer Theatre, the Black Swan Theatre, and the Portland Center for the Performing Arts.

Application Procedures: Send photograph and resume to Patricia Leonard, Personnel Asst.

▶ Internships

Contact: Patricia Leonard, Personnel Asst.

Type: Offers internships to college students.

Application Procedure: Send resume and cover letter to Patricia Leonard.

Organic Theater Company
3319 N. Clark
Chicago, IL 60657
Phone: (312)327-2427
Fax: (312)327-8947

Business Description: Has established a group of interdisciplinary theatre artists, including choreographers, writers, directors, designers, musicians, and performers. The group, dedicated to the creation of innovative plays and adaptations, is currently defining themselves as a collective attempting to renew their artistic vigor.

Human Resources: Jeff Neal, Gen. Mgr.

Application Procedures: Performers should send materials to the casting director. All other staff should send resume and cover letter to the artistic committee.

▶ Internships

Contact: Sarah Tucker, Literary Mgr.

Type: Offers unpaid internships in literary management, public relations, marketing, artistic administration, development, box office/front-of-house administration, or technical theater. Open to high school seniors, college students, and others. College credit is available. **Number Available Annually:** 2-6.

Application Procedure: Send a letter of interest to the literary manager.

PACT, Inc.
1111 McMullen Booth Rd.
Clearwater, FL 34619
Phone: (813)791-7060

Business Description: The company presents performing and visual arts and provides educational opportunities.

Employees: 50.

Human Resources: Christine Stevenson, Dir. of Personnel Services.

▶ Internships

Type: Offers unpaid internships in marketing, communications, development, and education departments. Open to high school seniors and graduates and college and graduate school students. Benefits include opportunities for full-time employment, college credit, and job placement assistance. **Number Available Annually:** 7.

Application Procedure: Send resume and cover letter to the director of personnel. In-person interview is recommended.

Pan Asian Repertory Theatre
Playhouse 46
St. Clement's Church
423 W. 46th St.
New York, NY 10036
Phone: (212)245-2660

Business Description: Presents American premieres of Asian works, adaptations of Western classics, and works by American playwrights. Also holds staged readings and training workshops.

Opportunities: Offers opportunities for performers and production staff.

Benefits: Benefits include medical insurance for full-time staff.

Application Procedures: Check for open call announcements in trade magazines or send resume/picture to Tisa Chang, Artistic Dir. 47 Great Jones St., New York, NY 10012.

▶ Internships

Contact: Russell Murphy.

Type: Offers paid internships to college and graduate students.

Application Procedure: Call (preferred) or send resume to Russell Murphy.

Paper Bag Players
Symphony Space
95th St. & Broadway
New York, NY 10025
Phone: (212)864-5400

Business Description: Founded in 1958, Paper Bag Players is a touring theatre company for children.

Employees: 25.

Opportunities: The organization is a rental company and offers administrative positions only. Requirements include college degree and previous experience.

Benefits: Benefits include medical insurance and life insurance.

Human Resources: Bob Bessoir, Dir. of Administration.

Application Procedures: Send resume to Joanne Cossa, Managing Dir.

▶ **Internships**

Type: Offers paid internships for college credit.
Applications Received: 2-3.

Application Procedure: Send resume to Joanne Cossa.

W hen hit with a layoff, the first risk workers face is panic. They roll up in a ball and don't do anything for weeks. Or they deny their loss of earnings by going on a spending sprees. Panic is normal, as are anger and tears. But it's crucial to get an early grip on your finances—to see how many months you can go without work.

Source: *Detroit Free Press*

Pasadena Playhouse

39 S. El Molino Ave.
Pasadena, CA 91101
Phone: (818)792-8672

Business Description: Founded in 1917 as a nonprofit educational center, the Pasadena Playhouse presents works by leading playwrights and new dramatists.

Benefits: Benefits include medical insurance and dental insurance.

Application Procedures: Performers may audition at casting calls or send resume and head shot to John Redmond, CFO.

▶ **Internships**

Type: Offers unpaid internships to college students.

Application Procedure: Write to John Redmond.

The Pearl Theatre Company

125 W. 22nd St.
New York, NY 10011
Phone: (212)645-7708
Fax: (212)645-7709

Business Description: Established in 1982, the Pearl Theatre Company is devoted to performance of the classics, from the Greek theatre to the present.

Application Procedures: Performers should request audition in April. Resume and head shot should be sent to Joanne Camp, Art. Assoc.

▶ **Internships**

Contact: Shepard Sobel, Artistic Dir.

Type: Offers paid internships in stage management, costume design, and theater administration. Open to high school graduates, college graduates, graduate students, and others. College credit is available and full-time employment is possible. Job placement and housing location assistance is provided.
Number Available Annually: 4.

Application Procedure: Applicants must write or phone before sending resume.

Application Deadline: May 1.

Peninsula Players

W. 4351 Peninsula Players Rd.
Fish Creek, WI 54212-9799
Phone: (414)868-3287

Business Description: A professional resident summer theatre.

Employees: 40.

▶ **Internships**

Contact: Todd Schmidt, Gen. Mgr.

Type: Offers office and production internships at $40-60/week to college students, graduates, and graduate students. Housing, meals, and travel expense reimbursement provided. Full-time employment possible. **Number Available Annually:** 8. **Applications Received:** 40.

Duties: Office interns assist with box office operation, production, publicity, and accounting. Production interns work in the costume department, carpentry, electrical, design, props, and stage management.

Application Procedure: Contact Todd Schmidt, Gen. Mgr.

Application Deadline: March 1.

Pennsylvania Stage Company

837 Linden St.
Allentown, PA 18101
Phone: (215)434-6110
Fax: (215)433-6086

Business Description: The Pennsylvania Stage Company produces new musicals and plays and recreates theatre classics.

Employees: 35.

Human Resources: Ellen Baltz, Co. Mgr.; Charles Richter, Art Dir.

Application Procedures: Open calls for performers are at the theatre in September; send materials ATTN: Casting.

▶ **Internships**

Type: Offers paid internships in acting and stage management and unpaid internships in production. Acting interns receive $150 per week for eight to nine months; stage management interns receive $150 per week for 37 weeks. Open to college graduates and graduate students. Benefits include college credit and the opportunity for full-time employment. **Number Available Annually:** 7.

Duties: Acting interns act and tour with the Outreach Program. Stage management interns assist the stage manager.

Application Procedure: Send resume and cover letter to Ellen Baltz, company manager.

Performance Space 122

150 1st Ave., 2nd Fl.
New York, NY 10009
Phone: (212)477-5829

Business Description: Presents new and experimental multi-media works by choreographers and performance artists.

Benefits: Benefits include medical insurance.

Human Resources: Dominick Belletta, Managing Dir.

Application Procedures: For technical positions, send resume to David Herrigel. Performers should send a proposal to Mark Russell, Dir.

▶ **Internships**

Type: Offers unpaid internships. College credit is available. **Number Available Annually:** 12.

Application Procedure: Send a resume and cover letter to the managing director.

Peridance Ensemble

Peridance Studio/Theatre
132 4th Ave.
New York, NY 10003
Phone: (212)505-0886

Business Description: A contemporary dance company.

Application Procedures: Performers may apply through a trial class or audition. Send resume to Denise Damon, Asst. Dir.

▶ **Internships**

Type: The company does not offer an internship program.

Perkins Productions Inc.

1633 N. Halsted St.
Chicago, IL 60614
Phone: (312)944-5626

Business Description: A theatre production company.

Application Procedures: For technical positions, send resume to Jim Jensen, general manager. For casting positions, check classified advertising in appropriate newspapers or send resume and photograph to Aimee Simpson, assistant to the producer.

▶ **Internships**

Type: The company does not offer an internship program.

Philadelphia Drama Guild

Robert Morris Bldg., 8th Fl.
100 N. 17th St.
Philadelphia, PA 19103
Phone: (215)563-7530

Business Description: The Guild produces new works and classics from a contemporary perspective.

Benefits: Benefits include a health maintenance organization (HMO) and Blue Cross and Blue Shield coverage.

Application Procedures: Send resume, cover letter, and head shot to Barbara Silvle, Casting Coord. and Company Mgr.

▶ **Internships**

Type: Offers paid internships to individuals interested in this field. **Number Available Annually:** 5.

Philadelphia Festival Theatre for New Plays

3900 Chestnut St.
Philadelphia, PA 19104
Phone: (215)222-5000
Fax: (215)222-8581

Business Description: An independent, nonprofit theatre that produces new plays by contemporary American playwrights.

Employees: 10.

Application Procedures: Performers should send resume and head shot with a self-addressed stamped envelope to Debbie Levin, Casting Dir.

▶ **Internships**

Contact: Andy Loose, Prod. Bus. Mgr.

Type: Offers unpaid marketing, development, press relations, and production internships for high school seniors and graduates, college students, and graduates. Duration is three or more months. Full-time employment is possible. College credit is available.

As a rule of thumb, you'll need one month of job search for every $10,000 in salary you seek, although older people or those in bad job markets may find that their search goes on much longer.

Source: *Detroit Free Press*

Piano Players Plus

PO Box 788
Scottsdale, AZ 85252
Phone: (602)831-2712

Business Description: An agency representing piano players, Dixieland bands, rock groups, string quartets, brass quintets, big bands, and soloists.

Application Procedures: Call or write to express an interest in auditioning. Contact Bob Thompson.

▶ **Internships**

Type: The company does not offer an internship program.

Pink Inc.

So Grand Studio
62 Grand St.
New York, NY 10013
Phone: (212)941-1949
Fax: (212)941-7606

Business Description: Pink Inc. is a performance ensemble. It operates a theatre space, called the So Grand Studio, presents theatrical collections twice a year, and an Artist-in-Residence program. Pink Inc. also conducts classes in Corporeal Movement Technique for both company and non-company members, and So Grand Studio provides toning and aerobic classes. The company's goal is to further the evolution of hybrid artforms through the continuing development of the director's works, its performances/installations, and through sponsoring other interdisciplinary artists.

Opportunities: Offers opportunities for performers and technical personnel.

Application Procedures: For technical positons, send resume to Christopher Eaves, Development Dir. For artistic positions, send resume, photos, and tapes (if appropriate) to Debra Roth, Artistic Dir.

▶ **Internships**

Contact: Debra Roth, Artistic Dir.

Type: Offers unpaid internships. College credit is available.

Application Procedure: Contact Debra Roth, Artistic Dir.

Pioneer Theatre Co.

University of Utah
Salt Lake City, UT 84112
Phone: (801)581-6356

Business Description: The professional company of the University of Utah, the Pioneer Theatre Co. produces plays, classics, and musicals.

Employees: 50.

Opportunities: Offers entry-level positions in fundraising or box office areas. College degree or previous experience necessary.

Benefits: Benefits include medical insurance, life insurance, dental insurance, and a pension plan.

Application Procedures: Send cover letter and resume to the personnel office of the university. Cover letter must include job number (each job corresponds with a job number). No unsolicited resumes accepted.

▶ Internships

Type: Offers paid acting internships to college students enrolled in the theatre program at the University of Utah. College credit is available. **Number Available Annually:** 4.

Application Procedure: Send application to the personnel office at the University of Utah. Applicants must audition for internships during their junior year.

Playhouse 91

316 E. 91st St.
New York, NY 10128
Phone: (212)831-2001

Business Description: Home of the Light Opera of Manhattan and the Jewish Repertory Theatre, the company presents contemporary plays, musicals, and operas.

Human Resources: Charles Timm, Owner.

Application Procedures: Send resume to Charles Timm, Owner.

▶ Internships

Type: The company does not offer an internship program.

Playhouse on the Square

51 S. Cooper
Memphis, TN 38104
Phone: (901)725-0776
Fax: (901)272-7530

Business Description: A professional theatre company dedicated to ensemble company work.

Employees: 23.

Application Procedures: Applicants should send resume, cover letter, and head shot (if applicable) with a self-addressed, stamped envelope to Mr. Jackie Nichols, Exec. Prod.

▶ Internships

Contact: Mr. Jackie Nichols, Exec. Prod.

Type: Offers acting, stage management, costume, technical, and administrative internships to college students and graduates, graduate students, and others. Pays $75/week for one year. Provides placement assistance, letters of recommendation, career counseling, and housing.

Playwrights Horizons Theatre

416 W. 42nd St.
New York, NY 10036
Phone: (212)564-1235

Business Description: Features new plays and musicals dedicated to American playwrights, composers, and lyricists.

Application Procedures: Send resume and a head shot to Toby Miller, Casting Resident.

▶ Internships

Contact: Mary Kay Hamalainen.

Type: Offers paid (stipend) internships to college students.

Application Procedure: Send resume to the attention of Mary Kay Hamalainen.

Portland Stage Company

PO Box 1458
Portland, ME 04104
Phone: (207)774-1043
Fax: (207)774-0576

Business Description: Established in 1974, the Portland Stage Company is a resident professional theatre that also provides educational services.

Employees: 30.

▶ Internships

Contact: Shoshana Bobkoff, Intern Dir.

Type: Offers seasonal paid internships to people with training in theater or those with college degrees. Accepts international applications. Interns are given formal training and placement assistance after completion of the internship. Full-time employment is possible.

Application Procedure: Contact the intern director for further information.

Posey School of Dance, Inc.

PO Box 254
Northport, NY 11768-0254
Phone: (516)757-2700

Employees: 10.

Opportunities: Entry-level opportunities available with varying requirements.

Benefits: Benefits include workers' compensation.

Application Procedures: Direct phone calls or letters of interest to Elsa Posey.

▶ **Internships**

Contact: Elsa Posey.

Type: Offers internships with varying requirements.

Application Procedure: Direct phone calls or letters of interest to Elsa Posey.

Pregones Theatre

295 St. Ann's Ave.
Bronx, NY 10454
Phone: (718)585-1202

Opportunities: Offers opportunities to those willing to make long-term employment commitment. Highly interested in Latino artists.

Benefits: Benefits include medical insurance, life insurance, dental insurance, and room and board.

Application Procedures: Send resume and photo to Judith Rivera, Assoc. Dir.

▶ **Internships**

Contact: Judith Rivera, Assoc. Dir.

Type: Offers paid and unpaid internships to college students. **Number Available Annually:** 2.

Application Procedure: Contact Judith Rivera by phone.

The management of the arts in America is no longer neatly divided between Broadway and Hollywood, or, for that matter, between what is called "commercial" and "serious" art. No longer can one expect to specialize in either live or electronic ventures, nor can one expect to settle down on one coast or the other, ignoring everything in between and outside.

Primary Stages

354 W. 45th St.
New York, NY 10036
Phone: (212)333-7471

Business Description: Founded in 1984, Primary Stages features works by new American playwrights.

Employees: 2.

▶ **Internships**

Contact: Casey Childs, Dist. Dir.

Type: Offers full-time, unpaid administrative and production internships for college credit.

Application Procedure: Send letter of interest to Casey Childs.

Professional Performing Arts Series

Queensborough Community College Theatre
222-05 56th Ave.
Bayside, NY 11364-1497
Phone: (718)613-6321

Business Description: Offers a diverse selection of music, theatre, dance, opera, and family entertainment.

Application Procedures: Performers normally work through agents, but press kits (photos, reviews) are accepted. Stage crew applicants should send resumes. Performers and stage crew applicants should send materials to the attention of Anthony Carobine, Dir. of Performing Arts.

▶ **Internships**

Type: The company does not offer an internship program.

Pulse Ensemble Theatre

432 W. 42nd St.
New York, NY 10036
Phone: (212)695-1596

Business Description: Presents new plays, revivals, dramas, classics, and comedies.

Application Procedures: Send resume and picture to Alexa Kelly, Artistic Dir.

▶ **Internships**

Type: Offers unpaid internships. College credit is available. **Number Available Annually:** 3.

Queens Theatre in the Park

Queens Council of the Arts
Flushing Meadows
Corona Park
Flushing, NY 11352
Phone: (718)760-0064

Business Description: Presents musicals, plays, dance, and music concerts.

Opportunities: Hires performance and technical staff.

Benefits: Benefits include medical insurance, life insurance, vision insurance, and savings plan.

Human Resources: Bob Foreman, Gen. Mgr.

Application Procedures: For performance positions, send resume in response to advertisements or audition through casting calls. For technical positions, send resume to Bob Foreman, Gen. Mgr.

▶ **Internships**

Type: Offers paid and unpaid internships for college credit.

Application Procedure: Send resume and cover letter.

RA Reed Productions Inc.
955 N. Columbia
Portland, OR 97217
Phone: (503)735-0003

Business Description: Involved in concert and event staging and scenery.

Opportunities: Hires scenic artists, carpenters, and welders on a part-time basis with the potential of advancement.

Human Resources: Rick Reed, Owner.

Application Procedures: Apply in person or contact and send resume to Rick Reed, Owner.

▶ **Internships**

Type: The company does not offer an internship program.

Radio Express Inc.
3575 Cahuenga Blvd. W
Los Angeles, CA 90068
Phone: (213)850-1003
Fax: (213)874-7753

Business Description: Engaged in radio program production.

Opportunities: Hires staff with previous experience in buying and selling tapes.

Benefits: Benefits include medical insurance, life insurance, dental insurance, and vision insurance.

Human Resources: Johnny Biggs, Mgr.

Application Procedures: Send resume and cover letter to company.

▶ **Internships**

Type: Offers internships to those with previous experience.

Repertorio Espanol (Spanish Theatre Repertory Company)
Gramercy Arts Theatre
138 E. 27th St.
New York, NY 10016
Phone: (212)889-2850

Business Description: Founded in 1968, the company presents classical and contemporary plays in Spanish, classical, and flamenco dance events. The group offers English simulcasts for many of its productions. It also tours to festivals around the country, to schools, community centers, churches, and settlement houses.

Opportunities: Offers opportunities for individuals with previous experience. Those interested should check press releases and posted notices for openings. Openings listed in *ArtSEARCH*.

Benefits: Benefits include medical insurance.

Application Procedures: Send samples to Gilberto Zaldivar, Producer.

▶ **Internships**

Type: Offers unpaid internships to those with previous experience.

Application Procedure: Applicants should contact their college advisors for information.

Richard Bull Dance/Theatre
Warren Street Performance Loft
46 Warren St.
New York, NY 10007
Phone: (212)732-3149

Business Description: A post-modern company that features choreographic improvisation.

Human Resources: Cynthia Nowak.

Application Procedures: For open dance auditions, check advertisements in *The Village Voice* newspaper. For technical or lighting positions, send resume.

▶ **Internships**

Type: The company does not offer an internship program.

Ron Smith's Celebrity Look-A-Likes

7060 Hollywood Blvd., Ste. 1215
Los Angeles, CA 90028
Phone: (213)467-3030

Application Procedures: Apply in person or send resume and demo tape.

▶ **Internships**

Type: The company does not offer an internship program.

Roundabout Theatre Company, Inc.

1530 Broadway
New York, NY 10036
Phone: (212)869-8400

Business Description: With a subscription audience of around 22,000, the Roundabout Theater Company is noted for successfully reviving the classics to repertory.

Opportunities: Offers opportunities for individuals with theatre education, administration, or production experience.

Benefits: Benefits include medical insurance.

Application Procedures: Send cover letter and resume to Ellen Gordon, Business Mgr.

▶ **Internships**

Type: Offers paid internships to college students and qualified adults. College credit available.

Application Procedure: Send cover letter and resume to Ellen Gordon.

Roy A. Somlyo Productions

234 W. 44th St.
New York, NY 10036
Phone: (212)764-6080
Fax: (212)764-6363

Business Description: Produces and manages musicals and plays on- and off-Broadway, on tour, and in London. Also produces television specials and markets programs within the entertainment industry.

▶ **Internships**

Contact: Roy A. Somlyo, President.

Type: Offers unpaid production internships to college sophomores, juniors, seniors, graduate students, and graduates. Applicants' primary goal should be in writing, producing, or managing shows. Benefits include the opportunity to meet professionals in the industry and the possibility of full-time employment in professional theater or broadcasting. **Number Available Annually:** 1. **Applications Received:** 40.

Duties: Reading and evaluating scripts, attending meetings and performances, and performing general office duties such as answering phones and running errands.

Application Procedure: Send cover letter, educational resume, and summary of previous employment or internships to Roy A. Somlyo.

St. Bart's Players

Theatre at St. Bartholomew's Church
109 E. 50th St.
New York, NY 10022
Phone: (212)751-1616

Business Description: Features revivals of Broadway musicals, plays, comedies, and mysteries.

Benefits: Benefits include medical insurance, life insurance, and dental insurance.

Human Resources: Chris Catt, Artistic Dir.

Application Procedures: Send resume and cover letter to Chris Catt, Artistic Dir.

▶ **Internships**

Type: Offers unpaid internships for college credit. **Number Available Annually:** 1-2 per year.

Application Procedure: Phone or send letter to Chris Catt.

St. Jean's Players

St. Jean's School Auditorium
173 E. 75th St.
New York, NY 10021
Phone: (212)288-1645

Business Description: Presents dramas, comedies, and musicals.

Human Resources: Steve Gavala, Contact.

Application Procedures: Notices of auditions are passed on by word-of-mouth. Those who belong to unions are welcome to apply and/or audition.

San Jose Repertory Theatre

PO Box 2399
San Jose, CA 95109-2399
Phone: (408)291-2266
Fax: (408)995-0737

Business Description: Established in 1980, the theatre produces both classical and contemporary theatre. Presents six shows per year and a touring show for young people.

Employees: 35.

▶ Internships

Contact: Benton Delinger, Prod. Mgr.

Type: Offers paid and unpaid internships in production, company management, and marketing. Open to college juniors and seniors, graduate students, and college graduates. Benefits include the possibility of college credit and placement and housing assistance. **Number Available Annually:** 3. **Applications Received:** 25 per year.

Application Procedure: Send resume to Benton Delinger.

Seattle Group Theatre

305 Harrison St.
Seattle, WA 98109
Phone: (206)441-9480

Business Description: Established in 1978, the Seattle Group Theatre is dedicated to promoting and producing multicultural theatre.

Employees: 12.

▶ Internships

Contact: Paul O'Connell, Producing Dir.

Type: Offers internships in such areas as administration, marketing, development, stage management, production/technical, directing, the literary department, and literary/dramaturg. College students, college graduates, and graduate students are eligible. College credit is available. Placement and housing assistance provided. **Number Available Annually:** 9. **Applications Received:** 75.

Duties: General administrative interns assist in the managing director in system maintenance, report completion, communication with the board, and volunteer program support. Public relations/marketing interns help design and write publications, create lobby displays and promotions, and assist in other various campaigns. Development interns work with potential contributors and fundraising campaigns. Stage management interns provide assistance to stage managers and help coordinate production during auditions, rehearsal, readings, workshops, and mainstage performance. Production/technical interns help technical directors and scenic designers. Directing interns assist the artistic director. Literary intern responsibilities include administrative tasks and supervision of dramaturgy work, playwrights lab scripts, and script reading. Literary/dramaturg interns assist the dramaturg/literary manager and perform administrative tasks.

Application Procedure: Contact Paul O'Connell.

Seattle Repertory Theatre

155 Mercer St.
Seattle, WA 98109
Phone: (206)443-2210

Business Description: Founded in 1963, the Seattle Repertory Theatre presents new plays, classical works, and musicals.

Officers: Benjamin Moore, Mng. Dir.

Benefits: Benefits include medical insurance, life insurance, dental insurance, and vision insurance.

Application Procedures: Casting notices for performers are posted in local newspapers. Those interested in administrative positions should send resume to Laura Penn, Assoc. Asst. Dir.

▶ **Internships**

Contact: Christie Bain, Intern Coord.

Type: Offers paid internships to those with experience. **Number Available Annually:** 26.

Second Stage Theatre

PO Box 1807
Ansonia Sta.
New York, NY 10023
Phone: (212)787-8302
Fax: (212)877-9886

Business Description: Established in 1979, the Second Stage produces new plays and revivals.

▶ **Internships**

Contact: Carol B. Fishman, Assoc. Prod.

Type: Offers unpaid internships. Positions include administrative assistant, asistants to the library manager, developmental assistant, and marketing intern. Open to college students, graduates, and graduate school students. Provides placement assistance and opportunities for full-time employment. College credit is available.

Application Procedure: Send cover letter, resume, and two letters of recommendation to the associate producer.

Settlement Music School

416 Queen St.
Philadelphia, PA 19147
Phone: (215)336-0400

Employees: 250.

Opportunities: Offers range of opportunities from clerical to faculty. Requirements vary depending on type of position.

Benefits: Benefits include medical insurance, life insurance, dental insurance, and vision insurance.

Application Procedures: Send resume and cover letter to Robert Capanna, Exec. Dir.

▶ **Internships**

Type: Offers internships in the pre-school program; includes a stipend.

Application Procedure: Send application to Robert Capanna, Exec. Dir.

Shubert Theatre

225 W. 44th St.
New York, NY 10036
Phone: (212)239-6200

Business Description: A professional Broadway theatre.

Opportunities: Hires entry-level staff in the production area. Previous experience and some college course work required.

Benefits: Benefits include medical insurance, life insurance, and savings plan.

Human Resources: Bill Canon, Office Mgr.

Application Procedures: Performers should inquire through their agents or send resume and head shot to company. Candidates interested in production positions should send resume to Wendy Orshan, Office Mgr.

▶ **Internships**

Contact: Christine Stubbs.

Type: Offers internships to college juniors and seniors for college credit. **Number Available Annually:** 1-2.

Application Procedure: Send resume to Christine Stubbs.

Sidewalks of New York

Sidewalks Theatre
40 W. 27th St.
New York, NY 10001
Phone: (212)481-3077

Business Description: A small, nonprofit organization that features classic period plays and contemporary works.

Application Procedures: Check for advertisements in newspaper and send in resume with cover letter. Unsolicited resumes are not accepted.

▶ **Internships**

Type: Offers unpaid internships. College credit is available.

Simon and Kumin Casting

1600 Broadway
New York, NY 10009
Phone: (212)245-7670

Business Description: Involved in casting for television, film, and theatre.

Employees: 5.

Opportunities: Hires entry-level office staff

with previous experience. New hires must start as interns.

Benefits: Benefits include medical insurance, life insurance, dental insurance, and vision insurance.

Human Resources: Alyssa Roth, Assoc. Casting Dir.

Application Procedures: Send resume and cover letter to Alyssa Roth, Assoc. Casting Dir.

▶ **Internships**

Type: Offers paid internships. **Number Available Annually:** 3-4.

Application Procedure: Send resume to Alyssa Roth.

Snug Harbor Cultural Center
Veterans Memorial Hall
1000 Richmond Terrace
Staten Island, NY 10301
Phone: (718)448-2500
Fax: (718)442-8534

Business Description: Runs performing and visual arts facilities, a children's museum, and a botanical garden.

Benefits: Benefits include medical insurance and a savings plan.

Human Resources: Gloria Riccardi, Dir. of Human Resources.

Application Procedures: For technical positions, send resume and cover letter. For performing positions, send tapes/press kit/videos and a self-addressed stamped envelope to Brian Rehr, Dir. of Performing Arts.

▶ **Internships**

Contact: Gloria Riccardi, Dir. of Human Resources.

Type: Offers unpaid internships to college students. College credit is available.

Application Procedure: Send resume and cover letter to Gloria Riccardi.

Society Hill Playhouse
Center for the Performing Arts, Inc.
507 S. 8th St.
Philadelphia, PA 19147
Phone: (215)923-0210
Fax: (215)923-1789

Business Description: Established in 1959,

Society Hill is a resident professional theatre that features contemporary works by American and European playwrights.

Application Procedures: Designers and technical staff should send resume and cover letter with a self-addressed, stamped envelope. Performers should send materials to the casting director. Open calls are in September and February.

▶ **Internships**

Contact: Susan Turlish, Program Dir.

Type: Offers unpaid technical, teaching, and public relations internships for college credit. Open to college juniors, seniors and graduate students. Benefits include job placement assistance, letters of recommendation, job counseling, seminars and workshops, and the opportunity for full-time employment.

Duties: Technical interns participate in theater projects, including lighting, setting, and sound. Teaching interns assist the program director with student counseling, preparing lessons, and student teaching. Public relations interns assist with fundraising, production promotion, and group sales.

Application Procedure: Contact the program director for further information. In-person interview required.

> **T**he most successful employees of the future will be mid-level decision makers who can use their own computer support systems. They will have specialized knowledge and expertise, and will be able to shift from one company to another, and industry to industry.
>
> Source: *Detroit Free Press*

Source Theatre Company
1835 14th St. NW
Washington, DC 20009
Phone: (202)462-1073
Fax: (202)462-0676

Business Description: The Source Theatre Company produces new and modern plays and reinterpretations of the classics.

Employees: 8.

▶ **Internships**

Contact: Bill Price, Production Coord.

Type: Offers unpaid internships including: administrative, publicity, stage management, house management, and technical interns. High school and college students and others are eligible. College credit is available. Placement and housing assistance are available. **Number Available Annually:** 20. **Applications Received:** 40.

Application Procedure: Contact Bill Price, Production Coord.

The person who mentions money first loses the negotiating edge. Ever play blackjack? You don't know what the dealer's hole card is, but your cards are face up. Who's got the advantage? The dealer. You can be the dealer if you're a shrewd negotiator. Don't give answers about compensation that pin you down. Asking the salary range for the position or responding in terms of total compensation (i.e., base plus profit-sharing/bonus/commission) gives you latitude.

Source: *Detroit Free Press*

Stage One: The Louisville Children's Theatre

425 W. Market St.
Louisville, KY 40202
Phone: (502)589-5946

Business Description: Stage One is a professional adult company that presents entertainment for young people and their families.

Employees: 30.

Human Resources: Moses Goldberg, Prod. Dir.; G. Jane Jarrett, Mng. Dir.

▶ Internships

Contact: Dan Herring, Education Dir.

Type: Offers full-time, paid internships in acting, administration, development, and marketing departments. Open to college sophomores, juniors, seniors, graduates, and graduate school students. Interns receive $80 to $100 per week Full-time employment possible. Interns have the opportunity to attend seminars/workshops and receive housing location assistance. College credit is available. **Number Available Annually:** 4.

Application Procedure: Send resume and cover letter and a list of three references to the education director.

Application Deadline: 2-3 months before start of the internship.

Stagewest

1 Columbus Center
Springfield, MA 01103
Phone: (413)781-4470
Fax: (413)781-3741

Business Description: Stagewest is a nonprofit resident theatre.

Employees: 15.

▶ Internships

Contact: Kate MaGuire, Managing Dir.

Type: Offers paid acting and production internships to college graduates and graduate students. College credit is available. Housing is provided at $200/month. Full-time employment possible. Placement assistance provided. **Applications Received:** 150.

Duties: Acting interns are involved in preparations for acting classes, workshops, children's shows, and technical work. Production interns perform running crew duties for mainstage and second stage productions.

Application Procedure: Contact Kate MaGuire, Managing Dir.

Application Deadline: May 1.

The Stamford Center for the Arts

61 Atlantic St.
Stamford, CT 06901
Phone: (203)326-4950

Business Description: The Stamford Center is involved in theatre, dance, and music performances.

Employees: 30.

▶ Internships

Contact: Theresa Gregory, Development Mgr.

Type: Offers unpaid theatre internships to college and foreign students. College credit is available. Placement assistance and job counseling provided. Full-time employment is possible. **Applications Received:** 100.

Application Procedure: Contact Theresa Gregory, Development Mgr., PO Box 15460, Stamford, CT 06901.

Steppenwolf Theatre Company

1650 N. Halsted St.
Chicago, IL 60614
Phone: (312)335-1888

Benefits: Benefits include medical insurance, life insurance, and dental insurance.

Application Procedures: Does not hold open auditions. Send resume and head shot to Phyllis Schuringa, Casting Dir.

▶ **Internships**

Type: Offers unpaid internships to college students. College credit is available.

Application Procedure: Contact Leslie Holland or Lisa Nowicki in the Educational Outreach Department.

Steven Scott Orchestra Inc.
Steven Scott Productions

200 W. 57th St., Ste. 303
New York, NY 10019-3211
Phone: (212)757-3299

Business Description: Involved in music directing, staging and lighting, music and entertainment consulting, and casting and entertainment booking.

Application Procedures: Those interested in entry-level positions should send resume and demo tape to company.

▶ **Internships**

Type: The company does not offer an internship program.

Studio Museum in Harlem

144 W. 125th St.
New York, NY 10027
Phone: (212)864-4500

Business Description: The studio is involved in exhibitions, programs, and education in the areas of African dance and music.

Employees: 40.

Opportunities: Offers opportunities for performers in African dance and music.

Benefits: Benefits are negotiated with contract performers.

Human Resources: Toni Lewis, Deputy Dir. for Admin.

Application Procedures: Send resume to the education deparment.

▶ **Internships**

Type: Offers internships for college credit in education and curatorial areas.

Application Procedure: Send resume and cover letter to the deputy dir. for programming.

Symphony Space

2537 Broadway
New York, NY 10025
Phone: (212)864-1414

Business Description: Presents low-cost film, dance, drama, and music events.

Opportunities: Hires performers and technical staff.

Human Resources: Denis Heron, Technical Dir.

Application Procedures: Performers should send resume and photograph to Isaiah Sheffer, Artistic Director. Technical applicants should send resume to Denis Heron, Technical Director.

▶ **Internships**

Contact: Denis Heron, Technical Dir.

Type: Offers internships for college credit.

Application Procedure: Send resume to Denis Heron.

Synchronicity Space

55 Mercer St.
New York, NY 10013
Phone: (212)925-8645

Business Description: A 40-week season is presented by five resident theatre companies.

Application Procedures: Send resume, cover letter, and head shot (if applicable) to John Smith Amato, Dir.

▶ **Internships**

Type: Offers paid and unpaid internships to college students.

Application Procedure: Contact John Smith Amato.

T. Schreiber Studio

83 E. 4th St.
New York, NY 10003
Phone: (212)420-1249

Business Description: The studio presents one-acts and full-length plays.

Human Resources: Terry Schreiber, Owner.

Application Procedures: Hires by audition only.

▶ **Internships**

Type: The company does not offer an internship program.

Tennessee Repertory Theatre
427 Chestnut St.
Nashville, TN 37203
Phone: (615)244-4878

Business Description: The professional theatre in residence at the Tennessee Performing Arts Center, Tennessee Repertory Theatre focuses primarily on new American musicals.

Benefits: Benefits include medical insurance and dental insurance.

Human Resources: Jennifer Orth, Company Mgr.

Application Procedures: Apply through auditon held every second week in June. One monologue and/or two songs required, depending on production.

▶ **Internships**

Type: Offers internships for college credit.

Thalia Spanish Theatre
41-17 Greenpoint Ave.
Sunnyside, NY 11104
Phone: (718)729-3880

Business Description: The theatre features Spanish operetta, classic and contemporary plays, and music and dance from Spain and Latin America.

Opportunities: Offers opportunities for Spanish-speaking performers.

Benefits: Benefits include medical insurance, life insurance, and dental insurance.

Application Procedures: Send resume and head shot to Silvia Brito, Artistic Dir.

▶ **Internships**

Type: The company does not offer an internship program.

Theatre 22
54 W. 22nd St.
New York, NY 10010
Phone: (212)243-2805

Business Description: Features modern American plays, Greek and Roman dramas, and 17th-19th century European works.

Opportunities: Hires set-up staff and runners. Preference is given to those who have volunteered at the theater.

Application Procedures: Apply in person.

▶ **Internships**

Type: The company has no formal internship program.

Theatre at Monmouth
Main St.
PO Box 385
Monmouth, ME 04259

Business Description: Produces classical works in Victorian theatre.

Employees: 42.

▶ **Internships**

Contact: Ms. George Carlson, Managing Dir.

Type: Offers acting, technical, and office internships. Interns earn $40/week. High school and college graduates, college and graduate students, and others are eligible. College credit is available. Placement assistance, housing, and meals are provided. Full-time employment possible. **Number Available Annually:** 10-14. **Applications Received:** 150.

Duties: Acting interns work in the front office in addition to their acting responsibilities. Technical interns work on stage and set design and do carpentry and electrical work. Office interns help with management, ordering, and publicity.

Application Procedure: Write to Ms. George Carlson. An in-person interview is recommended. No phone calls.

Application Deadline: March 1.

Theatre De La Jeune Lune
105 1st St. N.
Minneapolis, MN 55401
Phone: (612)332-3968
Fax: (612)332-0048

Business Description: A professional, modern theatre company.

▶ Internships

Contact: Ms. Kit Waickman, Business Dir.

Type: Offers unpaid production and administration internships. Educational credit is available. Full-time employment possible. Interns receive complimentary theatre tickets and housing assistance. **Number Available Annually:** 8. **Applications Received:** 30.

Duties: Production interns can specialize in such areas as costumes and props, stage management, or lighting design. Administrative interns assist management by working on marketing and development projects and assisting business office operations.

Application Procedure: Send letter and resume to Ms. Kit Waickman, Business Dir.

Theatre for the New City Foundation, Inc.

155 1st Ave.
New York, NY 10003
Phone: (212)254-1109

Business Description: The theatre is a nonprofit, off-Broadway company.

▶ Internships

Contact: Jerry Jaffe, Admin.

Type: Offers unpaid administrative and technical internships. High school students and individuals changing careers are eligible. College credit is available. Full-time employment possible. **Number Available Annually:** 2. **Applications Received:** 50.

Application Procedure: Contact Jerry Jaffe.

Theatre Off Park

224 Waverly Pl.
New York, NY 10014
Phone: (212)627-2556

Business Description: Presents a wide variety of entertainment, from new plays to workshops to full-scale productions.

Opportunities: Not hiring at this time.

Application Procedures: When performance and production positions are posted, send resume to Albert Harris, Artistic Dir.

▶ Internships

Contact: Albert Harris, Artistic Dir.

Type: Offers unpaid internships. College credit is available.

Application Procedure: Contact Albert Harris.

Theatre on the Square

450 Post St.
San Francisco, CA 94102
Phone: (415)433-6461
Fax: (415)362-5114

Business Description: Founded in 1982, Theatre on the Square is controlled by Reinis Productions, a company that produces about four new shows per year.

Benefits: Benefits include medical insurance, life insurance, dental insurance, and vision insurance.

Human Resources: John Reimis, Owner.

Application Procedures: Send resume and photograph to Joe Watson, Theatre Mgr.

According to the Association of Part-Time Professionals, 20 million Americans are working part-time. More than 4.5 million are part-time professionals, whose ranks have swelled more than 50 percent the past decade.

Source: *Detroit Free Press*

The Theatre-Studio

750 8th Ave.
New York, NY 10036
Phone: (212)719-0500

Business Description: Presents showcase productions of new plays, classics, readings, and workshops.

Opportunities: Offers volunteer positions only.

Application Procedures: Send resume and cover letter to A.M. Raychel, Artistic Dir.

▶ **Internships**

Type: Offers unpaid internships. **Number Available Annually:** 5.

Application Procedure: Send resume and cover letter to A.M. Raychel, Artistic Dir.

Theatre West Virginia

Box 1205
Beckley, WV 25802-1205
Phone: (304)256-6800
Toll-free: 800-666-9142

Business Description: Established in 1955, Theatre West Virginia offers two outdoor dramas and a musical that run in the summer. The theatre also has a touring program that includes acting, dance, and marionettes.

Application Procedures: Offers local auditions at conferences and colleges. Call or send resume and samples to Mirina Dolinger, Marketing Dir.

▶ **Internships**

Type: The company does not offer an internship program.

TheatreVirginia

2800 Grove Ave.
Richmond, VA 23221
Phone: (804)367-0840

Business Description: Established in 1954, TheatreVirginia produces dramas, comedies, and musicals.

▶ **Internships**

Contact: Nancy Sullivan, Dir. of Education and Outreach.

Type: Offers paid administrative and production internships. Interns earn $145-$170/week. Full-time employment possible. Placement and housing assistance provided. College graduates,

graduate students, and individuals changing careers are eligible. **Number Available Annually:** 11-13. **Applications Received:** 200.

Duties: Administrative interns work in development, arts administration, ticket operations, marketing/public relations, company management, or house management. Production interns work in scenic carpentry and artistry, properties, costume production, electrics, or sound.

Application Procedure: Contact Nancy Sullivan, Dir. of Education and Outreach.

Theatreworks

1305 Middlefield Rd.
Palo Alto, CA 94301
Phone: (415)323-8311
Fax: (415)323-3311

Business Description: Theatreworks presents live and culturally diverse theatre.

Employees: 20.

▶ **Internships**

Contact: Leslie Martinson, Operations Mgr.

Type: Offers internships to high school seniors and graduates, college students and graduates, and individuals changing careers. Full-time technical interns earn $100/week and apprentices earn $50/week. Part-time technical interns earn $50-$100/week. Part-time administrative interns are unpaid. College credit is available. Benefits include placement and housing assistance and complimentary show tickets. **Applications Received:** 30.

Duties: Technical theatre interns and apprentices assist in the construction and maintenance of scenes and costumes. Administrative interns work on special marketing, development, ticket services, or casting projects.

Application Procedure: Contact Leslie Martinson, Operations Mgr.

Tiny Mythic Theatre Company

145 Avenue of the Americas
Ground Fl.
New York, NY 10013
Phone: (212)647-0252

Business Description: Features work by young artists and directors.

Application Procedures: Send resume and a letter of interest and goals to Nicole Katz, Artistic Dir.

▶ **Internships**

Type: The company does not offer an internship program.

Todd-AO Corp.

172 Golden Gate Ave.
San Francisco, CA 94102
Phone: (415)928-3200

Business Description: Movie postproduction sound services.

Officers: John Sherwood, Pres.

Employees: 13.

Opportunities: Offers secretarial, production, performing, and executive positions. Previous experience and/or college degree required.

Benefits: Benefits include medical insurance and life insurance.

Application Procedures: Performing positions advertised in trade magazines, newspapers, and at job agencies. Performers should apply in person. Other applicants should send resumes to John Sherwood, Pres.

▶ **Internships**

Type: The company does not offer an internship program.

Triangle Theatre Company

316 E. 88th St.
New York, NY 10128
Phone: (212)860-7245

Business Description: Triangle Theatre Company is a subscription theatre producing shows and staged readings.

Employees: 10.

▶ **Internships**

Contact: Michael Ramach, Producing Dir.

Type: Offers paid and unpaid technical theatre and directing internships to high school

students and graduates; college students and graduates; graduate students; and others. College credit is available. Placement assistance provided. Full-time employment possible. **Number Available Annually:** 3.

Application Procedure: Send resume to Michael Ramach, Producing Dir.

You can also use "One day at a time" to keep you plugging away at your long-term goals. "One day at a time" can get you through any enterprise so big or complicated or long-range that it would discourage or terrify you to look at it in its entirety. Do you wonder how the great achievers and visionaries of the world accomplish so much? They do it one day at a time.

Source: *Detroit Free Press*

Vanco Stage Lighting Inc.

42 Gate Hill Rd.
Stony Point, NY 10980
Phone: (914)942-0075

Business Description: Provides theatrical and special event lighting services.

Opportunities: Hires entry-level staff to provide lighting for plays, concerts, and other events.

Benefits: Benefits include medical insurance.

Application Procedures: Send resume and cover letter to Phil Hirsch, Gen. Mgr.

▶ **Internships**

Type: The company does not offer an internship program.

Victory Gardens Theater

2257 N. Lincoln Ave.
Chicago, IL 60614
Phone: (312)549-5788

Business Description: The Victory Gardens Theatre was established in 1974 and concentrates on the work of local playwrights.

Employees: 11.

▶ **Internships**

Contact: Ms. Allyn M. Pokraka, Administrative Dir.

Type: Offers unpaid internships to college

seniors, graduates, graduate students, and others. Internships include artistic, management, marketing, and development. Educational credit is available and placement assistance provided. **Number Available Annually:** 12. **Applications Received:** 10-20.

Application Procedure: Send resume and cover letter to Ms. Allyn M. Pokraka, Administrative Dir.

Instead of advancing in your specialty, you transfer elsewhere in the company or take temporary assignments. These moves broaden your skills and your perspective, which might help promote you in the future.

Source: *Detroit Free Press*

Village Theatre Company

The Village Theatre
133 W. 22nd St.
New York, NY 10011
Phone: (212)627-8411

Business Description: Presents premieres of plays with political and social relevance.

Application Procedures: Send photo and/or resume to the attention of Marge Seenan, Prod.

▶ **Internships**

Type: The company does not offer an internship program.

Villar-Hauser Theatre Company

Greenwich Street Theatre
112 Charlton St.
New York, NY 10013
Phone: (212)255-3940

Business Description: The company represents small and independent works.

Application Procedures: Applicants should call or send resume with cover letter to Ludovica Villar-Hauser, Producing Artistic Dir. 286 Spring St., Rm. 304A, New York, NY 10013.

▶ **Internships**

Type: Offers unpaid technical and administrative internships to experienced, qualified individuals.

Application Procedure: Write to Ludovica Villar-Hauser at 286 Spring St., Rm. 304A, New York, NY 10013.

Vineyard Theatre

108 E. 15th St.
New York, NY 10003
Phone: (212)353-3874

Business Description: Presents drama and musical theatre, opera, and children's concerts. Has a resident chamber music ensemble.

Benefits: Benefits include medical insurance, life insurance, and dental insurance.

Application Procedures: Send resume, cover letter, and picture to Doug Aibel, Artistic Dir.

▶ **Internships**

Contact: Jon Nakagawa, Managing Dir.

Type: Offers paid and unpaid internships to college students.

Application Procedure: Send resume, cover letter, and picture to Jon Nakagawa, Managing Dir.

Virginia Stage Company

PO Box 3770
Norfolk, VA 23514
Phone: (804)627-6988

Business Description: A regional theatre company producing about five shows per year.

▶ **Internships**

Contact: Amanda Graham, Production Mgr.

Type: Offers paid and unpaid internships to college seniors, graduates, and graduate students. Administration and some stage management internships are unpaid. Costume construction, scenic construction, lighting/sound, and some stage management interns earn $175/week. College credit is available. Placement assistance provided. Full-time employment possible. **Number Available Annually:** 5-7. **Applications Received:** 50-75.

Application Procedure: Write to Amanda Graham, Production Mgr. No telephone calls.

Virginia Theatre

245 W. 52nd St.
New York, NY 10019
Phone: (212)840-8181

Business Description: A professional Broadway theatre.

Opportunities: Applicants for production positions need previous experience and/or some college course work.

Benefits: Benefits include medical insurance.

Human Resources: Sherman Warner, Prod. Mgr.

Application Procedures: Performers should contact their agents. Others send resume and cover letter to Sherman Warner, Prod. Mgr.

▶ Internships

Contact: Edward Strong, Prod. Partner.

Type: Offers internships for credit to college juniors and seniors. **Number Available Annually:** 1-2.

Application Procedure: Send resume and cover letter to Edward Strong.

Vortex Theatre Company

Sanford Meisner Theatre
164 11th Ave.
New York, NY 10011
Phone: (212)206-1764

Business Description: The Vortex Theatre Company presents works by gay and lesbian playwrights regarding gay and lesbian issues.

Application Procedures: Performers should watch casting notices for open positions. Performers and technical personnel should send resume and cover letter to Michael Serrato, Managing Dir.

▶ Internships

Type: Offers unpaid internships to college theatre students. **Number Available Annually:** 2.

Application Procedure: Send resume and cover letter to Michael Serrato.

Walnut Street Theatre Company

9th & Walnut Sts.
Philadelphia, PA 19107
Phone: (215)574-3550
Fax: (215)574-3598

Business Description: The Walnut Street Theatre Company began in 1809 as an equestrian circus, and became a National Historic Landmark in 1964. The theatre is now a center for the performing arts with a theatre company presenting a five-play subscription season. It emphasizes the importance of regional artists and not-for-profit performing companies.

Employees: 15.

▶ Internships

Contact: Kristin Hogan, Assistant Dir.

Type: Offers unpaid internships and paid apprenticeships to college graduates and those with equivalent experience. Positions available in acting, subscription, marketing, stage management, props, and painting. Benefits include training opportunities, placement, and housing assistance. **Number Available Annually:** 7. **Applications Received:** 200 per year.

Application Procedure: Write to Kristin Hogan.

Application Deadline: April 30.

It is significant that most major films are now produced by independent companies, even though financing is often provided by a major studio in return for distribution rights. Many such companies were formed by stars-turned-producers, such as Robert Redford, Jane Fonda, and Spike Lee. This has been a healthy way to get the creative process back under the control of the artists.

Source: *Jobs in Arts & Media Management*

Weill Recital Hall

154 W. 57th St.
New York, NY 10019
Phone: (212)247-7800

Business Description: An intimate performing arts company that features small music groups, solo artists, and trios.

Opportunities: Hires entry-level production staff.

Benefits: Benefits include medical insurance and dental insurance.

Application Procedures: Send resume to Lauren Scott, Dir. of Human Resources.

▶ **Internships**

Type: Offers paid internships.

Application Procedure: Contact Lauren Scott.

West Bank Downstairs Theatre Bar

407 W. 42nd St.
New York, NY 10036
Phone: (212)695-6909

Business Description: Features new works, full-length plays, stand-up comedy, one-acts, and music events.

Application Procedures: Apply in person or send resume, proposal, and head shot to Steve Olsen, Owner.

▶ **Internships**

Type: Offers unpaid internships.

Application Procedure: Contact Steve Olsen.

In all cases, the people with an edge will be those who know how to use a computer to do their jobs more efficiently, who can present ideas cogently, and who work well in teams.

Source: *U.S. News & World Report*

Westbeth Theatre Center

151 Bank St.
New York, NY 10014
Phone: (212)691-2272

Business Description: Westbeth Theatre Center produces its own plays, provides a no-rent or low-rent performing space to nonprofit organizations, and acts as a rehearsal and workshop facility for those in the theatrical community to rent.

Application Procedures: Check for open audition notices in *Backstage* magazine. Send resume and photographs to Tony Severon, Mgr.

▶ **Internships**

Type: Offers technical and management internships for college credit.

Application Procedure: Contact the Westbeth Theatre Center.

Westport Country Playhouse

PO Box 629
Westport, CT 06881
Phone: (203)227-5137

Business Description: Established in 1931, Westport Country Playhouse is a professional seasonal theatre.

Employees: 50.

Application Procedures: Hires only union actors; contact company by mail for an application.

▶ **Internships**

Contact: Julie A. Monahan.

Type: Offers paid internships to college students and graduates, graduate school students, and others. Interns receive $60 per week. Benefits include college credit, job placement assistance, and low-cost housing. **Number Available Annually:** 8. **Applications Received:** 50-100.

Application Procedure: In-person interview recommended.

Application Deadline: June 1.

Westside Repertory Theatre

252 W. 81st St.
New York, NY 10024-5728
Phone: (212)874-7290

Business Description: Presents original plays and full-length classical plays and one-acts.

Human Resources: Eleanor Tapscott, Artistic Dir.

▶ **Internships**

Type: The company does not offer an internship program.

Williamstown Theatre Festival

PO Box 517
Williamstown, MA 01267
Phone: (212)228-2286
Fax: (212)228-9091

Business Description: A summer theatre that presents new works and revivals.

Employees: 300. Number represents in-season employees.

Opportunities: Hires performers and production staff.

Application Procedures: Performers must send headshot and resume. Auditions are by invitation only. Production staff must acquire an application by writing to 100 E. 17th St., New York, NY 10003.

▶ **Internships**

Contact: Mary Lee, Internship Coordinator.

Type: Offers unpaid summer internships to college students and others. College credit is available. **Number Available Annually:** 50. **Applications Received:** April 15.

Duties: Duties include working in design, general management, production, sets, costumes, cabaret, props, electrics, or stage management.

Application Deadline: April 15.

The Wilma Theater
2030 Sansom St.
Philadelphia, PA 19103
Phone: (215)963-0249

Business Description: A professional, nonprofit company devoted to innovative theatre. The Wilma Theatre also runs a theatre school.

Employees: 13.

Opportunities: Hires performers and production staff.

Application Procedures: Performers must send a resume and a headshot to the casting director; production applicants must send resume and cover letter to the production manager.

▶ **Internships**

Type: Hires production interns, management/administration interns, and assistants to the director. Interview and significant theater experience required for assistant to director intern. Open to college juniors, seniors, and graduates. **Applications Received:** 10-20.

Wings Theatre Company
The Archive Bldg.
154 Christopher St.
New York, NY 10014
Phone: (212)627-2961

Business Description: A nonprofit off-Broadway company producing works by American playwrights featuring family and gay issues. Friday nights house late-night comedy troupes.

Human Resources: Michael Hillyer, Managing Dir.

Application Procedures: Company posts openings in newspapers. For technical positions, send resume and cover letter to Jeffery Zorrick, Artistic Dir.

▶ **Internships**

Type: The company does not offer an internship program.

Wisdom Bridge Theatre
1559 W. Howard
Chicago, IL 60626
Phone: (312)743-0486
Fax: (312)743-1614

Business Description: The Wisdom Bridge Theatre, founded in 1974, is dedicated to the work of women and minority playwrights and actors. The theatre is involved in student matinees, school and senior center workshops, and other community outreach programs.

Employees: 20.

Application Procedures: Performers are jobbed in for each show. The best time to request an audition is the summer. Send resume and head shot to Sharon Phillips, Admin. Head.

▶ **Internships**

Contact: Stan Winiarski, Outreach Assoc.

Type: Offers unpaid internships for business and operations, development, marketing and public relations, management, art, production and stage management, and other areas. Open to college seniors, graduates, and graduate school students. **Number Available Annually:** 12. **Applications Received:** 100-200.

Application Procedure: Send resume and cover letter to the attention of Stan Winiarski. An interview is required.

Application Deadline: June 1 for fall; November 1 for spring; and April 1 for summer.

Wolf Trap Foundation for the Performing Arts
1624 Trap Rd.
Vienna, VA 22182
Phone: (703)255-1906
Fax: (703)255-1905

Business Description: Handles programming for several theatres, educational programs, ticket sales, marketing, and public relations.

Human Resources: Dawn-Marie Nous.

Application Procedures: Applicants should

send resume to the program and production department.

▶ Internships

Type: Offers paid internships for individuals who have completed at least one year of college. Internships are offered in public relations, development, technical theatre, accounting, human resources, education, administration, and other areas. **Number Available Annually:** 20.

Application Procedure: Write to the attention of the Internship Program.

At the same time that whale-size firms are whacking away the blubber, a net of 1.9 million new jobs will be created this year, estimates Dun & Bradstreet, and 80 percent of them will be at companies with fewer than 100 employees. The 500 fastest-growing private companies identified this month by *Inc.* magazine have an average of 145 workers. Despite the rocky economy, many such outfits are thriving, often because they serve an ignored niche market or because they are being hired by downsizing giants to handle work that once was handled in-house.

Source: U.S. News & World Report

Women's Project and Productions

7 W. 63rd St.
New York, NY 10023
Phone: (212)873-3040
Fax: (212)873-3788

Business Description: Established in 1978, Women's Project and Productions is a nonprofit theatre that presents the work of female playwrights and directors.

Employees: 7.

▶ Internships

Contact: Tim Terramin, Asst. to Artistic Dir.

Type: Offers unpaid internships in such areas as management, development, and marketing.

Open to college students and graduates, graduate school students, and others. College credit is available. **Number Available Annually:** 6. **Applications Received:** 50.

Woodpeckers Tap Dance Center & Inter Arts Space

170 Mercer St.
New York, NY 10012
Phone: (212)219-8284

Business Description: Presents tap dance performances and theatre and jazz music events.

Human Resources: Elizabeth Gee, Studio Mgr.

Application Procedures: To audition, send resume to Brenda Bufalino, Artistic Dir.

Worcester Foothills Theater

074 Worcester Center
100 Front St.
Worcester, MA 01608-1402
Phone: (508)754-3314

Business Description: A nonprofit professional theatre.

Application Procedures: Interested performers should send resume and photo to Doug Landrum, Assoc. Prod. for Productions.

▶ Internships

Type: Offers unpaid internships to high school and college students. College credit is available. Placement and housing assistance provided. Interns receive free theatre tickets and parking reimbursement. Full-time employment possible. **Number Available Annually:** 10. **Applications Received:** 20-40.

Duties: Interns are responsible for public relations/marketing, administration/business, production, and stage management tasks.

Application Procedure: Those interested in administrative internships should write to Mr. Marshall Weiss; for technical internships, to Doug Landrum.

Yale Repertory Theatre

Yale Sta., Box 1903A
New Haven, CT 06520
Phone: (203)432-1515

Business Description: The professional arm of the Yale School of Drama, the theatre features classical and new plays, workshops, and readings.

Application Procedures: Send resume/ pictures with a self-addressed stamped envelope to the company manager, c/o Yale School Repertory Theatre, PO Box 208244, New Haven, CT 06520. Management and technical staff position openings are posted in *ArtSEARCH*.

▶ **Internships**

Type: Offers unpaid internships in technical design to students at the theatre. Students receive certificate upon completion.

Additional Companies

Actors' Playhouse
100 Seventh Ave. S.
New York, NY 10019
Phone: (212)691-6226

Actors Theatre of Louisville
316-320 W. Main St.
Louisville, KY 40202-4218
Phone: (502)584-1205

Ambassador Theatre
219 W. 49th St.
New York, NY 10036
Phone: (212)944-3700

Art & Work Ensemble
Synchronicity Space
55 Mercer St.
New York, NY 10013
Phone: (212)925-3960

Asia Society
Lila Acheson Wallace Auditorium
725 Park Ave.
New York, NY 10021
Phone: (212)517-2742

Astor Place Theatre
434 Lafayette St.
New York, NY 10003
Phone: (212)254-4370

Belasco Theatre
111 W. 44th St.
New York, NY 10036
Phone: (212)239-6200

The Big Apple Circus
35 W. 35th St., 9th Fl.
New York, NY 10001
Phone: (212)368-2500

Booth Theatre
222 W. 45th St.
New York, NY 10036
Phone: (212)239-6200

Broadhurst Theatre
235 W. 44th St.
New York, NY 10036
Phone: (212)239-6200

Broadway Theatre
53rd St. & Broadway
New York, NY 10036
Phone: (212)239-6200

Brooks Atkinson Theatre
256 W. 47th St.
New York, NY 10036
Phone: (212)719-4099

Centerfold Productions
Church of St. Paul and St. Andrew
263 W. 86th St.
New York, NY 10024
Phone: (212)866-4454

Cine Companies Inc.—Pacific Grip and Lighting
433 8th Ave. N.
Seattle, WA 98102
Phone: (206)622-8540

Circle-in-the Square/Downtown
159 Bleecker St.
New York, NY 10019
Phone: (212)307-2700

City Center
131 W. 55th St.
New York, NY 10109-3818
Phone: (212)581-7907

Coney Island, USA
Boardwalk & W. 12th St.
Brooklyn, NY 11224
Phone: (212)372-5159

Cort Theatre
138 W. 48th St.
New York, NY 10036
Phone: (212)239-6200

Dance Space Inc.
Evolving Arts Theatre
622 Broadway
New York, NY 10012
Phone: (212)777-8067

Ensemble Studio Theatre
549 W. 52nd St.
New York, NY 10019
Phone: (212)247-4982

Ethel Barrymore Theatre
243 W. 47th St.
New York, NY 10036
Phone: (212)239-6200

Eugene O'Neill Theatre
230 W. 49th St.
New York, NY 10036
Phone: (212)239-6200

Evolving Arts Theatre
Dance Space
622 Broadway
New York, NY 10012
Phone: (212)777-8067

Gershwin Theatre
51st St. West of Broadway
New York, NY 10019
Phone: (212)586-6510

Harold Clurman Theatre
412 W. 42nd St.
New York, NY 10036
Phone: (212)594-2370

Helen Hayes Theatre
240 W. 44th St.
New York, NY 10036
Phone: (212)944-9450

Hudson Guild Theatre
441 W. 26th St.
New York, NY 10001
Phone: (212)760-9800

Imperial Theatre
249 W. 45th St.
New York, NY 10036
Phone: (212)239-6200

Interart Theatre
Women's Interart Center
549 W. 52nd St.
New York, NY 10019
Phone: (212)246-1050

Interspace Inc. Technique Mirage
225 Rogers St. NE
Atlanta, GA 30317
Phone: (404)378-6654

Jean Cocteau Repertory
Bowerie Lane Theatre
330 Bowery
New York, NY 10012
Phone: (212)677-0060

Jewish Repertory Theatre
Playhouse 91
316 E. 91st. St.
New York, NY 10128
Phone: (212)831-2000

John Golden Theatre
252 W. 45th St.
New York, NY 10036
Phone: (212)239-6200

Joyce Theater
175 8th Ave.
New York, NY 10113
Phone: (212)242-0800

Kaleidoscope Dancers for Children
University Theatre, NYU
35 W. 4th St.
New York, NY
Phone: (212)998-5407

La Jolla Playhouse
Box 12039
La Jolla, CA 92039
Phone: (619)534-6760

La Mama, Etc.
74A E. 4th St.
New York, NY 10003
Phone: (212)254-6468
Fax: (212)254-7597

Lehman College Center for the Performing Arts
Bedford Park Blvd. W. & Paul Ave.
Bronx, NY 10468
Phone: (718)960-8833
Fax: (718)960-8935

Lincoln Center Theater
150 W. 65th St.
New York, NY 10023
Phone: (212)239-6200

Little People's Theatre Company
Courtyard Playhouse
39 Grove St.
New York, NY 10014
Phone: (212)765-9540

Longacre Theatre
220 W. 48th St.
New York, NY 10036
Phone: (212)239-6200

Lunt-Fontanne Theatre
205 W. 46th St.
New York, NY 10036
Phone: (212)575-9200

Lyceum Theatre
149 W. 45th St.
New York, NY 10036
Phone: (212)239-6200

Majestic Theatre
247 W. 44th St.
New York, NY 10036
Phone: (212)239-6200

Marquis Theatre
1535 Broadway & 45th St.
New York, NY 10036
Phone: (212)382-0100

Martin Beck Theatre
302 W. 45th St.
New York, NY 10036
Phone: (212)239-6200

Marymount Manhattan Theatre
Marymount Manhattan College
221 E. 71st St.
New York, NY 10021
Phone: (212)517-0475

Minetta Lane Theatre
18 Minetta Lane
New York, NY 10012
Phone: (212)420-8000

Minnesota Dance Alliance
528 Hennepin Ave., Ste. 600
Minneapolis, MN 55403
Phone: (612)340-1900
Fax: (612)340-9919

Minskoff Theatre
200 W. 45th St.
New York, NY 10036
Phone: (212)869-0550

Music Box Theatre
239 W. 45th St.
New York, NY 10036
Phone: (212)239-6200

Music Fair Group Inc.
176 Swedesford Rd.
Devon, PA 19333
Phone: (215)879-5900

Music Society
1801 W. St. Andrews
Midland, MI 48640
Phone: (517)631-1072

National Improvisational Theatre
222 8th Ave.
New York, NY 10011
Phone: (212)243-7224

New York State Theater
Lincoln Center
65th St. & Broadway
New York, NY 10023
Phone: (212)870-5570

**NYU Washington Square
Repertory Dance Company**
University Theatre
35 W. 4th St.
New York, NY 10012
Phone: (212)998-5278

Opera Company of Philadelphia
30 S. 15th St.
The Graham Bldg., 20th Fl.
Philadelphia, PA 19102
Phone: (215)981-1450
Fax: (215)981-1455

Orpheum Theatre
126 2nd Ave.
New York, NY 10003
Phone: (212)477-2477

Otrabanda Company
345 E. 5th St., Apt. 1C
New York, NY 10003

Palace Theatre
1564 Broadway & 47th St.
New York, NY 10036
Phone: (212)730-8200

Paper Mill Playhouse
Brookside Dr.
Millburn, NJ 07041
Phone: (201)379-3636

Peggy Spina Tap Company
Spina Loft
115 Prince St.
New York, NY 10012
Phone: (212)674-8885

Perry Street Theatre
31 Perry St.
New York, NY
Phone: (212)255-7190

Pittsburgh Civic Light Opera
719 Liberty Ave.
Pittsburgh, PA 15222
Phone: (412)281-3973
Fax: (412)281-5339

Plymouth Theatre
236 W. 45th St.
New York, NY 10036
Phone: (212)239-6200

Qwirk Production
1 Dream Theatre
232 W. Broadway
New York, NY 10013
Phone: (212)595-5673

Richard Rodgers Theatre
226 W. 46th St.
New York, NY 10036
Phone: (212)221-1211

Ridiculous Theatrical Company
Charles Ludlam Theatre
1 Sheridan Sq.
New York, NY 10014
Phone: (212)691-2271

Risa Jaroslow & Dancers
Arts at University Settlement
184 Eldridge St. at Rivington
New York, NY 10002
Phone: (212)674-9120

Royale Theatre
22 W. 45th St.
New York, NY 10036
Phone: (212)239-6200

Starstruck Entertainment Inc.
PO Box 121996
Nashville, TN 37212
Phone: (615)742-8835
Fax: (615)256-7686

The Tribeca Performing Arts Center
BMCC Campus
119 Chambers St., Rm S110B
New York, NY 10007
Phone: (212)346-8510

Union Square Theatre
100 E. 17th St.
New York, NY 10003
Phone: (212)505-9251

Village Gate/Top of the Gate
160 Bleecker St.
New York, NY 10012
Phone: (212)475-5120

Vivian Beaumont Theatre
150 W. 65th St.
New York, NY 10023
Phone: (212)362-7600

Walter Kerr Theatre
219 W. 48th St.
New York, NY 10036
Phone: (212)239-6200

Wave Hill
Wave Hill House/Armor Hall
675 W. 252 St.
Bronx, NY 10471
Phone: (718)549-3200

The Western Stage
156 Homestead Ave.
Salinas, CA 93901
Phone: (407)755-6990
Fax: (408)755-6954

Whitney Museum of American Art at Philip Morris
120 Park Ave. at 42nd St.
New York, NY 10003
Phone: (212)878-2453

Winter Garden Theatre
1634 Broadway & 50th St.
New York, NY 10019
Phone: (212)239-6200

WPA Theatre
519 W. 23rd St.
New York, NY 10011
Phone: (212)206-0523

CAREER
RESOURCES

CHAPTER TWENTY-THREE

Career Resources

The Career Resources chapter covers additional sources of job-related information that will aid you in your job search. It includes full, descriptive listings for sources of help wanted ads, professional associations, employment agencies and search firms, career guides, professional and trade periodicals, and basic reference guides and handbooks. Each of these sections is arranged alphabetically by organization, publication, or service name. For complete details on the information provided in this chapter, consult the introductory material at the front of this directory.

Sources of Help Wanted Ads

Advance Job Listings
PO Box 900
New York, NY 10020

Affirmative Action Register for Effective Equal Opportunity Recruitment
AAR, Inc.
8356 Olive Blvd.
St. Louis, MO 63132
Phone: (314)991-1335

Green, Warren H., editor. Published monthly. $15.00/year. Provides listing of state, university, and other publicly-funded positions directed to women, minorities, veterans, and handicapped job seekers.

American Dance Guild—Job Express Registry
American Dance Guild (ADG)
31 W. 21st St.
3rd Fl.
New York, NY 10010
Phone: (212)627-3790

Eleven times/year. $7.00/issue for members; $12.00/issue for nonmembers. Newsletter containing nationwide job listings for dance performers, choreographers, educators, administrators, and students of dance. Provides information on auditions, competitions, and awards.

Art Direction
10 East 39th St.
New York, NY 10016
Phone: (212)889-6500
Fax: (212)889-6504

Monthly. $27.50/year; $4.00/single issue.

Art SEARCH

Theatre Communications Group (TCG)
355 Lexington Ave.
New York, NY 10017
Phone: (212)697-5230

Biweekly. Employment bulletin.

Billboard Magazine

BPI Communications, Inc.
1515 Broadway
39th Fl.
New York, NY 10036
Phone: (212)764-7300

Timothy White, editor-in-chief. Weekly. $178.00/year. International magazine of music and home entertainment geared toward professionals in the music industry and related fields.

> **F**or twentysomethings not yet burdened with minivans and mortgages, the risks of signing on with a small company often pale beside the payoff. Small companies, it is true, are far more prone to going under. And one individual's decisions, right or wrong, can weigh heavily—and visibly—on the bottom line. On the other hand, the lack of a bureaucracy forces rapid professional development.
>
> Source: *U.S. News & World Report*

The Black Collegian

1240 S. Broad St.
New Orleans, LA 70125
Phone: (504)821-5694

Quarterly. $10.00/year; $5.00/year for students; $2.50/issue. Career and job-oriented publication for black college students.

Career Woman

Equal Opportunity Publications, Inc.
44 Broadway
Greenlawn, NY 11740

Three times/year. $13.00/year. Recruitment magazine for women. Provides free resume service and assists women in identifying employers and applying for positions.

Creative Register

American Center for Design (ACD)
233 E. Ontario
Ste. 500
Chicago, IL 60611
Phone: (312)787-2018
Fax: (312)649-9518

Monthly. Referral service bulletin.

CSI National Career Network

Computer Search International Corporation (CSI)
7926 Jones Branch Dr.
Ste. 120
McLean, VA 22102
Phone: (302)749-1635

Online database that contains job listings from potential employers and candidate resumes from executive recruiting firms. Covers more than 40 technical and managerial job categories.

Daily Variety

Daily Variety Ltd./Cahners Publishing Co.
5700 Wilshire Blvd.
Ste. 120
Los Angeles, CA 90036
Phone: (213)857-6600
Fax: (213)932-0393

Daily, except Saturday, Sunday, and most holidays. $119.00/year; $.75/single issue.

Dance Exercise Today

International Dance Exercise Association
2437 Morena Blvd.
2nd Fl.
San Diego, CA 92110

Directory of Internships

Ready Reference Press
PO Box 5249
Santa Monica, CA 90409
Phone: (213)474-5175

$95.00. Lists internship opportunities in many fields of interest, including, but not limited to arts, journalism, public relations, education, law, environmental affairs, business, engineering, and computer science. In addition, cites summer internship opportunities, work/study programs, and specialized opportunities for high school and undergraduate students. Indexed by subject, geography, and program.

Equal Opportunity Magazine

Equal Opportunity Publications
44 Broadway
Greenlawn, NY 11740

Three times/year. $13.00/year. Minority recruitment magazine. Includes a resume service.

GTM Newsletter

Guild of Temple Musicians (GTM)
Bet Shalom Congregation
201 9th Ave. N.
Hopkins, MN 55343
Phone: (612)933-8525
Fax: (612)933-3238

Three times/year. Free to members. Lists employment opportunities, educational opportunities, guild news, calendar of events, book reviews, and musical transcriptions.

How

F & W Publications, Inc.
1507 Dana Ave.
Cincinnati, OH 45207
Phone: (513)531-2222
Fax: (513)531-1843

Bimonthly. $41.00/year; $7.00/single issue.

International Musician

American Federation of Musicians
1501 Broadway
New York, NY 10036
Phone: (212)669-1330

Monthly. $60.00/year.

International Women's Writing Guild Network

International Womens Writing Guild (IWWG)
Box 810
Gracie Station
New York, NY 10028
Phone: (212)737-7536

Six times/year. Free to members. Lists employment opportunities, awards, and calendar of events. Helps women writers publish their work.

Internship and Job Opportunities in New York City and Washington, D.C.

The Graduate Group
86 Norwood Rd.
West Hartford, CT 06117
$27.50.

Internships: On-the-Job Training Opportunities for All Types of Careers

Peterson's Guides, Inc.
20 Carnegie Center
PO Box 2123
Princeton, NJ 08543-2123
Phone: (609)243-9111
Fax: (609)243-9150

Annual, December. $27.95, plus $3.00 shipping. Covers: 850 corporations, social service organizations, government agencies, recreational facilities (including parks and forests), entertainment industries, and science and research facilities which offer about 50,000 apprenticeships and internships in 23 different career areas. Entries include: Organization name, address, name of contact; description of internship offered, including duties, stipend, length of service; eligibility requirements; deadline for application and application procedures. Arrangement: Classified by subject (arts, communications, business, etc.). Indexes: Subject/organization name, geographical.

Job Contact Bulletin

Southeastern Theatre Conference (SETC)
University of North Carolina - Greensboro
506 Stirling St.
Greensboro, NC 27412
Phone: (919)272-3645

Bimonthly. Free for members. Includes

directory of affairs and news of conferences and conventions.

The Job HUNTER

University of Missouri-Columbia
Career Planning and Placement Center
100 Noyes Bldg.
Columbia, MO 65211

Biweekly. $75.00/year; $50.00/six months. Lists opportunities for college graduates with 0-3 years experience in many fields. Includes information on internships and summer jobs.

Jobs in Arts and Media Management: What They Are and How to Get One!

American Council for the Arts
1285 Avenue of the Americas
New York, NY 10019
Phone: (212)245-4510

Langley, Stephen, and Abruzzo, James. 1986. $19.95. Includes lists of about 150 sources of information on job opportunities in the arts, including organizations offering internships, job listings, graduate programs, and short-term study; professional groups concerned with theater, music, dance, opera, museum and gallery management, film, and telecommunication management. (Does not include popular music performing or music recording.) Entries include: For internships - Organization name, address, phone, description, requirements. For job referral associations and periodicals - Association or publisher name, address, fields covered, services offered, turn-around time, average number of jobs, cost of subscription or dues, comments. Arrangement: Classified by type of source.

Music Educators Journal

Music Educators National Conference
1902 Association Dr.
Reston, VA 22091-1597
Phone: (703)860-4000

Nine times/year. $41.00/year; $5.00/single issue.

The National Ad Search

National Ad Search, Inc.
PO Box 2083
Milwaukee, WI 53201

Fifty issues/year. $235.00/year; $145.00/six months; $75.00/three months. Contains listings of 'over 2,000 current career opportunities from over 72 employment markets.'

National Business Employment Weekly

Dow Jones and Company, Inc.
PO Box 300
Princeton, NJ 08543
Phone: (609)520-4000

Weekly. $199.00/year; $112.00/six months. Newspaper containing help-wanted advertising from four regional editions of the *Wall Street Journal*. Includes statistics and articles about employment opportunities and career advancements.

National Directory of Arts Internships

National Network for Artist Placement
935 West Ave. 37
Los Angeles, CA 90065
Phone: (213)222-4035

Biennial, odd years. $35.00, postpaid, payment with order. Includes about 800 internship opportunities in dance, music, theater, art, design, film, and video. Provides name of sponsoring organization, address, name of contact; description of positions available, eligibility requirements, stipend or salary (if any), application procedures. Classified by discipline.

National Directory of Internships

National Society for Internships and
Experiential Education
3509 Haworth Dr.
Ste. 207
Raleigh, NC 27609
Phone: (919)787-3263

Biennial, fall of odd years. $22.00, plus $2.50 shipping. Covers: Over 30,000 educational internship opportunities in 75 fields with over 2,650 organizations in the United States for youth and adults. Entries include: Organization name, address, phone, contact name, description of internship opportunities, including application procedures and deadlines, remuneration, and eligibility requirements. Arrangement: Classified by type of organization. Indexes: Geographical, organization name, career field.

National Employment Listing Service Bulletin

Sam Houston State University
College of Criminal Justice
Huntsville, TX 77341

Monthly. $30.00/year for individuals; $65.00/year for institutions/agencies.

New England Employment Week

PO Box 806
Rockport, ME 04856

The NonProfit Times

The NonProfit Times
PO Box 870
Wantagh, NY 11793-0870

Monthly. $39.00/year.

Opportunity Report

Job Bank, Inc.
PO Box 6028
Lafayette, IN 47903
Phone: (317)447-0549

Biweekly. $252.00/year. Lists 3,000-4,000 positions across the United States, from entry-level to upper management, in a variety of occupational fields. Ads are derived from newspapers, primarily in growth markets. Ads contain position description, employment requirements, and contact information.

Peterson's Job Opportunities for Business and Liberal Arts Graduates 1993

Peterson's
PO Box 2123
Princeton, NJ 08543-2123
Phone: (609)243-9111

Compiled by the Peterson's staff. 1993. $20.95 paperback. 300 pages. Lists hundreds of organizations that are hiring new business, humanities, and social science graduates in the areas of business and management. Explores how to match academic backgrounds to specific job openings. Provides information about opportunities for experienced personnel as well. Includes data on starting locations by city and state, summer jobs, co-op jobs, internships, and international assignments.

The Piano Quarterly

Box 815
Rader Rd.
Wilmington, VT 05363
Phone: (802)464-5149

Quarterly. $16.00/year; $5.00/single issue.

Placement Service Listing of Positions

College Art Association
275 7th Ave.
New York, NY 10001

Five times/year. Includes opportunities in academic institutions, museums, and foundations.

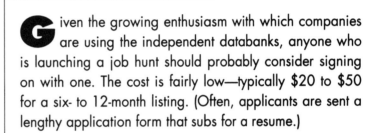

Given the growing enthusiasm with which companies are using the independent databanks, anyone who is launching a job hunt should probably consider signing on with one. The cost is fairly low—typically $20 to $50 for a six- to 12-month listing. (Often, applicants are sent a lengthy application form that subs for a resume.)

Source: *U.S. News & World Report*

Puppetry Journal

8005 Swallow Rd.
Macedonia, OH 44056

Spotlight on Dance

National Dance Association (NDA)
1900 Association Dr.
Reston, VA 22091
Phone: (703)476-3436
Fax: (703)476-9527

Three times/year. Free to members. Lists career opportunities. Includes reports on dance research, current information on dance education, professional preparation, and certification.

Summer Employment Directory of the United States

Peterson's Guides, Inc.
20 Carnegie Center
PO Box 2123
Princeton, NJ 08543-2123
Phone: (609)243-9111

Annual, December. $27.95, plus $3.00 shipping.

Covers: Camps, resorts, amusement parks, hotels, businesses, national parks, conference and training centers, ranches, and restaurants offering about 90,000 temporary summer jobs; listings are paid. Entries include: Name and address, length of employment, pay rate, fringe benefits, duties, qualifications, application deadline and procedure. Arrangement: Geographical, then by type of employer (camp, summer theater, etc.).

Tradition Magazine

National Traditional Music Association (NTMA)
PO Box 438
Walnut, IA 51577
Phone: (712)784-3001

Bimonthly. Free to members. Provides news about employment opportunities in traditional music; includes book, festival, and record reviews; offers current travel information.

Variety

Cahners Publishing Co.
475 Park Ave. S.
New York, NY 10016
Phone: (212)779-1100
Fax: (212)779-2706

Weekly. $100.00/year.

Westaf's National Job Bank

Western States Arts Federation
236 Montezuma Ave.
Santa FE, NM 87501
Phone: (505)988-1166
Fax: (505)982-9307

Biweekly. $15.00 for 6-issue subscription; $24.00 for 12-issue subscription; $36.00 for 24-issue subscription; sample issue free. Covers about 80-90 full- and part-time positions and temporary paid positions in visual, performing, and literary arts, arts education, and general arts administration. Entries include job title, salary, description of responsibilities, qualifications, application procedure and deadline, name and address of contact. Classified by field.

Where the Jobs Are: A Comprehensive Directory of 1200 Journals Listing Career Opportunities

Garrett Park Press
PO Box 190
Garrett Park, MD 20896
Phone: (301)946-2553

1989. $15.00; $14.00, prepaid. Contains list of approximately 1,200 journals that publish advertisements announcing job opportunities. Arranged alphabetically. Indexes: Occupational field.

Professional Associations

Actors' Equity Association (AEA)
165 W. 46th St.
New York, NY 10036
Phone: (212)869-8530
Fax: (212)719-9815

Membership: AFL-CIO. **Purpose:** Represents professional actors and stage managers. Maintains Actors' Equity Foundation that makes awards and grants to organizations or charities that work in the best interests of theatre. **Publication(s):** *Equity News*, monthly.

Actor's Fund of America
1501 Broadway
Ste. 518
New York, NY 10036
Phone: (212)221-7300
Fax: (212)764-0238

Membership: Human service organization of the entertainment industry. Activities: Sponsors survival jobs program to provide employment for those between engagements. Provides emergency financial assistance to those in need; makes available social services, counseling and psychotherapy, health and education services, and nursing home care and retirement housing. Conducts substance abuse programs and blood drives.

Affiliate Artists
37 W. 65th St.
New York, NY 10023
Phone: (212)580-2000

Membership: Professional singers, actors,

instrumentalists, mimes, and conductors. **Purpose:** To promote the career development of professional performing artists.

Alliance of Resident Theatres/New York (ART/NY)

131 Varick St.
Rm. 904
New York, NY 10013
Phone: (212)989-5257
Fax: (212)989-4880

Membership: Nonprofit professional theatres in New York City and interested theatre-related associations. Activities: Maintains job board and intern placement service, and provides career counseling. Promotes recognition of the nonprofit theatre community. Provides members with skills and information pertinent to their field. Facilitates discussion among the theatres; helps to solve problems of accessibility; serves as a public information source. Acts as advocate on behalf of members with government, corporate, and foundation funders to encourage greater support for New York's not-for-profit theatres. Operates a real estate project to assist theatres in the search for performance space. Sponsors seminars, roundtables, and individual consultations for members. Provides computer and financial assistance; operates small library.

American Association of Community Theatre (AACT)

c/o L. Ross Rowland
8209 N. Costa Mesa Dr.
Muncie, IN 47303
Phone: (317)288-0144

Membership: Community theatre organizations; individuals involved in community theatre. Activities: Maintains placement service and offers networking opportunities. Promotes community theatre. Sponsors Community Theatre Foundation, which provides travel funds so that theatre groups may participate in national festivals. Bestows awards. Publishes *AACT Directory of Community Theatres in the United States*, periodically.

American Association of Laban Movement Analysts (AALMA)

c/o Laban/Bartenieff Institute for Movement Studies
31 W. 27th St.
New York, NY 10001
Phone: (212)689-0740

Membership: Anthropologists, choreographers, dancers, dance instructors, actors, movement researchers, physical therapists, dance therapists, psychotherapists, management consultants, physical educators, and sports trainers. Activities: Provides job placement and training programs. Informs and demonstrates to other professionals the benefits of Laban Movement Analysis in their respective fields. Maintains library of audiotapes and videotapes.

American Center for Design (ACD)

233 E. Ontario
Ste. 500
Chicago, IL 60611
Phone: (312)787-2018
Fax: (312)649-9518

Membership: Design professionals, educators, and students. Activities: Offers placement service. Acts as informational, technical, and educational resource to the design community. Sponsors The 100 Show, an annual national design exhibition. Conducts workshops and seminars; bestows awards; provides specialized education. Maintains design gallery and 700 volume reference library.

American Classical League (ACL)

Miami University
Oxford, OH 45056
Phone: (513)529-7741
Fax: (513)529-7742

Membership: Teachers of classical languages in high schools and colleges. Activities: Maintains placement service. Promotes the teaching of Latin and other classical languages. Presents scholarship. Operates resource center to sell teaching aids to teachers of Latin and Greek.

American Conservatory Theatre Foundation (ACTF)
450 Geary St.
San Francisco, CA 94102
Phone: (415)749-2200
Fax: (415)771-4859

Activities: Operates placement service. Provides resources for the American Conservatory Theatre which functions as a repertory theatre and accredited acting school, offering a Master of Fine Arts degree. Holds national auditions for the MFA program in Chicago, IL, New York City, and Los Angeles, CA, usually in February. Holds student matinees, school outreach programs, and in-theatre discussions between artist and audiences. Conducts professional actor-training programs, a summer training congress, and a young conservatory evening academy program for children aged 8-18. Maintains biographical archives and 8000 volume library of plays. Offers children's services; provides speakers' bureau.

Third, start building your network. It's always easier to build one when you're working, because the topic of unemployment won't cloud your interaction. The easiest way is to involve yourself in an industry association, but don't overlook church groups, charities, and political organizations. Don't just join, participate. Make yourself known. Cultivate friendships, not just contacts.

Become known as a doer. I've run across folks who say they don't have time. Make time. It's your future at stake. No one said it would be easy.

Source: *Detroit Free Press*

American Council for the Arts (ACA)
1 E. 53rd St.
New York, NY 10022-4201
Phone: (212)223-2787

The council's activities emphasize advocacy, education, and private sector support. Maintains art library. **Publication(s):** Books on arts management, finance, law, marketing, and fundraising.

American Dance Guild (ADG)
31 W. 21st St., 3rd Fl.
New York, NY 10010
Phone: (212)627-3790

Membership: Teachers, performers, historians, critics, writers, and students in the field of dance, including ballet, modern dance, modern jazz dance, tap dance, and ethnological dance forms. **Purpose:** Sponsors professional seminars, workshops, and other projects. Initiates programs of national significance in the field. Maintains speakers' bureau; operates career counseling service and Job Express Registry, a monthly placement listing for people looking for work in the dance field. Makes available scholarships. **Publication(s):** *American Dance*, bimonthly. • *American Dance Guild—Job Express Registry*, eleven issues/year. • *Souvenir Journal*, annual. • Also publishes books and bibliographies on dance and dance education.

American Federation of Musicians of the United States and Canada (AFM)
Paramount Bldg.
1501 Broadway, Ste. 600
New York, NY 10036
Phone: (212)869-1330
Fax: (212)764-6134

Membership: AFL-CIO. Musicians interested in advancing the music industry. **Purpose:** Offers legal representation on issues dealing with breach of contract, job protection, and wage scale negotiations. **Publication(s):** *International Musician*, monthly.

American Federation of Television and Radio Artists (AFTRA)
260 Madison Ave.
New York, NY 10016
Phone: (212)532-0800

Membership: 75,000 television and radio artists. **Publication(s):** *AFTRA Magazine.* Quarterly.

American Guild of Musical Artists (AGMA)
1727 Broadway
New York, NY 10019
Phone: (212)265-3687

Membership: AFL-CIO. **Publication(s):** *AGMAzine*, five issues/year.

American Guild of Organists (AGO)

475 Riverside Dr., Ste. 1260
New York, NY 10115
Phone: (212)870-2310

Membership: Educational and service organization organized to advance the cause of organ and choral music and to maintain standards of artistic excellence of organists and choral conductors. **Purpose:** Offers professional certification in organ playing, choral and instrumental training, and theory and general knowledge of music. Sponsors competitions in organ performance and improvisation and two composition competitions. **Publication(s):** *American Organist*, monthly.

American Institute of Graphic Arts (AIGA)

1059 3rd Ave.
New York, NY 10021
Phone: (212)752-0813
Toll-free: 800-548-1634
Fax: (212)755-6749

Membership: Graphic designers, art directors, illustrators, packaging designers, and craftsmen involved in printing and allied graphic fields. **Purpose:** Sponsors exhibits and projects in the public interest. Annually awards medal for distinguished achievement in the graphic arts. Sponsors traveling exhibitions. Operates gallery. Maintains library of design books and periodicals; offers slide archives. **Publication(s):** *AIGA Journal of Graphic Design*, quarterly. • *AIGA Membership Directory*, biennial. • *AIGA News*, bimonthly. • *Graphic Design USA*, annual.

American Music Center

30 W. 26th St., Ste. 1001
New York, NY 10010
Phone: (212)366-5260

Promotes American music performance and acknowledgement. Serves as an information center for performing artists and managers.

American Society of Composers, Authors, and Publishers

1 Lincoln Plz.
New York, NY 10023
Phone: (212)595-3050

Clearinghouse in the field of music performing

rights. **Membership:** 35,000 composers, lyricists, and publishers. **Publication(s):** *Membership Directory*. Periodic. Also publishes *ASCAP in Action* • *Biographical Dictionary* • *How to Get Your Song Published* • *ASCAP-The Facts* • *ASCAP Copyright Law Symposium* and other books.

American Symphony Orchestra League

777 14th St. NW, Ste. 500
Washington, DC 20005
Phone: (202)628-0099
Fax: (202)783-7228

Membership: Symphony orchestras; associate members include educational institutions, arts councils, public libraries, business firms, orchestra professionals, and individuals interested in symphony orchestras. **Purpose:** Engages in extensive research on diverse facets of symphony orchestra operations and development. Provides consulting services for orchestras, their boards, and volunteer organizations. Sponsors management seminars and workshops for professional symphony orchestra administrative and artistic staff, volunteers, and prospective management personnel. Maintains employment services; collects and distributes resource materials, financial data, and statistical reports on many aspects of orchestra operations. Compiles statistics; bestows awards; sponsors educational programs; maintains resource center. **Publication(s):** *Orchestra/Business Directory*, annual. • *Symphony*, bimonthly. • Also publishes *Principles of Orchestra Management*, *The Gold Book: Director of Successful Projects for Volunteers, Orchestra, Education Programs*, and *Youth Orchestra Handbook* (resource books).

Associated Actors and Artistes of America

165 W. 46th St.
New York, NY 10036
Phone: (212)869-0358

Membership: International body consisting of 7 national unions within the performing arts field, each autonomous in its particular jurisdiction. Members are: Actors' Equity Association; American Federation of Television and Radio Artists; American Guild of Musical Artists; American Guild of Variety Artists;

Hebrew Actors' Union; Italian Actors' Union; Screen Actors Guild; Screen Extras' Guild.

Associated Writing Programs (AWP)

Old Dominion University
1411 N. 49th St.
Norfolk, VA 23529-0079
Phone: (804)683-3839

Membership: Writers; students and teachers in writing programs; editors, publishers, and creative and professional writers. Activities: Helps writers get published and find jobs; and enhances the quality of literary education. Operates placement service. Sponsors competitions.

Strategy: Until recently, most advice on career development focused on how to move up the corporate ladder. All that changed in the late 1980s, as corporate America began a series of cutbacks and layoffs that resulted in a broader, flatter hierarchy. Lateral moves were no longer taboo, and were even encouraged; some Fortune 500 corporations began using them as a way to keep valued employees challenged and motivated.

In fact, one of the trends in the personnel business is a new horizontal structure called "broad banding," in which employees are loosely organized into a few broad job categories, rather than the dozens of titles in traditional systems.

Source: *Working Woman*

Association for Theatre and Disability (ATD)

c/o William E. Rickert
Coll. of Liberal Arts
Wright State Univ.
Dayton, OH 45435

Membership: 150 individuals and organizations who work in the theatre with or as disabled persons; agencies promoting access to theatrical performances and drama activities. **Publication(s):** *ATD Newsletter.* 6x/year. • *Resources in Theatre and Disability.*

Association for Theatre in Higher Education (ATHE)

c/o Theatre Service
PO Box 15282
Evansville, IN 47716
Phone: (812)474-0549

Membership: Teachers, actors, students, directors, and other workers in all phases and at all levels of educational and community theatre. Activities: Operates placement service. Encourages excellence in postsecondary theatre training, production, and scholarship.

Association of Anglican Musicians (AAM)

c/o Susan Markley
Trinity Cathedral
310 W. 17th St.
Little Rock, AR 72206
Phone: (501)372-0294
Fax: (501)372-2147

Membership: Church musicians (laypersons or clergy) serving Episcopal and Anglican churches. Activities: Provides placement service. Encourages equitable compensation and benefits for professional church musicians. Works closely with seminaries toward the establishment and continuation of courses in music and the allied arts as they relate to worship and theology. Maintains biographical archives.

Association of Hispanic Arts (AHA)

173 E. 116th St.
New York, NY 10029
Phone: (212)860-5445

Provides technical assistance and educational seminars on Hispanic art. **Publication(s):** *AHA Hispanic Arts News.* 9 issues/year.

Association of Performing Arts Presenters

112 16th St. NW
Washington, DC 20036
Phone: (202)833-2787

Provides workshop and conferences to arts administrators and presenting organizations. **Publication(s):** *Bulletin.* Monthly. Trade newsletter. • *Inside Arts.* Quarterly. Articles focus on issues related to performing arts, trends, and industry personalities.

Choreographers Guild (CG)

256 S. Robertson
Beverly Hills, CA 90211
Phone: (213)275-2533

Membership: Choreographers united to promote their professional status and establish criteria for their responsibilities, salaries, and credentials. Activities: Operates placement service. Maintains library of records, video tapes, and Labanotations. Bestows awards; maintains hall of fame and biographical archives. Compiles statistics; conducts research.

Choreographers Theatre (CT)

94 Chambers St.
New York, NY 10007
Phone: (212)227-9067

Activities: Provides employment services, as well as a variety of production, administrative, and management services to the dance and arts community. Serves as the in-residence dance department of the New School for Social Research in New York City. Sponsors Laura Foreman Dance Performance Art Theatre which performs in New York City and on tour. Conducts symposia. Maintains tape library of original dance music, seminars, radio broadcasts, and interviews as well as videotapes of live performances. Division of Composers and Choreographers Theatre.

Council of Writers Organizations (CWO)

c/o WIW
220 Woodward Bldg.
733 15th St. NW
Washington, DC 20005
Phone: (202)347-4973

Membership: Twenty-four organizations representing 35,000 writers. Activities: Maintains referral service. Serves as an umbrella agency for organizations representing writers. Provides a means of sharing information among organizations and their members as well as a voice for professional writers.

Country Music Showcase International (CMSI)

110 Garfield St.
PO Box 368
Carlisle, IA 50047
Phone: (515)989-3748

Membership: Professional and amateur performers, agents, fan club presidents, journalists, and songwriters. Activities: Offers placement service. Works with communities and nonprofit organizations that wish to sponsor Country Classic's U.S.A., a stage show owned and produced by CMSI, by offering professional management and promotional services. Maintains small library. Sponsors festivals and competitions; bestows awards. Operates charitable program, educational programs, and speakers bureau. Maintains hall of fame, museum, and biographical archives. Compiles statistics.

D ancing Wheels, now under the auspices of the internationally known Cleveland Ballet, performs throughout the nation to a variety of audiences in theaters and schools, at local events, and on television. Its work has been choreographed to allow for the full participation of both partially disabled and able-bodied dancers.

Source: *Dance Magazine*

Dance Notation Bureau (DNB)

31 W. 21st St.
3rd Fl.
New York, NY 10010
Phone: (212)807-7899

Activities: Maintains placement service. Documents and preserves dance works through the use of graphic notation. Conducts research into movement related analysis techniques and programs. Maintains extension at Ohio State University, Columbus. Assists choreographers in copyrighting, licensing, and restaging of their dance works. Offers dance reconstruction service to members. Operates library of over 3000 notation scores of dance and movement, research, and analysis. Bestows annual Dance Service Award.

Dance Theatre Workshop

219 W. 19th St.
New York, NY 10011
Phone: (212)691-6500

Membership: Choreographers, artistic directors, and performing arts companies. Seeks to create and facilitate performance opportunities for choreographers, composers, and theatre artists and to stimulate the development of new and wider public audiences for the individual artist. **Publication(s):** *Poor Dancer's Almanac*. Published every five years. Manual and resource directory for artists. $10 for members; $15 for nonmembers. • *Poor Dancer's Almanac New(s)letter*. 3x/year. Contains announcements of special programs, offerings of discounted services, and articles by members and others.

Dance/USA

777 14th St., NW, Ste. 540
Washington, DC 20005
Phone: (202)628-0144

Membership: Professional modern dance, ballet, ethnic, jazz, and tap dance companies. **Publication(s):** *Update*. 7x/year. • *Journal*. Quarterly. Contains job listings.

Directors Guild of America (DGA)

7920 Sunset Blvd.
Hollywood, CA 90046
Phone: (310)289-2000
Fax: (310)289-2029

Membership: Independent. **Purpose:** Negotiates agreements for members. Bestows awards. **Publication(s):** *Directory of Members*, annual. • *Newsletter*, monthly.

Fastbreak Syndicate, Inc. (FSI)

PO Box 1626
Orem, UT 84059
Phone: (801)785-1300

Membership: Freelancers including writers, graphic artists, and photographers. Activities: Operates placement service. Seeks to enhance the profitability of freelance work and to facilitate the exchange of information and the marketing of finished works, using a computer network. Sponsors competitions for beginning freelancers; bestows awards. Maintains library and archive. Plans to conduct regional workshops and seminars.

Guild of Temple Musicians (GTM)

Bet Shalom Congregation
201 9th Ave. N.
Hopkins, MN 55343
Phone: (612)933-8525
Fax: (612)933-3238

Membership: Individuals involved in Jewish temple music including music directors, organists, choir directors, singers, and teachers. Membership is concentrated in the U.S., Canada, and Israel. Activities: Offers placement service. Conducts course in conjunction with School of Sacred Music, Hebrew Union College/Jewish Institute of Religion in New York City, leading to certification. Affiliated With: American Conference of Cantors.

Inter-American Music Council (CIDEM)

c/o Prof. Efrain Paesky
1889 F St. NW, 230-C
Washington, DC 20006
Phone: (202)458-3158
Fax: (202)458-3967

Membership: National music councils, music commissions, and musicians. Activities: Offers placement service. Promotes activity and study in musicology, folklore, and music education. Seeks to: establish centers for distribution of music by American composers; foster inter-American music festivals; support American activities in music by official and private organizations; solve problems related to copyrights and artistic property ownership. Sponsors competitions; bestows awards; maintains biographical archives.

International Association of Performing Arts Administrators

6065 Pickerel Dr.
Rockford, MI 49341
Phone: (616)874-6200

Publication(s): *Performing Arts Forum*. 10x/year. $25/year (free to members). Lists position openings.

International Tap Association (ITA)

3220 Connecticut Ave. NW
Ste. 112
Washington, DC 20008
Phone: (202)363-3960

Membership: Tap dancers, choreographers,

teachers, scholars, students, and interested individuals. Activities: Maintains placement service. Promotes the understanding, preservation, and development of tap dance as an art form. Sponsors educational programs and special projects. Encourages the creation of new performance venues, touring circuits, and presentation methods. Maintains biographical archives. Supports charitable programs including the Steve Condos Scholarship and Emergency Fund. Compiles statistics. Offers discount programs.

International Theatrical Agencies Association (ITAA)

c/o Hartland Talent Marketing
5775 Wayzetta Blvd.
Minneapolis, MN 55426
Phone: (612)545-8910
Fax: (612)541-1967

Membership: Theatrical agencies working to book entertainers and international acts into all live music venues. Activities: Provides placement service. Conducts educational seminars.

International Women's Writing Guild (IWWG)

Box 810
Gracie Station
New York, NY 10028
Phone: (212)737-7536

Membership: Women writers interested in expressing themselves through the written word professionally and for personal growth. Activities: Conducts talent bank, a job placement effort to place women in writing-related work. Participates in international network. Sponsors writing conferences and regional weekend writing workshops. Facilitates manuscript submissions to New York literary agents. Maintains health insurance program at group rates; offers legal referral services; bestows Artist of Life Award.

Jazz World Society (JWS)

c/o Jan A. Byrczek
250 W. 57th St.
Ste. 1212
New York, NY 10107
Phone: (212)713-0830

Membership: Professionals involved in jazz, including musicians, composers, record producers, distributors, collectors, and journalists; individuals who actively support jazz music. Activities: Provides placement service. Operates library of records, publications, books, and photographs. Sponsors competitions and jazz seminars. Presents awards; offers specialized education programs. Maintains hall of fame and biographical archives.

A lateral move often involves compromise in salary or title. To compensate, the job has to offer great training, experience, or exposure. You must be convinced that the position will help you develop valuable skills that will make you more marketable for your next big move.

Source: *Working Woman*

Louis Braille Foundation for Blind Musicians (LBF)

215 Park Ave., S.
New York, NY 10003
Phone: (212)982-7290

Activities: Offers placement services and helps obtain paid engagements. Purpose: 'To develop opportunities, vocational and avocational, for blind musicians and composers; to help blind musicians establish themselves professionally in their chosen field.' Auditions, evaluates, and counsels blind musicians and composers; provides dictation, transcription, and copyright services; and produces demonstration recordings. Sponsors 'showcase' concerts to present talented blind musicians to be judged by merit alone (in day care centers, old-age homes, and hospitals). When necessary, provides the blind musician with essentials for carrying on his professional activity (including wardrobe, union dues, publicity, and promotional help). Offers guidance in stage deportment and grooming. Provides braille transcriptions, musical instruments training, scholarship aid and any special equipment, based on financial need. Maintains concert bureau.

Musicians National Hot Line Association (MNHLA)

277 East 6100 South
Salt Lake City, UT 84107
Phone: (801)268-2000

Activities: Seeks to increase the employment of

musicians. Offers computerized search file to aid musicians and businesses in finding bands, and to help bands find musicians and gigs. Maintains computerized file of music educators looking for employment.

National Academy of Songwriters (NAS)

6381 Hollywood Blvd.
Ste. 780
Hollywood, CA 90028
Phone: (213)463-7178
Fax: (213)463-2146

Membership: Amateur and professional songwriters; others interested in the art, craft, and business of songwriting. Activities: Conducts placement service. Sponsors Songwriters Network, matching people who seek some type of collaboration; publishes bimonthly, *Open Ears*, tip sheet listing artists looking for songs. Conducts weekly song evaluation workshop and three semesters of workshops per year; offers ongoing, personalized counseling services; maintains legal panel and provides group legal services; operates bookstore of selected works and offers discounts; researches music-related questions for members; lobbies and testifies on legislative matters. Operates Songbank, a registry that provides evidence of original authorship of songs and acts as an interim alternative which takes less time and is less expensive than registration for federal copyright; maintains lead sheet service for songwriters who cannot write down the music they create. Bestows Helen King Award to best topical song. Operates Marilyn and Alan Bergman Library containing hundreds of works on all aspects of songwriting.

National Assembly of State Arts Agencies (NASAA)

1010 Vermont Ave., NW, Ste. 920
Washington, DC 20005
Phone: (202)347-6352

Membership: State arts councils.

National Association of Dramatic and Speech Arts (NADSA)

309 Cherokee Dr.
Blacksburg, VA 24060
Phone: (703)231-5805

Membership: Persons interested in educational, community, children's, and professional theatre. Area of interest is black and ethnic theatre and writers. Activities: Provides placement service. Bestows awards and sponsors annual Playwriting Contest.

National Association of Pastoral Musicians (NPM)

225 Sheridan St., NW
Washington, DC 20011
Phone: (202)723-5800
Fax: (202)723-2262

Membership: Parish clergy, parish musicians, music teachers, and others engaged or interested in Catholic church music. Activities: Offers placement service. Reviews current music; assists in parish music celebrations. Conducts research and specialized education programs. Operates Pastoral Press (publications division). Maintains speakers' bureau and library of 1000 volumes. Sponsors competitions; bestows awards.

National Association of Schools of Art and Design (NASAD)

11250 Roger Bacon Dr., No. 21
Reston, VA 22090
Phone: (703)437-0700

Purpose: Serves as the accrediting agency for educational programs in the visual arts and design. Aims are to: establish a national forum to stimulate the understanding and acceptance of the educational disciplines inherent in the creative arts in higher education in the U.S.; develop reasonable standards in areas of budget, faculty qualifications, faculty-student ratios, class time requirements, and library and physical facilities; evaluate, through the process of accreditation, schools of art and design and programs of studio art instruction in terms of the quality and results they achieve; assure students and parents that accredited art and design programs provide competent teachers, adequate equipment, and sound curricula; assist schools in developing their programs and encourage self-evaluation and continuing self-improvement. **Publication(s):** *Directory*, annual. • *Handbook*, biennial.

National Association of Schools of Dance

11250 Roger Bacon Dr., No. 21
Reston, VA 22090
Phone: (703)437-0700

Purpose: Serves as the accrediting agency for educational programs in dance. Provides prospective students with current, accurate information about schools offering instruction in dance. Seeks to establish standards in the field regarding budget, class time requirements, faculty qualifications, faculty-student ratios, and library and physical facilities. Fosters public understanding and acceptance of educational disciplines inherent in the creative arts in the nation's system of higher education. Encourages high-quality teaching, as well as varied and experimental methods and theories of dance instruction. Provides national representation in matters pertaining to dance and affecting member institutions and their goals. Encourages the collaboration of individuals and members in general assistance and counseling in program development and encourages self-evaluation and continuing efforts toward improvement. Evaluates dance schools and dance instruction programs through voluntary accreditation processes; assures students and parents that accredited programs offer competent instructors and adequate curricula and facilities.

National Association of Schools of Theatre

11250 Roger Bacon Dr., No. 21
Reston, VA 22090
Phone: (703)437-0700

Purpose: Accrediting agency for postsecondary educational programs in theatre. Provides prospective students with current, accurate information about schools offering instruction in theatrics. Seeks to improve educational practices and maintain high professional standards in theatre education. Counsels and assists institutions in developing their programs and engourages the cooperation of professional theatre groups and individuals in the formulation of appropriate curricula and standards.

National Association of Teachers of Singing (NATS)

2800 University Blvd., N.
Jacksonville, FL 32211
Phone: (904)744-9022

Membership: Singing and voice instructors in private studios, conservatories, schools, colleges, and other institutions. Activities: Provides a placement service for members. Encourages the highest standards of the vocal art and ethical principles in the teaching of singing. Promotes vocal education and research at all levels.

> The road to success has also been widened by a decade of radical changes in office life. The star businesses of the '80s were not corporate giants, long on control and conformity; they were freewheeling, entrepreneurial outfits that encouraged individuality. As companies like Ben & Jerry's and Microsoft became pop icons, their success gave millions of Americans the subversive idea that serious work did not demand total suppression of self. Employees began asking for flexible schedules and other rule bending because they knew that such arrangements worked elsewhere.
>
> Source: *Working Woman*

National Council for Culture and Art (NCCA)

1600 Broadway
Ste. 611C
New York, NY 10019
Phone: (212)757-7933

Membership: Artists, civic and business leaders, professional performers, and visual arts organizations. Activities: Offers placement services and employment opportunities. Sponsors art programs and spring and fall concert series. Operates Opening Night, a cable television show. Bestows annual Monarch Award and President's Award, and sponsors annual Monarch Scholarship Program. Provides children's services; conducts charitable program; maintains hall of fame. Plans to conduct Minority Playwrights Forum, Dance Festival U.S.A., Vocal and Instrumental Competition, Film and Video Festival, and Concerts U.S.A.

National Dance Association (NDA)

1900 Association Dr.
Reston, VA 22091
Phone: (703)476-3436
Toll-free: 800-321-0789
Fax: (703)476-9527

Membership: Public and private schools; college teachers of dance. **Purpose:** Promotes the development of sound philosophies and policies for dance as education through conferences, convention programs, special projects, and publications. Acts as advocate for better dance education programs through liaison activities with government, foundations, and special agencies. Provides reports and publications on dance research, career opportunities, current information on dance education, professional preparation, and certification. Maintains oral history archives of leaders in dance. Presents annual Heritage Award for outstanding contributions to the field of dance. Offers placement service and speakers' bureau; makes consultant referrals; sponsors seminars. **Publication(s):** *Dance Directory*, biennial. • *Focus on Dance*, biennial. • *Journal of Physical Education, Recreation, and Dance*, nine issues/year. • *Spotlight on Dance*, three issues/year. • *Update*, nine issues/year. • Also publishes books, pamphlets, and audio/visuals.

National Traditional Music Association (NTMA)

PO Box 438
Walnut, IA 51577
Phone: (712)784-3001

Membership: Individuals interested in the preservation, presentation, and perpetuation of traditional acoustic country, folk, honkytonk, ragtime, mountain, and bluegrass music celebrating contributions of U.S. settlers and pioneers; country music associations. Activities: Maintains placement service. Holds annual Old-Time Country Music Contest and Pioneer Exposition Festival to gather and disseminate information and foster appreciation of settling pioneer music, arts, crafts, recipes, stories, religious dogma, survival techniques, and lifestyles. Conducts international seminars and workshops; holds jam sessions; sponsors booths and offers hands-on music and craft experiences; operates charitable program; offers children's services. Sponsors championship contests in numerous categories, including:

Great Plains Story Telling; Hank Williams Songwriting; International Country Singer; Jimmie Rodgers Yodeling; Mid-West Horse Shoe Pitching; National Bluegrass Band; National Harmonica Playing. Bestows awards and prizes, including free recording studio time; free albums; guest appearances in Shreveport, LA and Nashville, TN; concert performances and tours abroad; free musical instuments. Programs are taped and televised by various local, national, and international stations. Established Pioneer Music Museum, MidAmerica Old-Time Fiddlers Hall of Fame, and Iowa Country Music Hall of Fame.

New England Theatre Conference (NETC)

50 Exchange St.
Waltham, MA 02154
Phone: (617)893-3120

Membership: Individuals and theatre-producing groups in New England who are actively engaged in or have a particular interest in theatre activity either professionally or as an avocation. Activities: Offers placement service. Activities include: auditions for jobs in New England summer and equity theatres; Theatrical Talent Registry (listing actors, directors, and technicians); five-day Drama Festival for community theatre groups; workshops on performance, administrative, and technical aspects of production; Annual Readers' Theatre Mini-Festival. Provides speakers' bureau and consultant services which are available for monthly programs or consulting on various aspects of theatre production. Divisions and committees hold workshops throughout the year geared to particular theatre areas. Maintains library and archives. Bestows: Annual Award for Outstanding Creative Achievement in the American Theatre; annual special awards and regional citations for theatre achievement nationally and regionally; annual John Gassner Memorial Play Writing Award for new one-act and full-length plays; annual Moss Hart Memorial Award for outstanding production of a full-length play with positive values; annual Community Theatre Drama Award for best play entered in annual drama festival.

Opera America
777 14th St., NW, Ste. 520
Washington, DC 20005
Phone: (202)347-9262

The organization's information service offers opera and musical theatre resources such as a computerized database and other files. Sponsors an annual conference. **Membership:** Opera and musical theatre management.

Performing Arts Resources
270 Lafayette St., Ste. 809
New York, NY 10012
Phone: (212)966-8658

Clearinghouse offering production/administration services, consultations, production services, and referral services. **Publication(s):** *Newsletter.* Quarterly.

Presbyterian Association of Musicians (PAM)
1000 E. Morehead St.
Charlotte, NC 28204
Phone: (704)333-9071

Membership: Organists, choir directors, singers, churches, clergy, directors of Christian education, and interested persons of all denominations. Activities: Acts as a clearinghouse for job referrals. Publishes *Guidelines for Committees Seeking to Employ Church Musicians in Presbyterian Churches.* PAM's objective is to develop use of music and the arts in the life and worship of individual congregations. Offers assistance in the areas of worship, music, and the arts. Conducts continuing education festivals; sponsors choir camps. Promotes the professional status of church musicians and recommends salaries and benefits to churches; certifies church musicians. Maintains biographical archives.

Screen Actors Guild (SAG)
7065 Hollywood Blvd.
Hollywood, CA 90028
Phone: (213)465-4600
Fax: (213)856-6603

Screen actors' labor union. **Membership:** 75,000. **Publication(s):** *Screen Actor.* Quarterly. Covers union activities, general interest topics, and includes book reviews and obituaries. $7.00/year for nonmembers. • *Screen Actor Hollywood.* Quarterly. Regional newsletter.

Covers official business of the guild and general interest topics.

Women Directors: The 80% Impact

Call them pragmatic: Women who sit on the boards of directors today are more likely to consider corporate women's advancement a business issue than a personal mission, says Catalyst, the New York-based research organization. In a new survey of 162 female directors of the Fortune 1000, 80 percent say they've had an impact on their companies' sensitivity to issues that affect women.

Comparing its research with a 1977 Burson-Marsteller study of 31 women directors, Catalyst found that the pool of women with business credentials has, not surprisingly, expanded. While the vast majority in 1977 came from academia, the arts, and nonprofits, more than 40 percent now have solid experience in the corporate sector.

Source: *Working Woman*

Show Business Association (SBA)
1501 Broadway
New York, NY 10036
Phone: (212)354-7600

Membership: Writers, performers, producers, editors, directors, designers, artists, and audiences in the entertainment field. Activities: Operates placement service. Participates in political campaigns and the drafting of related legislation; lobbies at city, state, and national levels; conducts training programs in the arts field. Sponsors competitions and bestows monetary awards annually for excellence; maintains biographical archives; compiles statistics. Maintains library of 24,000 volumes. Publications include: *How to Produce a Show and Film* (annual), *Angels* (listing of investors for shows, films, and art programs), *Summer Theatres* (annual), *Models Guide* (annual), and *Show Business* (weekly tabloid).

Society of Composers
PO Box 296
Old Chelsea Sta.
New York, NY 10013-0296
Phone: (718)899-2605

Membership: Professional composers.

Purpose: Concerned with the exchange of music and performers, the printing and recording of music, etc. **Publication(s):** *Journal of Music Scores.* Semiannual.

Southeastern Theatre Conference (SETC)

University of North Carolina - Greensboro
506 Stirling St.
Greensboro, NC 27412
Phone: (919)272-3645

Membership: Individuals and theatre organizations involved in university, college, community, professional, children's, and secondary school theatres. Activities: Offers job contact service; holds annual auditions for summer indoor and outdoor theatres, and fall auditions for professional theatres. Purpose is to bring together people interested in theatre and theatre artists and craftspeople from 10 southeastern states of the U.S. in order to promote high standards and to stimulate creativity in all phases of theatrical endeavor. Runs new play project and maintains central office for business and communication. Bestows awards. Maintains biographical archives; sponsors design competition; compiles statistics.

Theatre Communications Group (TCG)

355 Lexington Ave.
New York, NY 10017
Phone: (212)697-5230

Collects and publishes theatre operations information, with an emphasis on nonprofit, professional resident theatre companies. **Membership:** Theatre management. **Publication(s):** *Theatre Profiles.* Biennial. Surveys noncommercial theatres. • *Theatre Facts.* Provides financial and productivity information to members. • *Theatre Directory.* Listing of theatres, artistic directors, managing directors, and other information. • *American Theatre.* Monthly. Focuses on theatre as a profession and includes articles and information on acting, directing, government, management, and related topics. • *ArtSearch.* Provides job search information.

United Scenic Artists (USA)

575 8th Ave.
New York, NY 10018
Phone: (212)581-0300

Labor union providing contracts and benefits for professional scenic designers, scenic artists, costume and lighting designers, diorama and display workers, mural artists, and costume painters employed by TV, theatre, motion picture studios, and producers of commercials. **Membership:** 2,000. **Publication(s):** *Directory.* Monthly.

United States Institute for Theatre Technology (USITT)

10 W. 19th St., Ste. 5A
New York, NY 10011
Phone: (212)924-9088

Individuals, colleges, organizations, producing theatrical groups, manufacturers, and students in the U.S. and Canada interested in the advancement of theatre design and technology. **Membership:** 3,500. **Publication(s):** *Project Report.* Periodic. • *Theatre Design and Technology.* Quarterly. Features articles on theatrical lighting, acoustics, costuming, architecture, health, safety, and education. • *U.S. Institute for Theatre Technology-Annual Membership Directory.* • *Sightlines.* 10x/year. • Also publishes *AMX/DMX Standards* • *Directory of Software for Technical Theatre* • *Exhibition Catalogue* • *Theatre Words.*

United States National Institute of Dance (USNID)

38 S. Arlington Ave.
PO Box 245
East Orange, NJ 07019
Phone: (201)673-9225

Membership: Participants include dance teachers, students, colleges and universities, dance companies, and local and international dance teachers' organizations. Activities: Provides placement services and an international network of consultation and counseling services for dance teachers and dancers. Seeks to provide dance teachers with international variations and techniques for improving artistic qualities and teaching methods, and to establish a uniform method of teaching all forms of dance at the highest professional level. Offers children's services;

sponsors competitions. Conducts seminars, demonstrations, workshops, lectures, and certificate correspondence courses. Bestows awards. Affiliated with World Congress of Teachers of Dancing.

Western States Arts Federation (WESTAF)

236 Montezuma Ave.
Santa Fe, NM 87501-2641
Phone: (505)988-1166

Provides seminar, workshop, and conference information. **Membership:** State art agencies of the western United States. **Publication(s):** *The National Arts JobBank.* Provides job postings and placement information.

World Congress of Teachers of Dancing (WCTD)

c/o United States National Institute of Dance
38 S. Arlington Ave.
PO Box 245
East Orange, NJ 07019
Phone: (201)673-9225

Membership: Colleges, universities, professional dance schools, and teachers of dancing. Activities: Maintains placement service. Conducts educational programs and examinations; certifies teachers of dancing. Researches and disseminates information on the history and status of dance from local to international levels. Bestows honorary degrees, including Professor of Dance, Companion of Dance, and Danseur/Premier Danseuse Supreme. Sponsors competitions; operates speakers' bureau. A division of the United States National Institute of Dance.

Employment Agencies and Search Firms

Austin Employment Agency

71-09 Austin St.
Forest Hills, NY 11375
Phone: (718)268-2700

Employment agency.

Beautiful People International

3240 University Ave.
Madison, WI 53705
Phone: (608)238-6372

Places staff in variety of temporary assignments.

Bert Davis Associates, Inc.

400 Madison Ave.
New York, NY 10017
Phone: (212)838-4000

Executive search firm.

Blair Personnel of Parsippany, Inc.

1130 Rte. 46
Box 5306
Parsippany, NJ 07054
Phone: (201)335-6150

Employment agency. Focuses on regular and temporary placement.

Calvert Associates, Inc.

202 E. Washington St.
Ste. 304
Ann Arbor, MI 48104
Phone: (313)769-5413

Employment agency.

Capitol Search Employment Services

915 Clifton Ave.
Clifton, NJ 07013
Phone: (201)779-8700

Employment agency. Second location in Ridgewood, NJ.

Chaloner Associates

Box 1097
Back Bay Station
Boston, MA 02117
Phone: (617)451-5170
Fax: (617)451-8160

Executive search firm.

Claremont-Branan, Inc.

2150 Parklake Dr.
Ste. 212
Atlanta, GA 30345
Phone: (404)491-1292

Employment agency. Executive search firm.

Consultants and Designers Inc.
360 W. 31st St.
New York, NY 10001
Phone: (212)563-8400

Places staff in temporary positions.

Creative Options/Temporary Options
1730 K St., NW
Washington, DC 20006
Phone: (202)785-8367

Employment agency. Places staff on a regular and temporary basis.

I t's your property. Remember that your work experience still belongs to you, no matter who took credit in the short run.

This isn't simply a goody-goody statement to make you feel better. Besides adding to your expertise and experience, your work belongs to you because you can take credit for it on your resume.

So make sure you record the accomplishments from your internship on your resume and save documentation or examples that will prove you did the work.

It's always good to keep an up-to-date work journal and to save your work samples.

Source: *Detroit Free Press*

Fuller Williams Placement
406 W. 34th
Kansas City, MO 64111
Phone: (816)931-8236

Employment agency.

Helen Edwards and Staff Agency
2500 Wilshire Blvd.
Ste. 1018
Los Angeles, CA 90057
Phone: (213)388-0493

Employment agency.

Howard-Sloan Associates, Inc.
545 5th Ave.
New York, NY 10017
Phone: (212)661-5250
Fax: (212)687-5760

Executive search firm.

I.D.E.A. of Charleston, Inc.
PO Box 11100
Charleston, SC 29411
Phone: (803)723-6944

Employment agency. Places individuals on a temporary or regular basis.

Kathy Clarke Model and Talent Agency
2030 E. 4th St.
Ste. 102
Santa Ana, CA 92705
Phone: (714)667-0222

Employment agency.

LaserType
12788 Highway 9
Ste. 6
Boulder Creek, CA 95006
Phone: (208)338-9080

Employment agency.

The Pathfinder Group
295 Danbury Rd.
Wilton, CT 06897
Phone: (203)762-9418

Employment agency. Executive search firm. Recruits staff in a variety of fields.

Printers Placement
1609 Gessner
Box 904
Houston, TX 77080
Phone: (713)973-4904

Employment agency. Provides regular or temporary placement of staff.

Production Associates
5530 S. 79th, East Place
Tulsa, OK 74145
Phone: (918)622-7038

Employment agency.

Remer-Ribolow and Associates
275 Madison Ave.
Ste. 1605
New York, NY 10016
Phone: (212)808-0580

Employment agency.

RitaSue Siegel Associates, Inc.
18 E. 48th St.
New York, NY 10017
Phone: (212)308-0700
Fax: (212)308-0805

Executive search firm.

Staff Inc.
2121 Cloverfield Blvd.
Ste. 133
Santa Monica, CA 90404
Phone: (213)829-5447

Employment agency.

Career Guides

300 New Ways to Get a Better Job
Bob Adams, Inc.
260 Center St.
Holbrook, MA 02343
Phone: (617)767-8100
Fax: (617)767-0994

Baldwin, Eleanor. $7.95. Advocates a job search approach designed to meet the changing nature of the job market.

850 Leading USA Companies
Jamenair Ltd.
PO Box 241957
Los Angeles, CA 90024
Phone: (213)470-6688

Studner, Peter K. $49.95. Compatible with IBM and IBM-compatibles.

A-Job Hunting We Will Go
McGraw Hill Book Company
Continuing Education Program
1221 Avenue of the Americas
New York, NY 10020
Phone: (212)997-6572

Video cassette. 3/4' U-matic. 21 minutes. Part of a ten-part series entitled *The Career Development Video Series,* which offers a step-by-step approach to finding a job and planning a career.

Acting Professionally: Raw Facts About Careers in Acting
Mayfield Publishing Co.
1240 Villa St.
Mountain View, CA 94041
Phone: (415)960-3222
Fax: (415)960-0328

Robert Cohen. Fourth edition, 1990.

The Actor: A Practical Guide to a Professional Career
Donald I. Fine, Inc.
19 W. 21st St.
New York, NY 10010
Phone: (212)727-3270
Fax: (212)727-3277

Eve Brandstein and Joanna Lipari. 1987. Topics covered include auditions, networking, and restarting a stalled career.

Actor/Actress
Careers, Inc.
PO Box 135
Largo, FL 34649-0135
Phone: (813)584-7333

1992. Four page brief offering the definition, history, duties, working conditions, personal qualifications, educational requirements, earnings, hours, employment outlook, advancement, and careers related to this position.

Actors and Actresses
Chronicle Guidance Publications, Inc.
66 Aurora St. Extension
PO Box 1190
Moravia, NY 13118-1190
Phone: (315)497-0330
Toll-free: 800-622-7284

1991. Career brief describing the nature of the job, working conditions, hours and earnings, education and training, licensure, certification, unions, personal qualifications, social and psychological factors, location, employment outlook, entry methods, advancement, and related occupations.

The American Almanac of Jobs and Salaries

Avon Books
105 Madison Ave.
New York, NY 10016
Phone: (212)481-5600
Toll-free: 800-247-5470

John Wright, editor. Revised and updated, 1990. A comprehensive guide to the wages of hundreds of occupations in a wide variety of industries and organizations.

Breaking into the Music Business

Simon & Schuster, Inc
Simon & Schuster Bldg.
1230 Avenue of the Americas
New York, NY 10020
Phone: (212)698-7000
Toll-free: 800-354-4004

Alan H. Siegel. Revised edition, 1990. Describes the record deal; the artist-manager relationship; working with copyrights, demos, and the terminology used in the industry.

Seeking to link education with specific, real-world goals, companies are sending fewer managers to off-the-shelf programs—a change that may be causing many B-schools to lose participants. Corporate customers, which spend nearly $15 million a year on formal training programs for managers and professionals, are demanding that learning lead to immediate changes on the job. Some companies are sticking with business schools for custom programs, such as the one for Bell Atlantic at Wharton. The school now draws half its executive-education revenues from such custom programs. Others are designing their own in-house courses, often cherry-picking some of the best professors and consultants to teach them.

Source: *Business Week*

Career Choices for the 90's for Students of Art

Walker and Co.
720 5th Ave.
New York, NY 10019
Phone: (212)265-3632
Toll-free: 800-289-2553
Fax: (212)307-1764

1990. Describes alternative careers for students of art. Offers information about job outlook and competition for entry-level candidates. Includes a bibliography and an index.

Career Employment Opportunities Directory

Ready Reference Press
PO Box 5249
Santa Monica, CA 90409
Phone: (213)474-5175

Four-volume set. $190.00/set; $47.50/volume. Volume 1 covers the liberal arts and social sciences; Volume 2 covers business administration; Volume 3 covers engineering and computer sciences; Volume 4 covers the sciences. Directory of employers and career opportunities in each field. Provides information about company benefits and special programs. Indexed by subject and geography.

The Berkeley Guide to Employment for New College Graduates

Ten Speed Press
PO Box 7123
Berkeley, CA 94707
Phone: (415)845-8414

Briggs, James I. $7.95. 256 pages. Basic job-hunting advice for the college student.

Best of the National Business Employment Weekly

Consultants Bookstore
Templeton Rd.
Fitzwilliam, NH 03447
Phone: (603)585-2200
Fax: (603)585-9555

$5.00/booklet. Booklets summarizing the best articles from the *National Business Employment Weekly* on a variety of job hunting topics.

The Career Fitness Program: Exercising Your Options

Gorsuch Scarisbrick, Publishers
8233 Via Paseo del Norte
Ste. F-400
Scottsdale, AZ 85258

Sukiennik et al. 1989. $16.00. 227 pages. Textbook, with second half devoted to the job search process.

The Career Guide—Dun's Employment Opportunities Directory

Dun's Marketing Services
Dun and Bradstreet Corporation
Three Sylvan Way
Parsippany, NJ 07054-3896
Phone: (201)605-6000

Annual, December. $450.00; $385.00 for public libraries (lease basis). Covers: More than 5,000 companies that have a thousand or more employees and that provide career opportunities in sales, marketing, management, engineering, life and physical sciences, computer science, mathematics, statistics planning, accounting and finance, liberal arts fields, and other technical and professional areas; based on data supplied on questionnaires and through personal interviews. Also covers personnel consultants; includes some public sector employers (governments, schools, etc.) usually not found in similar lists. Entries include: Company name, location of headquarters and other offices or plants; entries may also include name, title, address, and phone of employment contact; disciplines or occupational groups hired; brief overview of company; discussion of types of positions that may be available; training and career development programs; benefits offered. Arrangement: Companies are alphabetical; consultants are geographical. Indexes: Geographical, Standard Industrial Classification code.

Career Information Center

Macmillan Publishing Co.
866 3rd Ave.
New York, NY 10022
Phone: (818)898-1391
Toll-free: 800-423-9534

Richard Lidz and Linda Perrin, editorial directors. Fifth edition, 1993. A multi-volume set that profiles over 600 occupations. Each occupational profile describes job duties, educational requirements, advancement possibilities, employment outlook, working conditions, earnings and benefits, and where to write for more information.

Career Information System (CIS)

National Career Information System
1787 Agate St.
Eugene, OR 97403
Phone: (503)686-3872

Includes information on job search techniques and self-employment options. Also provides extensive career planning information.

Career Opportunities for Writers

Facts on File, Inc.
460 Park Ave., S.
New York, NY 10016-7382

Rosemary Ellen Guiley. 1993. Sourcebook on over 100 careers for writers from various fields.

Career Opportunities in Art

Facts on File, Inc.
460 Park Ave., S.
New York, NY 10016-7382

Susan H. Haubenstock and David Joselit. 1993. Guidebook containing valuable information on obtaining practical employment in art-related fields. Includes contact information for degree programs as well as professional associations.

Career Opportunities in the Music Industry

Facts On File, Inc.
460 Park Ave., S.
New York, NY 10016
Phone: (212)683-2244
Toll-free: 800-322-8755

Shelly Field. 1990. Discusses approximately 80 jobs in music, including the performing arts, business, and education. Each job description provides basic career information, salary, employment prospects, advancement opportunities, education, training, and experience required.

Career Opportunities in Theater and the Performing Arts

Facts on File, Inc.
460 Park Ave., S.
New York, NY 10016-7382

Shelly Field. 1993. Guidebook offering complete career information for those entering the theater or any of the performing arts.

Career Placement Registry (CPR)

Career Placement Registry, Inc.
302 Swann Ave.
Alexandria, VA 22301
Phone: (703)683-1085
Fax: (703)683-0246

Online database that contains brief resumes of job candidates currently seeking employment. Comprises two files, covering college and university seniors and recent graduates, and alumni, executives, and others who have already acquired substantial work experience. Entries typically include applicant name, address, telephone number, degree level, function, language skills, name of school, major field of study, minor field of study, occupational preference, date available, city/area preference, special skills, citizenship status, employer name, employer address, description of duties, position/title, level of education, civil service register, security clearance type/availability, willingness to relocate, willingness to travel, salary expectation, and overall work experience. Available online through DIALOG Information Services, Inc.

Careering and Re-Careering for the 1990's

Consultants Bookstore
Templeton Rd.
Fitzwilliam, NH 03447
Phone: (603)585-6544
Fax: (603)585-9555

Krannich, Ronald. 1989. $13.95. 314 pages. Details trends in the marketplace, how to identify opportunities, how to retrain for them, and how to land jobs. Includes a chapter on starting a business. Contains index, bibliography, and illustrations.

Careers and the College Grad

Bob Adams, Inc.
260 Center St.
Holbrook, MA 02343
Phone: (617)767-8100
Fax: (617)767-0994

Ranno, Gigi. 1992. $12.95. 64 pages. An annual resource guide addressing the career and job-hunting interests of undergraduates. Provides company profiles and leads.

Careers in Clothing and Textiles

Glencoe Publishing Co.
866 3rd Ave.
New York, NY 10022-6299
Phone: (212)702-3276

Videotape that explores career possibilities in the manufacturing, designing, merchandising, and selling of clothes.

Chronicle Career Index

Chronicle Guidance Publications
PO Box 1190
Moravia, NY 13118-1190
Phone: (315)497-0330

Annual. $14.25. Provides bibliographic listings of career and vocational guidance publications and other resources. Arrangement: Alphabetical by source. Indexes: Occupation; vocational and professional information.

Seven Steps to Being the Best

1. Determine the world standards.
2. Use process mapping.
3. Communicate with employees as if your life depended on it.
4. Distinguish what needs to be done from how hard it is to do it.
5. Set stretch targets.
6. Never stop.
7. Pay attention to your inner self.

Source: *Fortune*

Career Strategies—From Job Hunting to Moving Up

Association for Management Success
2360 Maryland Rd.
Willow Grove, PA 19090

Six video cassettes. Kennedy, Marilyn Moats. $36.95/each. $203.70/set. 30 minutes each. Covers the following topics: planning the job hunt, networking, resumes, interviewing, negotiating salaries and benefits, and moving up on the job.

The College Board Guide to Jobs and Career Planning

The College Board
45 Columbus Ave.
New York, NY 10023-6992
Phone: (212)713-8000

Joyce S. Mitchell. 1990. Covers a variety of

careers. Each career profile contains information on salaries, related careers, education needed, and sources of additional information.

College Majors and Careers: A Resource Guide to Effective Life Planning

Garrett Park Press
PO Box 190C
Garrett Park, MD 20896
Phone: (301)946-2553

Paul Phifer. 1987. Lists 60 college majors, with definitions; related occupations and leisure activities; skills, values, and personal attributes needed; suggested readings; and a list of associations.

College Recruitment Database (CRD)

Executive Telecom System, Inc.
College Park North
9585 Valparaiso Ct.
Indianapolis, IN 46268
Phone: (317)872-2045

Online database that contains resume information for graduating undergraduate and graduate students in all disciplines at all colleges and universities for recruitment purposes. Enables the employer to create and maintain a private 'skill' file meeting selection criteria. Typical entries include student identification number, home and campus addresses and telephone numbers, schools, degrees, dates of attendance, majors, grade point averages, date available, job objective, curricular statement, activities/honors, and employment history. Available online through the Human Resource Information Network.

Coming Alive from Nine to Five

Mayfield Publishing
1240 Villa St.
Mountain View, CA 94041

Micheolzzi, Betty N. 1988. $12.95. In addition to general job-hunting advice, provides special information for women, young adults, minorities, older workers, and persons with handicaps.

The Complete Guide to Finding Jobs in Government

Planning/Communications
7215 Oak Ave.
Dept. CCI
River Forest, IL 60305
Phone: (708)366-5200

Lauber, Daniel. 1989. $14.95. 183 pages. A comprehensive resource for the governmental job market, featuring job-matching services; job hotlines; internships; sources of advertisements; and sources of local, state, federal, Canadian, and international opportunities.

Compu-Job

Cambridge Career Products
723 Kanawha Blvd., E.
Charleston, WV 25301

Menu-driven program designed to take the user through the job search process, from determining career alternatives to identifying openings, applying for employment, and interviewing.

CPC Annual

College Placement Council
62 Highland Ave.
Bethlehem, PA 18017

Annual, fall. Provides a directory of opportunities and employers in many fields, including health, engineering, sciences, computer fields, administration, and business. Offers job-hunting guidance.

Creating Careers in Music Theatre

Peter Lang Publishing, Inc.
62 W. 45th St.
New York, NY 10036
Phone: (212)302-6740

Glenn Loney and Meredith and William Boswell. 1988.

Dance: A Career for You

National Dance Association (NDA)
1900 Association Dr.
Reston, VA 22091
Phone: (703)476-3436

Suggests career opportunities as a teacher, therapist, performer, recreation leader, and choreographer. Describes employment opportunities, personal qualifications, training, knowledge, and skills required for a career in dance.

The Dancer Prepares: Modern Dance for Beginners

Mayfield Publishing Co.
1240 Villa St.
Mountain View, CA 94041
Phone: (415)960-3222
Fax: (415)960-0328

James Penrod, editor. Third edition, 1990.

To embed our values, we give our people 360-degree evaluations, with input from superiors, peers, and subordinates. These are the roughest evaluations you can get, because people hear things about themselves they've never heard before.

Source: *Fortune*

Dancers

Careers, Inc.
PO Box 135
Largo, FL 34649-0135
Phone: (813)584-7333

1993. Two-page occupational summary card describing duties, working conditions, personal qualifications, training, earnings and hours, employment outlook, places of employment, related careers, and where to write for more information.

The Dancer's Complete Guide to Healthcare and a Long Career

Bonus Books
160 E. Illinois St.
Chicago, IL 60611
Phone: (312)467-0580

Allan J. Ryan and Robert E. Stephens. 1988. Contains advice on starting, maintaining, and extending a career in dance. Includes information on training, diet, nutrition, and preventing and treating injuries.

Designer, Clothing

Careers, Inc.
PO Box 135
Largo, FL 34649-0135
Phone: (813)584-7333

1991. Two-page occupational summary card describing duties, working conditions, personal qualifications, training, earnings and hours, employment outlook, places of employment, related careers, and where to write for more information.

The Director's Voice

Theatre Communications Group
355 Lexington Ave.
New York, NY 10017
Phone: (212)697-5230

Arthur Bartow. 1988. Includes interviews with 21 directors who reveal their methods for collaborating with actors, designers, musicians, and playwrights. They also discuss how their training and early influences, as well as imagination and command of craft, impact their productions.

Effective Job Search Strategies

Robert Ehrmann Productions
4741 Calle Camarada
Santa Barbara, CA 93110

Video casssette. $150.00. 26 minutes. Two college seniors, one of whom is handicapped, are advised of job search strategies and resources by a college job counselor.

The Elements of Job Hunting

Bob Adams, Inc.
260 Center St.
Holbrook, MA 02343
Phone: (617)767-8100
Fax: (617)767-0994

Noble, John. $4.95. Concisely focuses on the key components of job hunting.

The Encyclopedia of Career Choices for the 1990s: A Guide to Entry Level Jobs

Walker and Co.
720 5th Ave.
New York, NY 10019
Phone: (212)265-3632
Toll-free: 800-289-2553
Fax: (212)307-1764

1990. Describes entry-level careers in a variety of industries. Presents qualifications required, working conditions, salary, internships, and professional associations.

Encyclopedia of Careers and Vocational Guidance

J. G. Ferguson Publishing Co.
200 W. Monroe, Ste. 250
Chicago, IL 60606
Phone: (312)580-5480

William E. Hopke, editor-in-chief. Eighth edition, 1990. Four-volume set that profiles 900 occupations and describes job trends in 76 industries. Includes career description, educational requirements, history of the job, methods of entry, advancement, employment outlook, earnings, conditions of work, social and psychological factors, and sources of further information.

The Experienced Hand: A Student Manual for Making the Most of an Internship

Carroll Press
43 Squantum St.
Cranston, RI 02920
Phone: (401)942-1587

Stanton, Timothy, and Ali, Kamil. 1987. $6.95. 88 pages. Guidance for deriving the most satisfaction and future benefit from an internship.

For the Working Artists: A Survival Guide

c/o Warren Christianson
935 W. Ave. 37
Los Angeles, CA 90065
Phone: (213)222-4035

Judith Luther and Eric Vollmer. Second edition, updated by Eric Vollmer, 1991.

Get a Better Job!

Peterson's
PO Box 2123
Princeton, NJ 08543-2123
Phone: (609)243-9111

Rushlow, Ed. 1990. $11.95. 225 pages. Counsels the reader on job search techniques. Discusses how to win the job by bypassing the personnel department and how to understand the employer's system for screening and selecting candidates. Written in an irreverent and humorous style.

High-Impact Telephone Networking for Job Hunters

Bob Adams, Inc.
260 Center St.
Holbrook, MA 02343
Phone: (617)767-8100
Fax: (617)767-0994

Armstrong, Howard. 1992. $6.95. Examines the challenges associated with phone networking, shows the reader how to use "positive errors" to generate referrals, and offers hints on how to deal with "getting the runaround". Includes advice on how to ask for the meeting and addresses long-distance job searches by phone.

Hot New Niche: Executive Temporaries

Consultants Bookstore
Templeton Rd.
Fitzwilliam, NH 03447
Phone: (603)585-2200
Fax: (603)585-9555

1991. $10.00. List of firms placing executives in temporary positions. Provides specialty and contact information.

How to Be a Working Actor: An Insider's Guide to Finding Jobs in Theatre, Film, and Television

M. Evans and Co.
216 E. 49th St.
New York, NY 10017
Phone: (212)688-2810

Mari Lyn Henry and Lynne Rogers. Second edition, 1989. Gives advice on putting together a portfolio, finding leads, and dealing with agents and managers. Covers unions, interviewing, auditions, and screen tests.

How to Find and Get the Job You Want

Johnson/Rudolph Educational Resources, Inc.
1004 State St.
Bowling Green, KY 42101

1989. $20.50. 160 pages. Aimed at the college student.

How to Get a Better Job in This Crazy World

Crown Publishers, Inc.
225 Park Ave., S.
New York, NY 10003
Phone: (212)254-1600

Half, Robert. $17.95.

Appear for all interviews, on campus and elsewhere, unless foreseeable events prevent you from doing so. And, if you can't make the interview because of an unforeseeable event, notify your career center or the employer at the earliest possible moment.

Source: *Planning Job Choices: 1994*

How to Get a Good Job and Keep It

VGM Career Horizons
4255 W. Touhy Ave.
Lincolnwood, IL 60646-1975
Phone: (708)679-5500

Bloch, Deborah Perlmutter. 1993. $7.95. Aimed at the recent high school or college graduate, this guide provides advice on finding out about jobs, completing applications and resumes, and managing successful interviews.

How to Get a Job

Business Week Careers
PO Box 5810
Norwalk, CT 06856-9960

Video cassette. $34.95. 70 minutes. Job search skills presented from the viewpoint of career planning and placement professionals, CEOs, and others.

How to Get and Get Ahead on Your First Job

VGM Career Horizons
4255 West Touhy Ave.
Lincolnwood, IL 60646-1975
Phone: (708)679-5500

Bloch, Deborah Perlmutter. 1988. $7.95. 160 pages. Details in step-by-step ways how to go about finding that first job, apply for it, write the winning resume, and manage the successful interview.

How to Get Hired Today!

VGM Career Horizons
4255 W. Touhy Ave.
Lincolnwood, IL 60646-1975
Phone: (708)679-5500

Kent, George, E. 1991. $7.95. Directed at individuals who know the type of job they are looking for. Focuses the reader on activities that are likely to lead to a job and eliminates those that won't. Shows how to establish productive contacts and discover, evaluate, and pursue strong job leads.

How to Get Interviews from Job Ads

Elderkin Associates
PO Box 1293
Dedham, MA 02026

Elderkin, Kenton W. 1989. $19.50. 256 pages. Outlines how to select and follow up ads to get the job. Includes unique ways to get interview offers and how to incorporate the use of a computer and a fax machine in arranging interviews. Illustrated.

How to Land a Better Job

VGM Career Horizons
4255 West Touhy Ave.
Lincolnwood, IL 60646-1975
Phone: (708)679-5500

Lott, Catherine S., and Lott, Oscar C. 1989. $7.95. 160 pages. Tells the job seeker how to enhance his or her credentials, overcome past weaknesses, uncover job leads, get appointments, organize an appealing resume, and score points in interviews. A special section devoted to getting a better job without changing companies covers the process of transferring departments and gives pointers on moving up to the boss's job.

How to Locate Jobs and Land Interviews

The Career Press, Inc.
180 5th Ave.
PO Box 34
Hawthorne, NJ 07507

French, Albert L. $9.95. Shows readers how to tap into the unadvertised, hidden job market and guides them through the resume, cover letter, and interview preparation process.

How to Market Your College Degree

VGM Career Horizons
4255 W. Touhy Ave.
Lincolnwood, IL 60646-1975
Phone: (708)679-5500

Rogers, Dorothy, and Bettinson, Craig. 1992. $12.95. Provides a guide to self-marketing as a key component of an effective job search. Helps job seekers to develop a strategic marketing plan that targets niches with needs that match their skills, differentiate themselves from the competition by positioning themselves against other candidates, evaluate their potential worth from the employer's perspective, and manage their careers as they move up the career ladder or into another field.

How to Seek a New and Better Job

Consultants Bookstore
Templeton Rd.
Fitzwilliam, NH 03447
Phone: (603)585-6544
Fax: (603)585-9555

Gerraughty, William. 1987. $5.95. 64 pages. Presents information on cover letters, resumes, and mailings. Includes a self-analysis, fifty-six questions asked by interviewers, and a variety of forms and lists.

How to Sell Yourself As an Actor

Sweden Press
Box 1612
Studio City, CA 91614
Phone: (818)995-4250

K. Callan. Second edition, completely revised, 1990.

In Their Own Words: Contemporary American Playwrights

Theatre Communications Group (TCG)
355 Lexington Ave.
New York, NY 10017
Phone: (212)697-5230

David Savran. 1988. Playwrights describe their early experiences in the theatre, their working methods, and their plays in various interviews.

Internships: 50,000 On-the-Job Training Opportunities for Students and Adults

Peterson's Guides, Inc.
PO Box 2123
Princeton, NJ 08543-2123
Phone: (609)243-9111
Toll-free: 800-338-3282

Brian C. Rushing, editor. Eleventh edition, 1991. Lists internship opportunities under five broad categories: communications, creative arts, human services, international affairs, and public affairs. Includes a special section on internships in Washington, DC. For each internship program, gives the name, phone number, contact person, description, eligibility requirements, and application procedure.

Job and Career Building

Ten Speed Press
PO Box 7123
Berkeley, CA 94707
Phone: (415)845-8414

Germann, Richard, and Arnold, Peter. $7.95. 256 pages.

The Job Bank Series

Bob Adams, Inc.
260 Center St.
Holbrook, MA 02343
Phone: (617)767-8100
Fax: (617)767-0994

$12.95/volume. There are eighteen volumes in the Job Bank Series, each covering a different job market. Volumes exist for the following areas: Atlanta, Boston, Chicago, Dallas/Fort Worth, Denver, Detroit, Florida, Houston, Los Angeles, Minneapolis, New York, Ohio, Philadelphia, Phoenix, San Francisco, Seattle, St. Louis, and Washington D.C. Each directory lists employers and provides name, address, telephone number, and contact information. Many entries include common positions, educational backgrounds sought, and fringe benefits provided. Cross-indexed by industry and alphabetically by company name. Profiles of professional associations, a section on the region's economic outlook, and listings of executive search and job placement agencies are included. Features sections on conducting a successful job search campaign and writing resumes and cover letters.

The Job Hunt

Ten Speed Press
PO Box 7123
Berkeley, CA 94707
Phone: (415)845-8414

Nelson, Robert. $3.95. 64 pages. A compact guide with a direct question-and-answer format with space for notations.

Although every recruiter and employer handles the interview in their own way, there are four basic questions the recruiter wants to answer: What job does the candidate want? Can the person do the job? Will the person do the job? Is the person compatible with the existing team?

Source: *Planning Job Choices: 1994*

The Job Hunter's Final Exam

Surrey Books, Inc.
230 E. Ohio St.
Ste. 120
Chicago, IL 60611
Phone: (312)661-0050

Camden, Thomas. 1990. $10.95. 140 pages. Helps job seeker quiz self about resumes, interviews, and general job-hunting strategies.

Job Hunters Survival Kit

The Guidance Shoppe
2909 Brandemere Dr.
Tallahassee, FL 32312
Phone: (904)385-6717

Includes two interactive software programs: *The Skill Analyzer* and *The Resume Writer*. $149.95.

Compatible with Apple II-plus, IIe, IIc; TRS—80 III/4; and IBM.

The Job Hunter's Workbook

Peterson's
PO Box 2123
Princeton, NJ 08543-2123
Phone: (609)243-9111

Taggart, Judith; Moore, Lynn; and Naylor, Mary. $12.95. 140 pages. Deals with such job-seeking topics as assessing personal strengths, networking, interviewing and answering interview questions, dealing with salaries and benefits, and preparing resumes, cover letters, and portfolios. A combination of self-assessment exercises, work sheets, checklists, and advice.

Job Hunting for Success

Ready Reference Press
PO Box 5249
Santa Monica, CA 90409
Phone: (213)474-5175

Set of three video cassettes. Aimed at the student job hunter. Focuses on the importance of knowing yourself, your interests, aptitudes, and other characteristics. Describes job openings in a variety of areas, including apprenticeship, clerical, on-the-job training, and summer employment. Helps prepare the student for the career planning and job search process.

Job Search: Career Planning Guidebook, Book II

Brooks/Cole Publishing Company
Marketing Dept.
511 Forest Lodge Rd.
Pacific Grove, CA 93950

Lock. 1992. 248 pages. Assists the reader in a production job search.

The Job Search Handbook

Bob Adams, Inc.
260 Center St.
Holbrook, MA 02343
Phone: (617)767-8100
Fax: (617)767-0994

Noble, John. $6.95. 144 pages. Identifies and provides advice on the essential elements of the job search, including networking, cover letters, interviewing, and salary negotiation. Aimed at first-time entrants to the job market, those looking for a job in a new field, and middle-level professionals looking to take their next step up.

Job Search: The Total System

Consultants Bookstore
Templeton Rd.
Fitzwilliam, NH 03447
Phone: (603)585-6544
Fax: (603)585-9555

Dawson, Kenneth, and Dawson, Sheryl. 1988. $14.95. 244 pages. A guide that shows how to link networking, resume writing, interviewing, references, and follow-up letters to land the job. Thirty resumes are included.

Jobs Rated Almanac: Ranks the Best and Worst Jobs by More Than a Dozen Vital Criteria

Pharos Books
200 Park Ave.
New York, NY 10166
Phone: (212)692-3863
Toll-free: 800-521-6600

Les Krantz. Second edition, 1992. Ranks 250 jobs by environment, salary, outlook, physical demands, stress, security, travel opportunities, and geographic location. Includes jobs the editor feels are the most common, most interesting, and the most rapidly growing.

Jobs! What They Are—Where They Are—What They Pay

Simon & Schuster, Inc.
Simon & Schuster Bldg.
1230 Avenue of the Americas
New York, NY 10020
Phone: (212)698-7000

Snelling, Robert O., and Snelling, Anne M. 1989. Describes duties and responsibilities, earnings, employment opportunities, training, and qualifications.

Journeying Outward: A Guide to Career Development

Delmar Publishers, Inc.
2 Computer Dr., W.
PO Box 15015
Albany, NY 12212-5015
Phone: (518)459-1150
Fax: (518)459-3552

Lynton, Jonathan. 1989. 224 pages. Examines the correct way to present oneself in the job search, covering appearance, interviewing, writing a resume, and completing a job application. Resume writing section illustrates models of various resume formats. Includes sections on planning the job search and working the plan.

Joyce Lain Kennedy's Career Book

VGM Career Horizons
4255 West Touhy Ave.
Lincolnwood, IL 60646-1975
Phone: (708)679-5500

Kennedy, Joyce Lain. Co-authored by Dr. Darryl Laramore. 1992. $17.95 paperback. $29.95 hardcover. 448 pages. Guides the reader through the entire career-planning and job-hunting process. Addresses how to find the kinds of jobs available and what to do once the job is secured. Provides a number of case histories to give examples.

Just Around the Corner: Jobs and Employment

Cambridge Career Products
723 Kanawha Blvd. E.
Charleston, WV 25301

Video cassette. Beta, VHS, 3/4' U-matic. 30 minutes. The many different aspects of work are explored in this series of 8 cassettes. Tips on good and bad job habits are given, how to fill out a job application, and how to act on a job interview are explained. Program titles: 1. Effective Job Behavior I. 2. Effective Job Behavior II. 3. Employment Agencies I. 4. Employment Agencies II. 5. Job Interviews I. 6. Job Interviews II. 7. Equal Employment Opportunity/Discrimination I. 8. Equal Employment Opportunity/Discrimination II.

Liberal Arts Jobs

Peterson's
PO Box 2123
Princeton, NJ 08543-2123
Phone: (609)243-9111

Nadler, Burton Jay. 1989. $9.95. 110 pages. Presents a list of the top 20 fields for liberal arts majors, covering more than 300 job opportunities. Discusses strategies for going after those jobs, including guidance on the language of a successful job search, informational interviews, and making networking work.

Making It in the New Music Business

Writer's Digest Books
1507 Dana Ave.
Cincinnati, OH 45207
Phone: (513)531-2222
Toll-free: 800-289-0963

James Riordan. Revised and updated, 1991. Covers how to make records and establish an audience.

All companies desire to hire the best people possible. In these years of limited hiring and reduced work forces, there are still many good jobs available. In any year, the best candidates get jobs offers; in fact, they usually have multiple offers. By preparing for your on-campus and on-site interviews as much as possible, you can place yourself among the best.

Source: *Planning Job Choices: 1994*

Moody's Corporate Profiles

Moody's Investors Service, Inc.
Dun and Bradstreet Company
99 Church St.
New York, NY 10007
Phone: (212)553-0300
Fax: (212)553-4700

Provides data on more than 5,000 publicly held companies listed on the New York Stock Exchange or the American Stock Exchange or NMS companies traded on the National Association of Securities Dealers Automated Quotations. Typical record elements: Company name, address, phone, D-U-N-S number, Moody's number, stock exchange, line of business analysis, annual earnings and dividends per share, and other financial and stock trading data. Available through DIALOG Information Services, Inc.

The Music Business: Career Opportunities and Self-Defense

Crown Publishers, Inc.
225 Park Ave. S.
New York, NY 10003
Phone: (212)254-1600

Dick Weissman. New, revised, updated edition, 1990.

Music Careers

Careers, Inc.
PO Box 135
Largo, FL 34649-0135
Phone: (813)584-7333

1992. Four-page brief offering the definition, history, duties, working conditions, personal qualifications, educational requirements, earnings, hours, employment outlook, advancement, and careers related to this position.

Music Composer

Vocational Biographies, Inc.
PO Box 31
Sauk Centre, MN 56378-0031
Phone: (612)352-6516

1987. Four-page pamphlet containing a personal narrative about a worker's job, work likes and dislikes, career path from high school to the present, education and training, the rewards and frustrations, and the effects of the job on the rest of the worker's life. The data file portion of this pamphlet gives a concise occupational summary, including work description, working conditions, places of employment, personal characteristics, education and training, job outlook, and salary range.

Musician, Instrumental

Careers, Inc.
PO Box 135
Largo, FL 34649-0135
Phone: (813)584-7333

1991. Two-page occupational summary card describing duties, working conditions, personal qualifications, training, earnings and hours, employment outlook, places of employment, related careers, and where to write for more information.

Musicians, Instrumental

Chronicle Guidance Publications, Inc.
66 Aurora St. Extension
PO Box 1190
Moravia, NY 13118-1190
Phone: (315)497-0330
Toll-free: 800-622-7284

1988. Career brief describing the nature of the job, working conditions, hours and earnings, education and training, licensure, certification, unions, personal qualifications, social and psychological factors, location, employment outlook, entry methods, advancement, and related occupations.

Network Your Way to Job and Career Success

Consultants Bookstore
Templeton Rd.
Fitzwilliam, NH 03447
Phone: (603)585-6544
Fax: (603)585-9555

Krannich, Ron, and Krannich, Caryl. 1989. $11.95. 180 pages. Based on a comprehensive career planning framework, each chapter outlines the best strategies for identifying, finding, and transforming networks to gather information and obtain advice and referrals that lead to job interviews and offers. Includes exercises, sample interviewing dialogues, and a directory of organizations for initiating and sustaining networking activities.

Occupational Outlook Handbook

Bureau of Labor Statistics
441 G St., NW
Washington, DC 20212
Phone: (202)523-1327

Biennial, May of even years. $22.00 hardcover. $17.00 paperback. Contains profiles of various occupations, which include description of occupation, educational requirements, market demand, and expected earnings. Also lists over 100 state employment agencies and State Occupational Information Coordinating Committees that provide state and local job market and career information; various occupational organizations that provide career information. Arranged by occupation; agencies and committees are geographical. Send orders to: Superintendent of Documents, U.S. Government Printing Office, Washington, D.C. 20402 (202-783-3238).

Online Hotline News Service

Information Intelligence, Inc.
PO Box 31098
Phoenix, AZ 85046
Phone: (602)996-2283

Online database containing five files, one of

which is Joblines, which features listings of employment and resume services available in voice, print, and online throughout North America. Joblines focuses on the online, library automation, and information-related fields.

The Only Job Hunting Guide You'll Ever Need

Poseidon Press
Simon and Schuster Bldg.
1230 Avenue of the Americas
New York, NY 10020
Phone: (212)698-7290

Petras, Kathryn, and Petras, Ross. 1989. $10.95. 318 pages. Covers the full range of the job search process.

Real job satisfaction comes from finding a job that fits a variety of your specifications, your values, interests, and skills. You have to envision yourself going to work every day at each of the institutions. How would you feel there? Do you like the lifestyle you would live if you take the position? Would the job make you feel competent, yet challenged? Would it leave you time for friends, family, and yourself? Is the compensation enough to support your lifestyle?

Source: *Planning Job Choices: 1994*

Only You Can Decide: The First Key to Career Planning and Job Hunting

McGraw Hill Book Company
Continuing Education Program
1221 Avenue of the Americas
New York, NY 10020
Phone: (212)997-6572

Video cassette. 3/4' U-matic. 28 minutes. Part of a ten-part series entitled *The Career Development Video Series*, which offers a step-by-step approach to finding a job and planning a career.

Opportunities in Acting Careers

National Textbook Co.
4255 W. Touhy Ave.
Lincolnwood, IL 60646-1975
Phone: (708)679-5500
Toll-free: 800-323-4900

Dick Moore. Revised edition, 1993. Describes acting positions in show business; discusses how much actors earn, unions, working with agents, and schools. Gives advice on how to get started. Includes a bibliography.

Opportunities in Music Careers

National Textbook Co.
4255 W. Touhy Ave.
Lincolnwood, IL 60646-1975
Phone: (708)679-5500
Toll-free: 800-323-4900

Robert Gerardi. 1991. Includes a bibliography.

Opportunities in Performing Arts Careers

VGM Career Books
4255 W. Touhy Ave.
Lincolnwood, IL 60646-1975
Phone: 800-323-4900

Bonnie Bjorguine Bekken. 1991. Overviews the exciting world of performing arts, including opportunities in classical and popular music; theater, television, and movie acting; dance; performance art; and teaching and therapy. Also offers information on developing a portfolio and preparing for auditions.

Opportunities in Writing Careers

National Textbook Co.
4255 W. Touhy Ave.
Lincolnwood, IL 60646-1975
Phone: (708)679-5500
Toll-free: 800-323-4900

Elizabeth Foote-Smith. 1989. Describes writing career opportunities. Covers articles, novels, short stories, nonfiction books, reviews, and interviews. Also includes information on playwrights, poets, journalists, and broadcasters. Discusses educational preparation. Includes a bibliography.

Out of Work but Not Alone

Self-Help Clearinghouse
Publications Dept.
St. Clares - Riverside Medical Center
Pocono Rd.
Denville, NJ 07834
Phone: (201)625-9565

1984. $9.00.

The Overnight Job Change Strategy

Ten Speed Press
PO Box 7123
Berkeley, CA 94707
Phone: (415)845-8414

Asher, Donald. 1993. Subtitled *How to Plan a Comprehensive, Systematic Job Search in One Evening.* Incorporates sales and marketing techniques into a six-stage job search process.

The Perfect Job Reference

Consultants Bookstore
Templeton Rd.
Fitzwilliam, NH 03447
Phone: (603)585-2200
Fax: (603)585-9555

Allen, Jeffrey, G. 1990. $9.95. Step-by-step methods for securing a written or verbal recommendation.

Playing for Pay: How to be a Working Musician

Writer's Digest Books
1507 Dana Ave.
Cincinnati, OH 45207
Phone: (513)531-2222

James R. Gibson. 1990. Written for the freelance musician. Discusses how to market your music, how to locate clients, and how to book and play the jobs. Toll-free/Additional Phone Number: 800-543-4644.

Professional's Job Finder

Planning/Communications
7215 Oak Ave.
River Forest, IL 60305-1935
Phone: (708)366-5297

$15.95. Discusses how to use sources of private

sector job vacancies in a number of specialties and state-by-state, including job-matching services, job hotlines, specialty periodicals with job ads, salary surveys, and directories. Covers a variety of fields from healthcare to sales. Includes chapters on resume and cover letter preparation and interviewing.

Rejection Shock

McGraw Hill Book Company
Continuing Education Program
1221 Avenue of the Americas
New York, NY 10020
Phone: (212)997-6572

Video cassette. 3/4' U-matic. 28 minutes. Part of a ten-part series entitled *The Career Development Video Series*, which offers a step-by-step approach to finding a job and planning a career. Provides viewers with ways to handle frustration, anxiety, and despair in job hunting.

The Right Place at the Right Time

Ten Speed Press
PO Box 7123
Berkeley, CA 94707
Phone: (415)845-8414

Wegmann, Robert G. $11.95. 192 pages. A comprehensive approach to career planning and job seeking developed to find the right job in the new economy.

Singers

Chronicle Guidance Publications, Inc.
66 Aurora St. Extension
PO Box 1190
New York, NY 13118-1190
Phone: (212)497-0330

1990. Career brief describing the nature of the job, working conditions, hours and earnings, education and training, licensure, certification, unions, personal qualifications, social and psychological factors, location, employment outlook, entry methods, advancement, and related occupations.

Skills in Action: A Job-Finding Workbook

University of Akron
Adult Resource Center
Akron, OH 44325

Selden, J.H. $5.50. 75 pages. Workbook format;

aimed at job seekers looking for initial or transitional employment.

Super Job Search: The Complete Manual for Job-Seekers and Career-Changers

Jamenair Ltd.
PO Box 241957
Los Angeles, CA 90024
Phone: (213)470-6688

Studner, Peter. $22.95. 352 pages. A step-by-step guidebook for getting a job, with sections on getting started, how to present accomplishments, networking strategies, telemarketing tips, and negotiating tactics.

W omen who embark on modeling careers have two dreams sharp in their minds: to be on the cover of *Vogue*, *Harper's Bazaar*, or *Elle*, and to land a major makeup contract. Few realize either dream. Were they to come true, they would most likely occur within the first year or two of modeling. The arbiters of beauty tend to make up their minds fairly fast, separating the faces of destiny from the faces of ordinariness.

Source: *The New York Times*

Supporting Yourself as an Artist

Oxford University Press
200 Madison Ave.
New York, NY 10016
Phone: (212)679-7300

Deborah A. Hoover. Second edition, 1989. Assists artists in identifying organizations and individuals that can provide the financial and nonfinancial support needed to survive.

Taking Charge of Your Career Direction

Brooks/Cole Publishing Company
Marketing Dept.
511 Forest Lodge Rd.
Pacific Grove, CA 93950

Lock. 1992. 377 pages. Provides guidance for the job search process.

U.S. Employment Opportunities: A Career News Service

Washington Research Associates
7500 E. Arapaho Plaza
Ste. 250
Englewood, CO 80112
Phone: (303)756-9038
Fax: (303)770-1945

Annual; quarterly updates. $184.00. List of over 1,000 employment contacts in companies and agencies in the banking, arts, telecommunications, education, and 14 other industries and professions, including the federal government. Entries include: Company name, name of representative, address, description of products or services, hiring and recruiting practices, training programs, and year established. Classified by industry. Indexes: Occupation.

> **R**emember, choose the job with features that most closely match your needs and wants. Reevaluate occasionally. Values, interests, and skills change, and your job priorities will change, too.
>
> Source: *Planning Job Choices: 1994*

VGM's Careers Encyclopedia

National Textbook Co.
4255 W. Touhy Ave.
Lincolnwood, IL 60646-1975
Phone: (708)679-5500
Toll-free: 800-323-4900

Third edition, 1991. Profiles 200 occupations. Describes job duties, places of employment, working conditions, qualifications, education and training, advancement potential, and salary for each occupation.

What Color Is Your Parachute?

Ten Speed Press
PO Box 7123
Berkeley, CA 94707
Phone: (415)845-8414

Bolles, Richard N. 1993. $12.95 paperback. $18.95 hardcover. Subtitled: *A Practical Manual for Job-Hunters and Career-Changers*. One of the best-known works on job hunting, this book provides detailed and strategic advice on all aspects of the job search.

Where Do I Go from Here with My Life?

Ten Speed Press
PO Box 7123
Berkeley, CA 94707
Phone: (415)845-8414

Crystal, John C., and Bolles, Richard N. $11.95. 272 pages. A planning manual for students of all ages, instructors, counselors, career seekers, and career changers.

Where the Jobs Are: The Hottest Careers for the '90s

The Career Press, Inc.
180 5th Ave.
PO Box 34
Hawthorne, NJ 07507

Satterfield, Mark. 1992. $9.95. Provides a look at current trend in the job market and the industries that offer the greatest opportunity for those entering the work force or making a career change. Contains advice on career pathing opportunities and breaking into the field.

Where to Start Career Planning

Peterson's
PO Box 2123
Princeton, NJ 08543-2123
Phone: (609)243-9111

Lindquist, Carolyn Lloyd, and Miller, Diane June. 1991. $17.95. 315 pages. Lists and describes the career-planning publications used by Cornell University's Career Center, one of the largest career libraries in the country. Covers more than 2,000 books, periodicals, and audiovisual resources on topics such as financial aid, minority and foreign students, overseas employment and travel, resources for the disabled, second careers, study-and-work options, summer and short-term jobs, women's issues, and careers for those without a bachelor's degree. Includes a bibliographic title index.

Who's Hiring Who?

Ten Speed Press
PO Box 7123
Berkeley, CA 94707
Phone: (415)845-8414

Lathrop, Richard. $9.95. 268 pages. Provides advice on finding a better job faster and at a higher rate of pay.

Work in the New Economy: Careers and Job Seeking into the 21st Century

The New Careers Center
1515 23rd St.
Box 297-CT
Boulder, CO 80306

1989. $15.95.

The Working Actor: A Guide to the Profession

Viking Penguin
375 Hudson St.
New York, NY 10014
Phone: (212)366-2000

Katinka Matson, editor. Revised edition, 1993.

Writer

Careers, Inc.
PO Box 135
Largo, FL 34649-0135
Phone: (813)584-7333

1992. Four-page brief offering the definition, history, duties, working conditions, personal qualifications, educational requirements, earnings, hours, employment outlook, advancement, and careers related to this position.

Writers, Artistic and Dramatic

Chronicle Guidance Publications, Inc.
PO Box 1190
Moravia, NY 13118-1190
Toll-free: 800-622-7284

1989. Occupational brief describing the nature of the job, working conditions, hours and earnings, education and training, licensure, certification, unions, personal qualifications, social and psychological factors, location, employment outlook, entry methods, advancement, and related occupations.

Your Own Way in Music: A Career and Resource Guide

St. Martin's Press, Inc.
175 5th Ave.
New York, NY 10010
Phone: (212)674-5151

Nancy Uscher. 1990.

Professional and Trade Periodicals

American Dance

American Dance Guild
31 W. 21st St., 3rd Fl.
New York, NY 10010-6807
Phone: (212)627-3790

Editor(s): Ann Vachon and Karen Deaver. Bimonthly. Presents information for those interested in dance. Contains news about the activities of schools, companies, and individuals; governmental and foundation grants; the activities of arts councils; dance reviews; and association news.

American Recorder

American Recorder Society
472 Point Rd.
Marion, MA 02738
Phone: (508)748-1734
Fax: (508)748-1928

Benjamin Dunham, editor. Quarterly. Magazine containing articles, reports, and reviews for the avocational and professional recorder player. Music for recorder in most issues.

American Theatre

Theatre Communications Group
355 Lexington Ave.
New York, NY 10017
Phone: (212)697-5230
Fax: (212)983-4847

Jim O'Quinn, editor. Monthly (combined issues May/June and July/August). Magazine containing news, features, and opinion on American and international theatre. Full-length play published seven times a year.

Audition News

Chicago Entertainment Company
6272 W. North Ave.
Chicago, IL 60639
Phone: (312)637-4595

Monthly. $24.95/year. Provides listings of Midwest job openings in acting, singing, dancing, and production.

Wouldn't it be nice if the world were orderly and you could control your career future so that things would happen according to plan? No, it would not be nice. And it is not possible. Your success and your career happiness will depend upon how well you respond to new problems as they occur.

Source: *Planning Job Choices: 1994*

Bass Player

Miller-Freeman Publications/GPI Group
20085 Stevens Creek Blvd.
Cupertino, CA 95014
Phone: (408)446-1105
Fax: (408)446-1088

Six issues year.

Career Opportunities News

Garrett Park Press
PO Box 190 C
Garrett Park, MD 20986-0190
Phone: (301)946-2553

Calvert, Robert, Jr., and French, Mary Blake, editors. Bimonthly. $30.00/year; $4.00 sample issue. Each issue covers such things as resources to job seekers, special opportunities for minorities, women's career notes, and the current outlook in various occupations. Cites free and inexpensive job-hunting materials and new reports and books.

Casting Call

Mel Pogue Enterprises
3365 Cahuenga
Hollywood, CA 90068
Phone: (213)874-4012

Biweekly. $36/year, $1/single issue. Lists show business positions.

The Chicago Reader

11 E. Illinois
Chicago, IL 60611
Phone: (312)838-0350

Weekly. Provides a listing of Chicago theatre productions.

Dance Magazine

33 W. 60th St.
New York, NY 10023-7990
Phone: (212)245-9050
Fax: (212)956-6487

Richard Philp, editor-in-chief. Monthly. $24.95/year. Performng arts magazine featuring all forms of dance with profiles, news, photos, reviews of performances, and information on books, videos, films, schools, health, and technique.

Dance/USA Journal

Dance/USA
777 14th St., NW
Washington, DC 20005
Phone: (202)628-0144

Quarterly. $30/year for nonmembers (free to members). Lists positions for dancers, administrators, trainers, and others in the field.

Designer

University and College Designers Association
210 N. Ironwood Dr.
South Bend, IN 46615-2518
Phone: (219)288-8232

Editor(s): Bill Noblitt. Quarterly. Focuses on different areas of visual communication design, including graphics, photography, signage, films, and other related fields. Reviews communication and design technologies and techniques. Recurring features include information on the Association's educational programs and other activities.

Down Beat

Maher Publications, Inc.
180 W. Park Ave.
Elmhurst, IL 60126
Phone: (708)941-2030
Fax: (708)941-3210

John Ephland, managing editor. Monthly. $18.00/year; $1.75/issue. Magazine edited for the learning musician.

Drama-Logue

PO Box 38771
Los Angeles, CA 90038-0771

Serves as a major source for West Coast theatre, film, and television jobs.

Dramatists Guild—Newsletter

Dramatists Guild
234 W. 44th St.
New York, NY 10036
Phone: (212)398-9366
Fax: (212)944-0420

Editor(s): Jason Milligan. Eight issues/yr. Contains news of Guild activities, including symposia, seminars, regional theater activity, playwriting contests and workshops, and playreading units. Offers information on organizations which are looking for new plays. Features business advice columns and articles by established playwrights.

Hot Line News

Musicians National Hot Line Association
277 E. 6100 S.
Salt Lake City, UT 84107
Phone: (801)268-2000

Editor(s): Nancy W. Zitting. Six issues/yr. Carries news of individual musicians and groups, and addresses ways to stay employed in music. Carries brief autobiographical sketches and lists of employment needs and opportunities. Recurring features include a column titled Spotlight.

International Musician

American Federation of Musicians
1501 Broadway, Ste. 600
New York, NY 10036
Phone: (212)869-1330
Fax: (212)302-4374

Stephen R. Sprague, editor. Monthly. $60.00/year. Tabloid for labor union musicians.

Journal of Career Planning and Employment

College Placement Council, Inc.
62 Highland Ave.
Bethlehem, PA 18017
Phone: (215)868-1421

Four issues/year. Free to members. Can be used to provide assistance to students in planning and implementing a job search.

Kennedy's Career Strategist

Marilyn Moats Kennedy Career Strategies
1153 Wilmette Ave.
Wilmette, IL 60091

Twelve issues/year. $89.00/year. Offers job search guidance.

Managing Your Career

Dow Jones and Co.
420 Lexington Ave.
New York, NY 10170

College version of the *National Business Employment Weekly*. Excludes job openings, but provides job-hunting advice.

Music Faculty Vacancy List

CMS Publications
PO Box 8208
Missoula, MT 59807
Toll-free: 800-729-0235

Monthly. $25/year. Provides listing of positions in college music teaching and performance positions in orchestras.

Music Notation News

Music Notation Modernization Association
PO Box 241
Kirksville, MO 63501
Phone: (816)665-8098
Fax: (816)627-4744

Editor(s): Thomas S. Reed. Quarterly. Serves as the official organ of the association, which is devoted to "finding ways to improve the basic system of musical notation for greater simplicity and efficiency in reading, writing, and printing music."

New Theatre Quarterly

110 Midland Ave.
Port Chester, NY 10573
Phone: (914)937-9600
Fax: (914)937-4712

Clive Barker and Simon Tussler, editors. Quarterly. International forum for theatrical scholarship and practice.

New York Opera Newsletter

PO Box 278
Maplewood, NJ 07040
Phone: (201)378-9549

11x/year. $40/year. Lists open positions for singers and musicians with opera companies and symphony orchestra choruses.

There's a slow but steady movement toward becoming "portfolio people," and individuals who market their skills and services to many employers on a contract basis.

The portfolio concept is taking hold because employers do not want as many full-time employees as they did before. Today, contract workers make up 24 percent of the corporate payroll. This proportion is expected to increase to 40 percent in this decade.

Source: *Planning Job Choices: 1994*

The Newsletter of the International Theatre Institute of the United States, Inc.

International Theatre Institute of the United States, Inc.
220 W. 42nd St.
New York, NY 10036
Phone: (212)944-1490
Fax: (212)944-1506

Louis A. Rachow, editor. Quarterly. Reports on the activities of ITI/Worldwide, ITI/US, and the theatre professionals who are served by ITI's international programs.

Occupational Outlook Quarterly

U.S. Government Printing Office
Superintendent of Documents
Washington, DC 20402
Phone: (202)783-3238

Quarterly. $6.50/year; $2.50/single issue.

Contains articles and information about career choices and job opportunities in a wide range of occupations.

Performing Arts

Performing Arts Network
3539 Motor Ave.
Los Angeles, CA 90034

Jeffrey Hirsch, editor. Monthly. In-theatre magazine for all major theatres in California and Texas.

Performing Arts Forum

International Association of Performing Arts Administrators
6065 Pickerel Dr.
Rockford, MI 49341
Phone: (616)874-6200

10x/year. $25/year (free to members). Lists job openings.

Spotlight Casting Magazine

PO Box 3270
Hollywood, CA 90078
Phone: (213)462-6775

Weekly. $40/year. Provides help wanted ads for actors, singers, dancers, technicians, and other show business positions.

Symphony Magazine

American Symphony Orchestra League
777 14th St. NW, Ste. 500
Washington, DC 20005
Phone: (202)628-0099
Fax: (202)783-7228

Faythe Benson, managing editor. Six issues/year. $35.00/year; $6.00/issue. Magazine with news and articles for symphonic orchestra managers, trustees, volunteers, and musicians.

Theatre Crafts

Theatre Crafts Assn.
135 5th Ave.
New York, NY 10010
Phone: (212)677-5997
Fax: (212)677-3857

Patricia Mackay, editor and publisher. Ten issues/year. $30.00/year; $3.00/issue. Magazine focusing on artistic production and the performing arts.

Theatre Facts

Theatre Communications Group
355 Lexington Ave.
New York, NY 10017
Phone: (212)697-5230

Provides financial and productivity information to members.

THEatre JOBLIST: The National Employment Service Billboard for Theatre Arts

THEatre Service
PO Box 15282
Evansville, IN 47716-0282
Phone: (812)474-0549

11x/year. $45/year for nonmembers; $30/members. Lists positions for technicians, designers, and college teachers.

Theatre Profiles

Theatre Communications Group
355 Lexington Ave.
New York, NY 10017
Phone: (212)697-5230

Biennial. Survey of noncommercial theatres.

Theatrical Calendar

Celebrity Service International, Inc.
1780 Broadway, Ste. 300
New York, NY 10019
Phone: (212)757-7979
Fax: (212)397-4626

Frank Gehrecke, editor. Biweekly. Provides information about current shows, weekly openings, previews, tryouts, rehearsals, future plans, road companies, and off- and off-off-Broadway plays. Listings contain the names of the producer, press agent, general manager, director, and stars. Recurring features include a listing of theaters outside the New York area.

The Washington International Arts Letter

Allied Business Consultants
PO Box 12010
Des Moines, IA 50312
Phone: (515)255-5577

10x/year. Features grants, awards, and residency programs in a variety of areas including administration, architecture, design, film, television, radio, music, performing arts, photography, research, training, visual arts, and writing.

The Writer

The Writer Inc.
120 Boylston St.
Boston, MA 02116-4615
Phone: (617)423-3157

Sylvia K. Burack, editor. Monthly. $24.75/year; $32.75/year for foreign subscribers. Magazine for free-lance writers. Publishing practical information and advice on how to write publishable material and where to sell it.

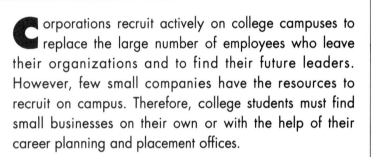

Corporations recruit actively on college campuses to replace the large number of employees who leave their organizations and to find their future leaders. However, few small companies have the resources to recruit on campus. Therefore, college students must find small businesses on their own or with the help of their career planning and placement offices.

Source: *Planning Job Choices: 1994*

Writers Club Newsletter

Jacklyn Barlow
67 Aberdeen Circle
Leesburg, FL 34788
Phone: (904)742-1224

Editor(s): Jacklyn Barlow. Bimonthly. Serves as a forum for writers wishing to share experiences, resources, writing problems, and successes.

Writer's Digest

F&W Publications
1507 Dana Ave.
Cincinnati, OH 45207
Phone: (513)531-2222
Fax: (513)531-1843

Bruce Woods, editor. Monthly. $24.00/year; $2.50/issue. Professional magazine for writers.

Basic Reference Guides

The 100 Best Companies to Work for in America

Signet/NAL Penguin
1633 Broadway
New York, NY 10019

Levering, Robert; Moskowitz, Milton; and Katz, Michael. 1985. $5.95. 477 pages. Describes the best companies to work for in America, based on such factors as salary, benefits, job security, and ambience. The authors base their 'top 100' rating on surveys and personal visits to hundreds of firms.

101 Careers: A Guide to the Fastest-Growing Opportunities

John Wiley & Sons, Inc.
605 3rd Ave.
New York, NY 10158
Phone: (212)850-6000
Fax: (212)850-6088

Michael Harkavy, author. $14.95. 352 pages. Provides listing of the best-paying job prospects. Includes occupational overviews, descriptions of fast-growing areas, salary information, and resource listings.

AACT Directory of Community Theatres in the United States

American Association of Community Theatre (AACT)
c/o L. Ross Rowland
8209 N. Costa Mesa Dr.
Muncie, IN 47303
Phone: (317)288-0144

Periodic.

AAM Directory

Association of Anglican Musicians (AAM)
c/o Susan Markley
Trinity Cathedral
310 W. 17th St.
Little Rock, AR 72206
Phone: (501)372-0294
Fax: (501)372-2147

Periodic.

ACD Membership Directory

American Center for Design (ACD)
233 E. Ontario
Ste. 500
Chicago, IL 60611
Phone: (312)787-2018
Fax: (312)649-9518

Annual.

Acting From the Ultimate Consciousness

Putnam Publishing Group, Inc.
200 Madison Ave.
New York, NY 10016
Phone: (212)951-8400

Eric Morris. 1992.

Acting Step by Step

Resource Publications, Inc.
160 E. Virginia St., Ste. 290
San Jose, CA 95112
Phone: (408)286-8505

Marshall Cassady. 1988. Includes bibliographical references.

Actor

Warner Books, Inc.
Time & Life Bldg.
1271 Avenue of the Americas
New York, NY 10020
Phone: (212)522-7200

Pamell Hall, editor. 1994.

The Actor and The Text

Applause Theatre Book Publishers
211 W. 71st St.
New York, NY 10023
Phone: (212)595-4735

Cicely Berry. Revised edition, 1992.

The Actor's Book of Classical Monologues

Penguin Books
375 Hudson St.
New York, NY 10014
Phone: (212)366-2000

Stefan Rudnicki, editor. 1988.

ALMA Directory

Association of Laban Movement Analysts (ALMA)
c/o Laban/Bartenieff Institute for Movement Studies
31 W. 27th St.
New York, NY 10001
Phone: (212)689-0740

Annual.

American Dance Guild Membership Directory

American Dance Guild
31 W. 21st St.
New York, NY 10010
Phone: (212)627-3790

America's Fastest Growing Employers

Bob Adams, Inc.
260 Center St.
Holbrook, MA 02343
Phone: (617)767-8100
Fax: (617)767-0994

Smith, Carter. 1992. $14.95. Identifies firms with the most rapid growth in employment opportunities. Provides contact information, recent sales figures, current employees, and a breakdown of common positions sought by the firms profiled.

The Anchor Companion to the Orchestra

Doubleday and Co., Inc.
1540 Broadway
New York, NY 10036-4094
Phone: (212)354-6500
Toll-free: 800-223-6834

Norman Del Mar. 1987. Contains entries on musical instruments, orchestral performance, and musical arrangement.

Annual Report

Actors' Fund of America
1501 Broadway
Ste. 518
New York, NY 10036
Phone: (212)221-7300
Fax: (212)764-0238

Includes membership listing and financial report.

The Art of Making Dances

Princeton Book Co., Publishers
12 W. Deleware Ave.
PO Box 57
Pennington, NJ 08534
Phone: (609)737-8177
Toll-free: 800-326-7149

Doris Humphrey, author; Barbara Pollack, editor. 1991.

ATHE Membership Directory

Association for Theatre in Higher Education (ATHE)
c/o THEatre Service
PO Box 15282
Evansville, IN 47716
Phone: (812)474-0549

Annual.

Sixty-four percent of undergraduate schools said that their programs were designed to train a student for educational stage management; 50 percent said students were being prepared for graduate programs in stage management; and 68 percent felt that their programs trained students for stage management on a professional level. 68 percent of those who answered indicated that their programs accomplished all three goals.

Source: Theatre Crafts

The Back Stage Handbook for Performing Artists

Waton-Guptill Publications, Inc.
1515 Broadway
New York, NY 10036
Phone: (212)764-7300

Sherry Eaker, editor. 1991.

The Best Companies for Women

Simon and Schuster
Simon and Schuster Bldg.
1230 Avenue of the Americas
New York, NY 10020

1989. $8.95.

The Business of Design

Van Nostrand Reinhold Co., Inc.
115 5th Ave.
New York, NY 10003
Phone: (212)254-3232
Toll-free: 800-842-3636

Ian Linton. 1988. Includes an index.

Chamber Music America Membership Directory

Chamber Music America
545 8th Ave.
New York, NY 10018
Phone: (212)244-2772

Annual, spring. $20.00, postpaid. Covers: Over 700 member ensembles, presenters, festivals, and training programs; over 3000 associate members, including managers, publishers, arts organizations, instrument manufacturers, libraries and individuals. Entries include: For members - Name, address, phone, name of contact, activities, awards. For associates - Name, address. Arrangement: Separate geographical sections for ensembles, presenters, festivals and training programs; associate members are classified by type of organization, then alphabetical. Indexes: General, ensemble format.

Often what stops people from pursuing a particular job is the feeling that "I'm not good enough to apply for that job." They imagine the other applicants to be more qualified. However, you need not ever be the perfect candidate for a certain job or career. In fact, there is no such thing as the perfect candidate. Seldom does anyone have all of what the job calls for. There is only the imperfect person—YOU—the individual who has some of what is needed for the job and can learn the rest on the job or get additional schooling.

Source: *Planning Job Choices: 1994*

Choreographing the Stage Musical

Routledge, Chapman & Hall, Inc.
29 W. 35th St.
New York, NY 10001-2291
Phone: (212)244-3336

Margot Sunderland, editor. 1990.

Contemporary Theatre, Film, and Television

Gale Research Inc.
835 Penobscot Bldg.
Detroit, MI 48226
Phone: (313)961-2242
Fax: (313)961-6241

Annual. $110.00. Covers: In ten volumes, about 5,800 leading and up-and-coming performers, directors, writers, producers, designers, managers, choreographers, technicians, composers, executives, dancers, and critics in the United States and Great Britain. Entries include: Name, home and/or agent or office addresses, personal and career data, writings, awards, other information. Arrangement: Alphabetical. Indexes: Cumulative name index also covers entries in *Who's Who in the Theatre* editions 1-17 and in *Who Was Who in the Theatre*.

The Dance Handbook

Macmillan Publishing Co.
866 3rd Ave, 7th Fl.
New York, NY 10022
Phone: (617)423-3990
Toll-free: 800-257-5755

Allen Robertson, editor. 1990.

DGA Directory of Members

Directors Guild of America (DGA)
7920 Sunset Blvd.
Hollywood, CA 90046
Phone: (310)289-2000
Fax: (310)289-2029

Annual.

Directory of Minority Arts Organizations

Civil Rights Division
National Endowment for the Arts
1100 Pennsylvania Ave., NW
Rm. 812
Washington, DC 20506
Phone: (202)682-5454

Irregular; latest edition February 1987. Free. Covers: Almost 1,000 performing groups, presenters, galleries, art and media centers, literary organizations, and community centers with significant arts programming which have leadership and constituency that is predominantly Asian-American, Black, Hispanic, Native American, or multiracial. Entries include:

Organization name, address, phone, name and title of contact, description of activities. Arrangement: Geographical. Indexes: Organization name, activity.

Directory of Opera/Musical Theatre Companies and Workshops in the U.S. and Canada

Central Opera Service
Metropolitan Opera
Lincoln Center for the Performing Arts
New York, NY 10023
Phone: (212)957-9871

$12.00, plus $1.65 shipping. Covers: About 1,100 theater and musical workshops and companies. Entries include: Company or theater name, address, phone, name of director or administrator; name of auditorium, capacity, stage size, stage type; budget classification or type of company. Arrangement: Geographical.

Directory of Summer Chamber Music Workshops, Schools and Festivals

Chamber Music America
545 8th Ave.
New York, NY 10018
Phone: (212)244-2772
Fax: (212)244-2776

Biennial, spring of even years. $10.00. Covers: Over 100 chamber music workshops and schools for students, young professionals, and adult amateurs; summer concert series. Entries include: For workshops and schools - Name, location or address, description of program and participants sought, procedure for auditions, type of accommodations and recreational facilities, dates, age requirements. Arrangement: Separate geographical sections for workshops and concert series.

Dramatics Magazine Summer Theatre Directory Issue

International Thespian Society
3368 Central Pkwy.
Cincinnati, OH 45225
Phone: (513)559-1996

Annual, February. $3.50, postpaid. Publication includes: List of over 150 study and performance opportunities in summer schools and summer theater education programs. Entries include:

Organization, school or group name, address, phone, name of contact; description of program, dates, requirements, cost, etc. Arrangement: Geographical.

Dramatist Sourcebook

Theatre Communications Group
355 Lexington Ave.
New York, NY 10017
Phone: (212)697-5230

Gillian Richards and Linda MacColl, editors. 1993. Written for playwrights. Filled with more than 700 entries describing script submission policies of more than 225 theatres, playwriting contests, publishing outlets, developmental workshops, conferences, and service organizations that aid playwrights.

Dramatists Guild Quarterly Directory Issue

Dramatists Guild
234 W. 44th St.
New York, NY 10036
Phone: (212)398-9366

Annual. Available to members only. Publication includes: Broadway and off-Broadway producers; off-off-Broadway groups; agents; regional theaters; sources of grants, fellowships, residencies; conferences and festivals; sponsors of playwriting contests; and sources of financial assistance. Entries include: For producers - Name, address, credits, types of plays accepted for consideration. For groups - Name, address, contact name, type of material accepted for consideration, future commitment, hiring criteria, response time. For agents - Name, address. For theaters - Theater name, address, contact name, submission procedure, types of plays accepted for consideration, maximum cast, limitations, equity contract, opportunities, response time. Arrangement: Contests are by deadline; others are classified.

Film Producers, Studios, Agents & Casting Directors Guide

Lone Eagle Publishing Co.
9903 Santa Monica Blvd., Ste. 204
Beverly Hills, CA 90212
Phone: (310)471-8066

Susan Avallone, editor. Third edition, 1992.

FSI Directory of Professional Freelancers

Fastbreak Syndicate, Inc. (FSI)
PO Box 1626
Orem, UT 84059
Phone: (801)785-1300

Annual. Also cited as *Professional American Freelancers.*

Fundamentals of Music

Prentice-Hall, Inc.
Rte. 9W
Englewood Cliffs, NJ 07632
Phone: (201)592-2000
Toll-free: 800-634-2863

Raymond Elliott. Fourth edition, 1989. Covers the basic elements of music: rhythm, melody, and harmony.

Cooperative education, internships, practicums, and similar programs are designed to provide students with relevant work experience, but they're also an avenue to full-time employment after graduation. Employers often hire those who have co-oped or served an internship with them.

Source: *Planning Job Choices: 1994*

GTM Directory

Guild of Temple Musicians (GTM)
Bet Shalom Congregation
201 9th Ave. N.
Hopkins, MN 55343
Phone: (612)933-8525
Fax: (612)933-3238

Semiannual.

The Harvard Guide to Careers

Harvard University Press
79 Garden St.
Cambridge, MA 02138
Phone: (617)495-2600
Fax: (617)495-5898

Martha P. Leape and Susan M. Vacca, editors. 1991. $12.95. 222 pgs. Handbook providing information on the career search process from career exploration to writing resumes and interviewing.

Honk If You're a Writer: Unabashed Advice, Undiluted Experience, & Unadulterated Inspiration for Writers & Writers-to-Be

Simon & Schuster Trade
Simon & Schuster Bldg.
1230 Avenue of the Americas
New York, NY 10020
Phone: (212)698-7000

Arthur Plotnik, editor. 1992.

Instrumentalist Directory of Summer Music Camps, Clinics, and Workshops Issue

Instrumentalist Company
200 Northfield Rd.
Northfield, IL 60093
Phone: (708)446-5000
Fax: (708)446-6263

Annual, March. $2.50. Publication includes: List of nearly 250 summer music camps, clinics, and workshops in the United States; limited Canadian and foreign coverage. Entries include: Camp name, location, name of director, opening and closing dates, tuition fees, courses offered. Arrangement: Geographical.

International Association of Performing Arts Administrators Membership Directory

International Association of Performing Arts Administrators
6065 Pickerel Dr.
Rockford, MI 49341
Phone: (616)874-6200

Annual. Free to members.

International Who's Who in Music and Musicians Directory

Gale Research Inc.
835 Penobscot Bldg.
Detroit, MI 48226
Phone: (313)961-2242
Fax: (313)961-6241

1988. $120.00. Covers almost all countries and represents a variety of musical interests. Contains approximately 10,000 biographical entries; includes data on orchestras, musical organizations, competitions, music libraries, and colleges and other educational establishments.

The Jazz Musician

Saint Martin's Press Inc.
175 5th Ave.
New York, NY 10010
Phone: (212)674-5151

Tony Scherman, editor. 1993.

Jobs '94

Simon & Schuster
Simon & Schuster Bldg.
Rockefeller Center
1230 Ave. of the Americas
New York, NY 10020
Phone: (212)698-7000

Kathryn and Ross Petras, authors. Annual. $15.00. 685 pages. Job guide providing company information, including salaries, working conditions, and job security. Lists the top companies in selected industries. Provides employment forecasts by region and career.

Jobs in Arts and Media Management

ACA Books
American Council for the Arts
1 E. 53rd St.
New York, NY 10022-4201
Phone: (212)228-2787
Toll-free: 800-321-4510
Fax: (212)223-4415

Stephen Langley, James Abruzzo, authors. $21.95. 279 pages. Provides information on jobs in the entertainment industry. Includes information on resumes, how to make contacts, and how to negotiate a contract.

The Master Musician

Zondervan Publishing House
5300 Patterson Ave. SE
Grand Rapids, MI 49530
Phone: (616)698-6900
Toll-free: 800-272-3480
Fax: (616)698-3235

John M. Talbot, editor. 1992.

Modern Dance in Germany and the United States: Cross Currents & Influences

Gordon & Breach Science Publishers, Inc.
270 8th Ave.
New York, NY 10011
Phone: (212)206-8900

Isa Partsch-Bergsohn, editor. 1993.

MTNA Directory of Nationally Certified Teachers

Music Teachers National Association (MTNA)
617 Vine St.
Ste. 1432
Cincinnati, OH 45202
Phone: (513)421-1420
Fax: (513)421-2503

Annual. Free.

Music Business Handbook & Career Guide

Sherwood Co.
PO Box 4198
Thousand Oaks, CA 91359
Phone: (805)379-6820

David Baskerville. Fifth edition, 1990.

Those with a bachelor's degree in the arts and letters often become marketable in alternative careers when they have chosen the proper electives and obtained career-related work experiences. Two or three courses in an area of specialization, such as computer science, marketing, finance, or personnel administration, can enhance one's chances for employment considerably.

Source: *Planning Job Choices: 1994*

Musical America International Directory of the Performing Arts

ABC Consumer Magazines, Inc.
825 7th Ave.
8th Fl.
New York, NY 10019
Phone: (212)887-8383
Fax: (212)586-1364

Annual, December. $75.00. Covers: U.S., Canadian, and international orchestras, musicians, singers, performing arts series, dance and opera companies, festivals, contests, foundations and awards, publishers of music, artist managers, booking agents, music magazines, and service and professional music organizations. Entries include: Name of organization, institution, address, phone, fax, telex, key personnel; most entries include name of contact, manager, conductor, etc. For orchestras - Number of concerts and seats. Other entries show similar details as appropriate. Arrangement: Geographical. Indexes: Alphabetical and by category.

Musical Theater Choreography

Watson-Guptill Publications
1515 Broadway
New York, NY 10036
Phone: (212)764-7300
Toll-free: 800-451-1741
Fax: (212)536-5359

Robert Berkson, editor. 1990.

J ob availability by geographical region is highly variable. While most of the country is not in a hiring mode, certain regions offer more opportunities than others. According to Dr. Patrick Scheetz of the Collegiate Employment Research Institute, the better areas are the southeastern and northcentral, followed by the southwestern regions. On the lower end of the scale are the southcentral, northwestern, and last is the northeastern region of the country.

Source: *Planning Job Choices: 1994*

National Association of Artists' Organizations Directory

National Association of Artists'
Organizations
National Union Bldg.
918 F St., NW
Washington, DC 20004
Phone: (202)347-6350
Fax: (202)347-7376

Annual, May. $20.00. Covers: About 200 state and regional art agencies, art service organizations, performance network sponsors; about 300 artists' organizations. Entries include: Organization, agency, or individual name, address, phone, name of contact, discipline, services, size of budget. Arrangement: Geographical. Indexes: Organization name.

National Directory of Addresses and Telephone Numbers

Omnigraphics, Inc.
2500 Penobscot Bldg.
Detroit, MI 48226
Phone: (313)961-1340

Annual. Covers about 223,000 corporations,

federal, state, and local government offices, banks, colleges and universities, associations, labor unions, political organizations, newspapers, magazines, television and radio stations, foundations, postal and shipping services, hospitals, office equipment suppliers, airlines, hotels and motels, accountants, law firms, computer firms, foreign corporations, overseas trade contacts, and other professional services. Entries include company, organization, agency, or firm name, address, phone, fax, toll-free phone.

National Directory of Nonprofit Organizations

Gale Research Inc.
835 Penobscot Bldg.
Detroit, MI 48226
Phone: (313)961-2242
Fax: (313)961-6241

Annual. $225.00. Covers: Over 210,000 nonprofit organizations with incomes over $100,000. Entries include: Organization name, address, phone, annual income, IRS filing status, activity description. Arrangement: Alphabetical. Indexes: Area of activity, income, geographical.

Nationwide Music Record Industry Toll Free Directory

CDE
Box 310551
Atlanta, GA 30331
Phone: (404)344-7621

Annual, January. $50.00; payment must accompany orders from individuals. Covers: Several hundred record companies, record services, record suppliers, wholesalers, music publishers, and videotape wholesalers, suppliers, and producers with toll-free (800) phone numbers. Entries include: Company name, address, toll-free phone number. Arrangement: Alphabetical.

NATS Membership Directory

National Association of Teachers of Singing
(NATS)
2800 University Blvd., N.
Jacksonville, FL 32211
Phone: (904)744-9022

NETC Membership Directory

New England Theatre Conference (NETC)
50 Exchange St.
Waltham, MA 02154
Phone: (617)893-3120

Annual.

New York Casting and Survival Guide and Datebook: The New York Performer's Handbook

Peter Glenn Publications
17 E. 48th St.
New York, NY 10017
Phone: (212)688-7940

Peter Glenn and Chip Brill, editors. Annual, September. $15.00. Covers: About 10,000 services and facilities for actors, models, and performers in the New York area, including agents in New York and Los Angeles, theaters, producers and casting agencies, casting personnel in advertising agencies, music clubs, typing services, schools, unions, health food stores, apartment and roommate referral agencies. Entries include: Company name, address, phone, and contact. Arrangement: Classified by service.

New York Theatrical Sourcebook

Broadway Press
12 W. Thomas St.
PO Box 1037
Shelter Island, NY 11964-1037
Phone: (516)749-3266
Toll-free: 800-869-6372
Fax: (516)749-3266

David Rodger, publisher. Annual, November. $30.00. 560 pages. Covers over 2,500 suppliers of products and services for film, television, theater, designers, and craftspeople.

Non-Profit's Job Finder

Planning Communications
7215 Oak Ave.
River Forest, IL 60305-1935
Phone: (708)366-5200
Fax: (708)366-5280

Daniel Lauber, editor. 1992. $14.95. 306 pgs. Provides over 1,001 sources of job, internship, and grant opportunities.

NYC/On Stage: Directory to the Performing Arts

Theatre Development Fund, Inc.
1501 Broadway
New York, NY 10036

Eve Rodriguez, editor. 103 pages. Guide to theatre, dance, and music companies, as well as artists and performing arts centers in New York. Includes public transportation directions.

The Official Southwest Talent Directory

Cobb-Rendish Publishing
2908 McKinney Ave.
Dallas, TX 75204
Phone: (214)754-4729

Annual. $25.00/single issue.

On Performing: A Handbook for Actors, Dancers, Singers on the Musical Stage

McGraw-Hill, Inc.
1221 Avenue of the Americas
New York, NY 10020
Phone: (212)512-2000
Toll-free: 800-722-4726

David Craig. 1987.

Orchestra/Business Directory

American Symphony Orchestra League
777 14th St., NW
Ste. 500
Washington, DC 20005
Phone: (202)628-0099
Fax: (202)783-7228

Annual.

Peterson's Job Opportunities for Business and Liberal Arts Graduates

Peterson's
PO Box 2123
Princeton, NJ 08543-2123
Phone: (609)243-9111

Compiled by the Peterson's staff. 1993. $20.95 paperback. 300 pages. Lists hundreds of organizations that are hiring new business, humanities, and social science graduates in the areas of business and management. Explores how to match academic backgrounds to specific job openings. Provides information about opportunities for experienced personnel as well.

Includes data on starting locations by city and state, summer jobs, co-op jobs, internships, and international assignments.

The Practical Director

Focal Press
80 Montvale Ave.
Stoneham, MA 02180
Phone: (617)438-8464
Fax: (617)438-1979

Mike Crisp, editor. 1993.

A Primer for Choreographers

Waveland Press, Inc.
PO Box 400
Prospect Heights, IL 60070
Phone: (708)634-0081

Lois Ellfeldt. 1988. An introductory text for choreographers. Covers spacial relationships, visual images, settings, and accompaniment.

Employers perceive "researching the company" as a critical factor in the evaluation of applicants because it reflects interest and enthusiasm. In the interview, it shows that you understand the purpose of this process and establishes a common base of knowledge from which questions can be asked and to which information can be added, thus enabling both applicant and interviewer to evaluate the position match more accurately.

Source: *Planning Job Choices: 1994*

Regional Theater Directory: A National Guide to Employment in Regional Theatres

American Theatre Works, Inc.
PO Box 519
Dorset, VT 05251
Phone: (802)867-2223

Jill Charles, C. Barrack Evans, and Gene Sirotof, editors. Annual, May. $14.95. Covers: Regional theater companies with employment opportunities in acting, design, production, and management. Entries include: Company name, address, phone, name and title of contact; type of company, activities, and size of house; whether union affiliated, whether nonprofit or commercial; year established; hiring procedure

and number of positions hired annually, season; desrciption of stage; internships, description of artistic policy and audience. Arrangement: Geographical. Indexes: Company name, type of play produced. Also includes: Lists of theater organizations, casting agencies, and other services.

Regional Theatre Directory

Theatre Directories
PO Box 519
Dorset, VT 05251
Phone: (802)867-2223
Fax: (802)867-0144

Jill Charles, editor. $14.95. 172 pages. Listing of equity and nonequity theatres. Describes hiring and casting procedures. Lists internship opportunities. Includes resource lists and book reviews.

Relationships Between Score & Choreography in Twentieth-Century Dance: Music, Movement, Metaphor

The Edwin Mellen Press
415 Ridge St.
PO Box 450
Lewiston, NY 14092
Phone: (716)754-2266

Paul Hodgins, editor. 1992.

The Rock Musician

Saint Martin's Press
175 5th Ave.
New York, NY 10010
Phone: (212)674-5151

Tony Scherman, editor. 1993.

The Songwriter's and Musician's Guide to Making Great Demos

Writer's Digest Books
1507 Dana Ave.
Cincinnati, OH 45207
Phone: (513)531-2222

Harvey Rachlin. 1990. Includes an index.

Songwriter's Market

Writer's Digest Books
1507 Dana Ave.
Cincinnati, OH 45207
Phone: (513)531-2222

Annual, September. $19.95, plus $3.00 shipping.

Covers: 2,000 music publishers, jingle writers, advertising agencies, audiovisual firms, radio and television stations, booking agents, and other buyers of musical compositions and lyrics; also lists contests, competitions, and workshops. Entries include: Buyer's name and address, phone, payment rates, submission requirements, etc. Arrangement: Classified by type of market.

Stern's Performing Arts Directory

Danad Publishing Company
33 W. 60th St.
New York, NY 10023
Phone: (212)245-8937

Annual, September. $65.00. Covers: Over 20,000 dance performers and performing groups, managers and artists' representatives, support personnel and services, funding sources, sponsors, booking organizations, dance and music education organizations. Entries include: Company, institution, or personal name, address, phone, cable, telex, names of key personnel. Arrangement: Classified by product or service.

Summer Theater Directory

American Theatre Works, Inc.
PO Box 519
Dorset, VT 05251
Phone: (802)867-2223

Jill Charles, Debra J. Bromley, and Gene Sirotof, editors. Annual, December. $13.95. Summer theater companies which offer employment opportunities in acting, design, production, and management; and summer theater training programs. Entries include: Company name, address, phone, name and title of contact; type of company, activities and size of house; whether union affiliated, whether nonprofit or commercial; year established; hiring procedure and number of positions hired annually, season; description of stage; internships; description of company's artistic goals and audience. Arrangement: Geographical. Indexes: Company name.

The Summer Theatre Directory

American Theatre Association
1010 Wisconsin Ave., NW
6th Fl.
Washington, DC 20007

$3.50. Includes information on openings, apprenticeships, and application procedures.

The Technique of Acting

Bantam Books
666 5th Ave.
New York, NY 10103
Phone: (212)765-6500

Stella Adler. 1990.

Theatre Companies of the World

Greenwood Press, Inc.
88 Post Rd. West
Westport, CT 06881
Phone: (203)226-3571

1986. $115.00. Covers: Theatre companies worldwide; Volume 1 covers companies in Africa, Asia, Australia/New Zealand, Canada, Eastern Europe, Latin America, the Middle East, and Scandinavia; volume 2 covers the United States (although less than 15 companies are included) and Western Europe. Companies are selected on the basis of international reputation, historical importance, innovative technology, theatre tradition, and experimental drama.' Entries include: Theatre company name, address, history and background, significant productions, description of performance facility, source of funding, purpose and plans. Arrangement: Geographical.

Research shows that employers are searching harder for candidates with proven track records in solving specific problems unique to their organizations. Therefore, a general resume of accomplishments won't garner as much attention. Today, you must be prepared to research the needs of an organization and tailor your resume to show how your past accomplishments meet the employer's criteria.

Source: *Planning Job Choices: 1994*

Theatre Directory

Theatre Communications Group
355 Lexington Ave.
New York, NY 10017
Phone: (212)697-5230

Listing of theatres; theatre personnel such as artistic and managing directors; board chairs; and other theatre-related information.

Theatre Member Directory

Alliance of Resident Theatres/New York
(ART/NY)
131 Varick St.
Rm. 904
New York, NY 10013
Phone: (212)989-5257
Fax: (212)989-4880

Periodic.

Tourist Attractions and Parks Talent and Carnival Guide Issue

Kane Communications, Inc.
7000 Terminal Square
Ste. 210
Upper Darby, PA 19082
Phone: (215)734-2420
Fax: (215)734-2423

Annual, April. $7.50. Publication includes: List of carnivals and promoters and talent agencies providing entertainers, musicians, and other acts for festivals, carnivals, fairs, amusement parks and similar facilities or events. Entries include: For carnivals - Name, location, description. For agencies -Name, address, phone, name of contact, references. Indexes: Type of act.

> **F**orty-four percent of teachers polled do not use a text when teaching stage management. Of those who do, over 50 percent favor Stern's *Stage Management Guidebook of Practical Techniques*, with Gruver's *The Stage Management Handbook* as a distant second choice.
>
> Source: *Theatre Crafts*

U.S. Employment Opportunities: A Career News Service

Washington Research Associates
7500 E. Arapaho Plaza
Ste. 250
Englewood, CO 80112
Phone: (303)756-9038
Fax: (303)770-1945

Annual; quarterly updates. $184.00. List of over 1,000 employment contacts in companies and agencies in the banking, arts, telecommunications, education, and 14 other industries and professions, including the federal government. Entries include: Company name, name of representative, address, description of products or services, hiring and recruiting practices, training programs, and year established. Classified by industry. Indexes: Occupation.

USA Jazz Directory

Jazz World Society (JWS)
c/o Jan A. Byrczek
250 W. 57th St.
Ste. 1212
New York, NY 10107
Phone: (201)713-0830

Periodic.

Ward's Business Directory of U.S. Private and Public Companies

Gale Research Inc.
835 Penobscot Bldg.
Detroit, MI 48226
Phone: (313)961-2242
Fax: (313)961-6241

1991. Four volumes. Volumes 1-3 lists companies alphabetically and geographically; $930.00/set. Volume 4 ranks companies by sales with 4-digit SIC code; $655.00. $1,050.00/complete set. Contains information on over 85,000 U.S. businesses, over 90% of which are privately held. Entries include company name, address, and phone; sales; employees; description; names of officers; fiscal year end information; etc. Arrangement: Volume 1 and 2 in alphabetic order; Volume 3 in zip code order within alphabetically arranged states.

Who's Who in Music

Mid-South Management, Inc.
Box 1051
Vicksburg, MS 39181
Phone: (601)636-6893

Irregular. $40.00, plus $2.00 shipping. Covers: About 20,000 musicians, singers, music associations, broadcasting organizations, record companies, producers, representatives, and others in the Black music industry. Entries include: Individual, organization, or company name, address, phone, key personnel. Arrangement: Alphabetical. Indexes: Subject.

Working Actors: The Craft of Televison, Film, & Stage Performance

Focal Press
Butterworth Publishers
80 Montvale Ave.
Storeham, MA 02180
Phone: (617)438-8464
Fax: (617)438-1479

Richard A. Blum. 1989.

Writer's A-Z

Writer's Digest Books
1507 Dana Ave.
Cincinnati, OH 45207
Phone: (513)531-2222

Kirk Polking, Joan Bloss, and Colleen Cannon, editors. 1990. Includes a bibliography.

The Writer's Handbook

The Writer's Magazine
120 Boylston St.
Boston, MA 02116
Phone: (617)423-3157

Sylvia K. Burack, editor. Revised edition, 1993. Annual. Contains information on getting published, writing techniques, and working with agents and editors. Describes specialized writing markets and lists publishers, writers' organizations, and literary agents.

Writer's Market: Where to Sell What You Write

Writer's Digest Books
1507 Dana Ave.
Cincinnati, OH 45207
Phone: (513)531-2222
Fax: (513)531-4744

Annual, September. $25.95, plus $3.00 shipping. Covers: More than 4,000 buyers of books, articles, short stories, plays, gags, verse, fillers, and other original written material. Includes book and periodical publishers, greeting card publishers, play producers and publishers, audiovisual material producers, author agents, and others. Entries include: Name and address of buyer, phone, payment rates, editorial requirements, reporting time, how to break in. Arrangement: Classified by type of publication.

Writing Effectively with Your PC: Computer Tools, Tips, and Tricks for Modern Writers

Random House, Inc.
201 E. 50th St.
New York, NY 10022
Phone: (212)751-2600

Larry Magid, editor. 1993.

The Young Performer's Guide: How to Break into Show Business

Betterway Publications, Inc.
PO Box 219
Crozet, VA 22932
Phone: (804)823-5661

Brian A. Padol and Alan Simon, authors. $14.95. 309 pages. Provides information on aspects of show business including how to enter the field and how to understand its potential for success and failure. Describes the roles of agents, managers, and tools of the trade.

MASTER INDEX

Master Index

The Master Index provides comprehensive access to all four sections of the Directory by citing all subjects, organizations, publications, and services listed throughout in a single alphabetic sequence. The index also includes inversions on significant words appearing in cited organization, publication, and service names. For example, "Ward's Business Directory of U.S. Private and Public Companies" could also be listed in the index under "Companies; Ward's Business Directory of U.S. Private and Public."